THE FINGER OF GOD

Reconsiderations
in Southern African
History

Richard Elphick, Editor

THE FINGER OF GOD

Enoch Mgijima, the Israelites, and the Bulhoek Massacre in South Africa

Robert R. Edgar

University of Virginia Press

Charlottesville and London

University of Virginia Press
© 2018 by the Rector and Visitors of the University of Virginia
All rights reserved
Printed in the United States of America on acid-free paper

First published 2018

9 8 7 6 5 4 3 2 1

Library of Congress Cataloging-in-Publication Data
Names: Edgar, Robert R., author.
Title: The finger of God : Enoch Mgijima, the Israelites, and the Bulhoek massacre
    in South Africa / Robert R. Edgar.
Other titles: Reconsiderations in southern African history.
Description: Charlottesville : University of Virginia Press, 2018. | Series:
    Reconsiderations in southern African history | Includes bibliographical
    references and index.
Identifiers: LCCN 2017057359| ISBN 9780813941028 (cloth ; alkaline paper) |
    ISBN 0813941024 (cloth ; alkaline paper) | ISBN 9780813941035 (e-book)
Subjects: LCSH: Israelites (South Africa)—History. | Christian sects—
    South Africa—History—20th century. | Mgijima, Enoch, 1868–1929. |
    Millennialism—South Africa—History—20th century. | Bulhoek Massacre,
    Bulhoek, South Africa, 1921. | Massacres—South Africa—History—20th
    century.
Classification: LCC BR1450 .E34 2018 | DDC 236.9—dc23
LC record available at https://lccn.loc.gov/2017057359

Cover art: Enoch Mgijima in the crimson robe he wore at Israelite services.
(Author's collection)

To those who died at Marikana

And he gave unto Moses, when he had made an end of communing with him upon Mount Sinai, two tables of testimony, tables of stone, written with the finger of God.

—Exodus 31:18

I am not here to fight anybody or to cause only bloodshed, but if the finger of God has pointed out that "This" must be the place, no earthly place, no earthly force can prevent it. I did not call this gathering here every follower of mine came of his own free will. It may be the fulfillment of the Scriptures that say, "All my people will gather together for that journey to the promised land." And if this is the place, Bullhoek, no earthly power can interfere.

—Extract from a letter from Enoch Mgijima, mid-May 1921

Contents

Illustrations follow page 92.

Acknowledgments

No one will ever accuse me of rushing my scholarship to print. This study started as a graduate seminar paper at UCLA under the direction of Edward Alpers, and it has gradually evolved into its current form. Hence I have a lengthy list of people and institutions to thank.

My original research in 1973–74 was funded by a Fulbright-Hays dissertation grant. In South Africa I was assisted by staff at the National Library of South Africa in Cape Town and Pretoria, the University of Cape Town library, the Jaeger Library at Witwatersrand University, the Cory Library at Rhodes University, the South African Police Archive, the South African Defence Force Archive, and the National Archives in Cape Town and Pretoria. I have a fond memory of the Pretoria archive, which was then located in the Union Buildings and featured a tearoom that served a divine *melktart*. Among all the dedicated people who assisted me, I would like to single out Cory Library's Michael Berning and Sandy Rowoldt and Witwatersrand University's Anna Cunningham and Michelle Pickover, who were to assist me for decades to come on this and other projects. I vividly remember the Cory librarians alerting me to a file of rare *Abantu Batho* clippings on the Bulhoek massacre in 1994. At Rhodes University I was affiliated with the Institute for Social and Economic Research.

During my research in the Queenstown area I was hosted by Rev. Martin and Doris Eberle at Shiloh Mission Station near Whittlesea. Whites were not allowed to stay in black areas overnight, but mission stations were exempted from the rule. The Israelites were very helpful to me in setting up interviews and welcoming me to their services. In particular I would like to thank A. V. Ndlangisa, J. J. Mbayi, Albert Mgijima, and Gideon Ntloko. I have been fortunate in maintaining a friendship with Gideon that has extended to his children.

My primary academic position over the years has been at Howard University, where I enjoyed the backing of the Department of African Studies and some tolerant chairs, Bob Cummings, Sulayman Nyang, and Mbye Cham, who gave me free rein to tackle some unorthodox projects that most departments would have looked askance at. I have benefited from a supportive faculty and inspiring students. I also appreciate my affiliation with the Department of History at Stellenbosch University.

To whip this study into shape I have been fortunate to have readers who have made a valiant effort to check facts, reorganize the structure, and breathe life into my prose. Thanks to Helen Hopps, Andre Odendaal, Jeff Peires, MaryLouise Peires, Ben Carton, Chris Saunders, Rick Elphick, and Charles Villa Vicencio. A special thanks to Maria Kail for translating sources in German script and George Roupe for meticulously editing my manuscript.

Parts of several chapters have appeared in journals. An earlier version of chapter 1 was published as "The Prophet Motive: Enoch Mgijima and the Origins of the Israelite sect in South Africa" in the *International Journal of African Historical Studies* 15, no. 3 (1982): 201–20, while parts of chapter 6 were published as "The Ash-Heap of History: Reflections on Historical Research in Southern Africa" in *African Studies Quarterly* 9, no. 4 (2007), 47–61.

I acknowledge a debt to the League of Extraordinary Gentlemen who have not found a cure for the common cold and do not lose any sleep over it.

Finally, I want to thank my wonderful son, Leteane, who wakes up every day with an infectious smile, which makes it difficult for me to be the grumpy old man I aspire to be.

THE FINGER OF GOD

Introduction

South Africa is known throughout the world as a country where the most fierce forms of colour discrimination are practiced, and where peaceful struggles of the African people for freedom are violently suppressed. It is a country torn from top to bottom by fierce racial strife and where the blood of African patriots frequently flows. Almost every African household in South Africa knows about the massacre of our people at Bulhoek in the Queenstown district where detachments of the army and police, armed with artillery, machine-guns, and riles, opened fire on unarmed Africans.

—**Nelson Mandela** (1962)

Rough wet winds
parch my agonized face
as if salting the wounds of
Bulhoek
Sharpeville
Soweto

—**Mafika Gwala, "Tap-Tapping"** (1979)

Modern South African history has been punctuated with periodic bursts of government brutality. One of the earliest examples, the Bulhoek massacre, shook the morning of 24 May 1921. A force of eight hundred white policemen and soldiers confronted an African prophet, Enoch Mgijima, and some three thousand of his followers called the Israelites, who refused to leave their holy village of Ntabelanga ("the Mountain of the Rising Sun"), located about fifteen miles southwest of Queenstown in eastern Cape Province, where they had been gathering since early 1919 to await the end of the world. While the Israelites maintained they were there to pray and worship in peace, the white authorities viewed them as illegally squatting on land that was not theirs. After many months of fruitless negotiations with the Israelites, government officials finally sent out an armed force to Bulhoek to expel them. They had hoped the Israelites would agree to leave without a fight, but if it came to that, the police and soldiers were prepared to use their modern weapons.

The outcome of the battle was a foregone conclusion. The police arrived with rifles, machine guns, and cannon, while the Israelites carried only knobkerries, swords, and spears. After a twenty-minute skirmish nearly two hundred Israelites lay dead and many more were wounded. This event came to be known as the "Bulhoek massacre."

From the establishment of the Union of South Africa in 1910 to the present government in 2012, Bulhoek was but one of many occasions on which the government used brute force to crush people it cast as its "enemies." Port Elizabeth (1920), Bulhoek (1921), Bondelswarts (Namibia) (1922), Duncan Village (1952), Ngquza Hill (1960), Sharpeville (1960), Soweto (1976), Langa (1985), Queenstown (1985), Winterveld (1986), Bhisho (1992), and Marikana (2012) are all part of the lexicon of repression in which the state—before and after 1994—sanctioned its forces to slaughter its opponents. What distinguishes Bulhoek is that the government directed its power at a community of faith, whereas in the other cases, the government faced off against opponents voicing political and economic grievances.[1]

The Finger of God addresses the questions of how and why the Israelites and the South African government confronted each other on the morning of 24 May 1921. Specifically, this study asks why Mgijima prophesied that the end of the world was imminent and what led him to summon his followers to his holy village of Ntabelanga. Why did negotiations between the Israelites and the government break down? And why did the South African government ultimately regard the Israelite encampment as a challenge to its rule and send armed men to expel them?

A Land of Prophets and Prophetesses

Prophetic movements have left an indelible mark on South Africa's historical landscape. As Solomon Plaatje, a founder of South Africa's African National Congress, observed in his classic work *Native Life in South Africa*, "South Africa is a land of prophets and prophetesses."[2] Nowhere was this more true than in the eastern Cape, where in the century before Enoch Mgijima was called to prophecy, a wave of inspirational Xhosa visionaries appeared as European settlers began conquering their peoples' land and threatening their autonomy and offered explanations that spoke to their spiritual needs. These nineteenth-century prophets, working cooperatively with political leaders, conveyed varying visions about how to respond to the arrival of Europeans and the conquest of their land and whether to embrace or to reject Christianity and Western culture. Some prophets, such as Nxele and Mlanjeni, rejected the European presence and wielded their spiritual powers to mobilize resistance against colonial expansion. Others, such as Ntsikana, preached a different message—accommodating Christianity and translating Christian beliefs into terms that made sense to people who were grappling with the implications of European intrusions.

Although many Africans were exposed to the Christian message, few converted to the faith. As British conquest in the eastern Cape was nearly completed and after an outbreak of lung sickness decimated Xhosa cattle herds, Nongqawuse, a teenaged Gcaleka Xhosa prophetess, appeared on the scene in 1856, preaching a message of renewal in which the ancestors would intervene to restore African autonomy and prosperity and drive out Europeans.[3] After her uncle and the Gcaleka chief Sarhili validated her message by calling on their people to kill their cattle and destroy their grain, tens of thousands died of starvation, and many of the survivors were forced to abandon their land and seek employment in white areas.

By the early twentieth century, Enoch Mgijima and other prophets were operating in a radically changed environment, one in which whites had conquered huge chunks of African land in the eastern Cape and were establishing a colonial presence that entrenched their rule. Yet they had not dispossessed the Mgijimas of their lands. Chapter 1 narrates how Mgijima's Hlubi people arrived in the eastern Cape with other refugees who sought sanctuary among the Gcaleka Xhosa before casting their lot with the British. Known as Mfengu, some of these refugees entered into a triple covenant in which they swore allegiance to the British, converted to Christianity, and embraced mission education. The Mgijimas were among those rewarded with grants of land that they hoped would be their promised land. At first Mfengu families such as the Mgijimas prospered, but by the early twentieth century, many saw their economic and political fortunes declining and were receptive to new ideas and leaders. In addition, a number of black Christian converts were critically questioning how white missionaries were defining their new faith, especially their condemnation of many African cultural practices, and were establishing their own churches with their own leaders and interpreting their faith in different ways. Enoch Mgijima was an independent evangelist who received a vision from God in April 1907 that eventually led him to break with the Moravian and Wesleyan Methodist missionaries who had invited him to preach at their mission stations.

Although steeped in Christian theology, Mgijima drew inspiration from the Old Testament book of Exodus, which narrates the story of the Hebrews' exile, captivity, flight, wandering in the wilderness, and search for a promised land. Seeing the parallels with his life experiences, he crafted a liberation theology for his followers, known as the Israelites.

Chapter 2 delves into the theological connection Mgijima made with an African American prophet, William Saunders Crowdy, and his Church of God and Saints of Christ. One of the ways that black South African Christians carried on a rich transatlantic exchange with African Americans was that they drew parallels with how African American Christians had established their own church institutions and leadership to cope with white oppression and discrimination and express their spirituality. While Mgijima could have reached out to African American churches such as the African Methodist Episcopal Church, which had recently established missions in southern Africa, he chose to join a denomination that gave him free rein for his prophetic leadership and a theology based on Exodus and its central ritual observance, the Passover. Indeed, some African American and black South African religious groups such as the Israelites so closely identified with the Old Testament that they regarded themselves as black Jews.[4]

Chapter 2 narrates Crowdy's prophetic life and his message and how his group established itself in the United States and then spread to South Africa and brought Mgijima into its fold. Mgijima's apocalyptic moment came in 1919 when he called on his followers to move to Ntabelanga to prepare for the coming millennium. This chapter assesses the political and economic factors and natural disasters such as drought and the Spanish influenza pandemic of 1918 that fueled their expectations.

Understanding the Massacre

The heart of this study unfolds in chapters 3 and 4. They focus on the years 1920 and 1921 as the Israelites gathered at their holy village and set off a prolonged series of confrontations with government officials, first at the local and then at the national level. These culminated in the Bulhoek massacre. Because secular authorities and the leaders of millennial movements hold vastly different worldviews, they create such negative perceptions of each other that they almost inevitably end up clashing rather than resolving their differences. Hence the state pressure on the Israelites to leave Ntabelanga reinforced their self-image as a group persecuted for their expectation that Jehovah was on their side. For their part, white officials interpreted Israelite intransigence as a challenge to government authority.

Chapter 3 deals with the first phase of the confrontation, which stretched from early 1919 to the end of the following year. After Mgijima summoned his followers to Ntabelanga and it became apparent they intended to stay at their sacred site indefinitely, a Cape Province Native Affairs official and the Queenstown magistrate defined the problem in legal terms. Officials issued summonses for Israelite "strangers" to appear in court for illegally squatting on Crown land. None honored them. In the ensuing months, as Ntabelanga became a self-sufficient, autonomous community that aroused fear in both black and white neighbors, Mgijima and his adherents transgressed a fundamental understanding that whites held about proper race relations—that blacks had to show deference to white settler authority.

Chapter 4 covers the second phase of the stand-off, which began after the government dispatched almost one hundred police officers to intimidate the Israelites into backing down in December 1920. A large force of Israelite men stood their ground and forced the police to retreat. From then until the massacre on 24 May 1921 relations continued to deteriorate between the Israelites and government officials as well as with moderate Africans, white and African farmers, and the Native Affairs Commission, which the state had established to liaise with Africans on a range of issues. The government perceived the Israelites as threatening black-white relations nationally and interpreted their ritual practices such as marching and wielding swords during services as a sign that they were plotting a general uprising. In the end, officials weighed their options and decided they had no choice but to use brute force to put an end to the Israelite resistance.

Something that stands out about the South African government's perception of the Israelites was its utter lack of comprehension of what millennial movements were about. That should not be surprising, since it was not until after World War II that social scientists began critically examining millennial movements of the past and present and gaining an understanding of how and why they emerge. As a result, we have become aware of how common end-of-time movements were in early Christianity[5] as well as how often these kinds of groups clashed with secular authorities during the era of colonial rule and still clash with them in modern times.[6]

Thus the South African government in 1921 was not unique in misinterpreting the intentions of the Israelites. Most modern-day governments still have a fundamental misunderstanding of the dynamics of millennial movements and erroneously assume that they are motivated by violent or self-destructive impulses. They find it difficult to comprehend that these kinds of religious movements might be passive and are not necessarily prone to aggressive behavior.

They also negotiate with millennial groups in a way that can lead to violent showdowns. An example of a government mishandling a situation like Bulhoek is how the American government dealt with David Koresh and the Branch Davidians, who took over a compound at Mount Carmel near Waco, Texas, to await Christ's Second Coming. Convinced the Branch Davidians had a sinister plan to purchase gun parts with the intent of building up an arsenal of dangerous weapons, the U.S. government's Bureau of Alcohol, Tobacco, and Firearms (ATF) engaged in a shootout with Koresh's group on 28 February 1993, resulting in the deaths of four ATF agents and six Branch Davidians. The FBI then took over the operation and laid siege to the compound for fifty-one days. FBI negotiators had such contempt for Koresh and the Branch Davidians that they did not seriously examine their beliefs or consider an alternative way of dealing with them other than through force. They ignored the advice of several religious studies scholars who had established their own theological dialogue with Koresh and who were convinced that he would have given up peacefully if he had been allowed to complete an exposition on the book of Revelation. Ultimately the U.S. attorney general, Janet Reno, believing that the Branch Davidians were mistreating children and preparing to blow themselves up and kill as many government agents as possible, approved an attack on 19 April 1993. Tear gas pumped into the compound set off a conflagration that killed Koresh and seventy-six of his congregants.[7]

The Legacy of Bulhoek

Chapter 5 explores how the Bulhoek massacre has reverberated in South Africa for almost a century. The Sharpeville massacre in which police mowed down demonstrators protesting pass laws on 21 March 1960 is the best known of South African massacres and has received both national and international recognition. The date 21 March is now South Africa's Human Rights Day and the United Nations' International Day for the Elimination of Racial Discrimination.[8] However, Bulhoek has been the subject of much discussion and debate in South Africa about the lessons that can be drawn from it and how it should be remembered and memorialized.

In the massacre's immediate aftermath, white and black commentators generally took diametrically opposing sides in assessing the blame for the massacre. Although a few African newspaper editors sided with the government, accepting its contention that the Israelites' religious beliefs were a cover for fomenting armed rebellion, most black opinion, represented by the South African Native National Congress (SANNC), the precursor of the African National Congress, and black labor unions, sympathized with the Israelites. *Abantu Batho,* the mouthpiece of the SANNC, editorialized that the massacre did not have to be the inevitable outcome of the Israelite-government showdown and that the government should have explored other alternatives to resolve the issue.[9] Would the government have treated a white religious group in the same callous fashion? As *Abantu Batho* saw it, the government was just as fanatical as the Israelites. How and why, it asked, did the Israelite defiance of the government escalate from being a simple case of trespassing to become a major threat to the state?[10]

Most whites, on the other hand, sympathized with the government's crackdown on the Israelites and pinned the blame for the massacre on a combination of African inability to evolve beyond so-called primitive, heretical religious beliefs. A letter to the *Cape Times* highlighted the Israelites' misreading of biblical truths. The Bible had become "a most dangerous book . . . in the hands of these natives—the Old Testament. If you taught these people that those miracles of the Bible had really happened in the past, what was to prevent their believing that they were to happen again?"[11] The writer Sarah Gertrude Millin, in her sympathetic portrait of Jan Smuts, the prime minister at the time of the Bulhoek massacre, also pointed to the excessive religiosity of Africans: "The African natives like religion. There are over two hundred fifty Christian sects among them, and many profess Mohammedanism. They were delighted with the comprehensive character of the new religion, and they added to it a bit of native belief, and so trebly assured salvation."[12] She blamed the Israelites for waging a campaign of "terror and terrorization" against its opponents, whether black or white.[13]

Chapter 5 also looks at the lessons the government drew from the massacre and how it dealt with a spate of other prophetic and millennial movements that appeared around the country, especially in the eastern Cape. The government viewed them with suspicion but refrained from using force. In the case of Nontetha Nkwenkwe, another eastern Cape visionary, officials attempted to silence her by declaring her mentally ill and institutionalizing her in several mental asylums.

Finally, chapter 5 treats how the government, before and after 1994, has remembered and memorialized the massacre. In the years before 1994 the official perspective on the massacre was inscribed in museum displays that justified the government's version, while supporters of the freedom movement enshrined Bulhoek as a part of their heroic struggle against white oppression. To encourage a dramatically different narrative about the South African past, the post-apartheid government erected a memorial at the massacre's site and has promoted it on one of its heritage trails.

Reflections on Research

One of the challenges of reconstructing the Bulhoek story was identifying sources that reveal Israelite perspectives. Most of the written documents I retrieved came from government archives that preserve the official perspective. Historians trying to get at black perspectives have to read such documents against the grain by asking probing questions and by creating alternative archives based on oral testimonies, music, and visual evidence from photographs and artwork and other manifestations of material culture.

While conducting research on Mgijima and the Israelites in the Queenstown area in 1974, I constructed a counternarrative by collecting the memories and written histories of the Israelites themselves, especially those who were at Bulhoek the day of the massacre and their descendants. However, because of apartheid's racial divide, the Israelites at first were understandably reserved toward me since blacks were generally suspicious of whites. Who else but a white police detective would raise questions about their personal lives and an explosive event in the past? However, the Israelites had had prior experience interacting with white anthropologists. Once I began attending Israelite services and their first commemoration of the Bulhoek massacre on 24 May 1974, they gradually welcomed me. I was fortunate to interview about a dozen Israelite men and women who had been present at the massacre and to receive accounts several Israelites wrote for me about their group's history and their prophet's life. Their voices provided a radically different picture of what transpired. This does not mean that a historian uncritically accepts oral accounts, but oral evidence is an important antidote to the overwhelming preponderance of written, especially official, sources, which follow their own logic.

Because the official view often prevails in historical accounts of millennial movements, their perspective can sway even the most independent-minded historian. In South Africa I initially searched for primary documentation at the national archive in Pretoria, which contains records of the central government.[14] My experience there validated the judgment of the editors of *Refiguring the Archive* that "archives are often both documents of exclusion and monuments to particular configurations of power."[15] Although official files contain a wealth of information on government dealings with the Israelites, they reveal very little about the group's history, motivations, and religious beliefs. The same is true of white newspapers, missionary journals, private papers, and diaries that I consulted. The vocabulary the South African government (and the white press) consistently used to demonize the Israelites included words such as fanatical, deluded, mad men, irrational, misguided, strange, subversives, and lawbreakers. Relying on these sources can easily lead one to place the onus for the carnage at Bulhoek on Israelite fanaticism and their uncompromising stance and to conclude that they were laying the groundwork for a general uprising.

Historians depending exclusively on the official side inevitably see events through the eyes of the state. Hence D. H. Dikobe, a historian for the Documentation Services Directorate of the South African National Defense Force, wrote a series of articles on the Bulhoek massacre relying exclusively on government—in particular defense force—records.[16] His conclusion not surprisingly was that the government's approach to the Israelites, including the use of force, was justified. Clifton Crais, who treated the Israelites sympathetically in *The Politics of Evil*, relied heavily on trial transcripts to conclude that the Israelites were arming themselves and preparing for an armed rebellion against the government.[17] My own reading is that the Israelites were not planning an uprising and that their "weapons," such as swords and drills, were an integral part of their rituals.

Researching Mgijima and the Israelites and Nontetha Nkwenkwe over an extended period also led me to some unconventional personal experiences after 1994 that I reflect on in chapter 6. The first took place in 1995 when I initiated a search for the Israelites' most revered relic, their Ark of the Covenant that police seized after the massacre. The Ark had gone missing for over seven decades until a fortuitous circumstance allowed me to identify the museum in Grahamstown where it was being stored and to set in motion a process to return it to the Israelites. The second was tracking down the grave of Nontetha Nkwenkwe, who died in a state mental hospital in Pretoria and had been buried anonymously in a pauper's grave, and helping to arrange for her remains to be exhumed and returned to her home village in 1998. The final case happened in 2000 when Israelite elders tasked me with searching for the grave of Charles Mgijima, the Israelite prophet's brother, who died in a Kimberley prison in 1924 and was buried in a local cemetery. They wanted to find his grave so they could bring his remains home.

My experiences raise questions about how we historians go about our research. Who is our audience and what should our relationship be with the wider community? Should we be primarily responsible to our craft and interact with other professional historians, or should we directly engage with the individuals, groups, and communities we write about? My own view is that we should do both, and that those of us who work on South Africa's past have a special obligation to use our talents and training to address injustices and wrongs that the government perpetrated throughout much of the twentieth century—and even into the twenty-first. Because the government often meticulously documented its actions, historians can apply their skills to mine official archives for documents that the average person is unable or reluctant to consult. Until the 1990s, most black South Africans viewed state archives as hostile or alien territory.

1 The Promised Land

The origins of Enoch Mgijima's confrontation with the government extend back to dramatic transformations that drove Africans to search for secure "promised lands." One of these developments involved the "turbulent times" of the Mfecane, an early nineteenth-century eruption of political conflicts and widespread migrations in southern Africa. The other experience—of war and violent conquest—was unleashed by British colonists seizing African land in the eastern Cape.

The first development emerged from the often violent centralization and fragmentation of chiefdoms.[1] Historians are still assessing the causes of these momentous changes, among them increasingly hostile competition over trade routes from Delagoa Bay and the Cape interior, population growth resulting in environmental stresses, and fierce struggles over cattle and grazing land. These conflicts propelled movements of people from present-day South Africa to as far north as Zambia, Malawi, and Tanzania. On the way, these migrants remade their ethnic identities.[2] Near the epicenter of this turmoil in what is now KwaZulu Natal, some groups, including Mgijima's family, fled their ancestral homes southward along the Indian Ocean coast, where they began to be assimilated into isiXhosa-speaking communities.

The second experience, triggered by colonists encroaching on the lands of isiXhosa-speaking groups living between the Kei and Sunday Rivers, severely disrupted the eastern Cape for many decades. The first European newcomers were Boer cattle keepers who trekked into the region in the early eighteenth century. Their desultory struggles with Xhosa cattle keepers over grazing pastures sparked a few heated skirmishes in which the balance of power did not change. The arrival of British forces in 1806, however, altered everything. Throughout the nineteenth century they gradually conquered most of southern Africa, and in the eastern Cape their military might was decisive. After they exerted "a proper degree of terror" to subjugate Chief Ndlambe's Xhosa in 1812, the British army ruthlessly prosecuted wars in 1819, 1834–35, 1846–47, and 1850–53 that opened up land for white settlement.[3] Although imperial officials in London resolved to return some territory to Xhosa following the 1834–35 war, white wool farmers living in the eastern Cape since the early 1820s successfully lobbied to overturn this decision in the next decade.

The end result was the disintegration of Xhosa sovereignty into factional strife, which the British manipulated, in part to forge strategic military alliances with groups like Mgijima's Mfengu people, who gave their soldiers and loyalty to the crown in three wars in return for grants of land.

Exile

The Mgijimas were among the families displaced by the upheavals of the Mfecane. Their journey to the eastern Cape began in the foothills of the Ukahlamba/Drakensberg when family members joined the Hlubi diaspora after Matiwane's Ngwane smashed Chief Mthimkulu's Hlubi chiefdom around 1819 in what the Hlubi call the *izwekufa*, "the destruction of the nation."[4] The Hlubi splintered into a number of groups. One headed north to the Highveld and joined the many groups contesting for power. Some found sanctuary among Moshoeshoe's Basotho kingdom, while others continued further, crossing the Orange River into what became known as the Herschel district. Another band under Chief Langalibalele also migrated into Sotho-speaking areas before heading back to the east, where they established a base in the Estcourt area. Yet another group moved southwest to Griqualand East around Qumbu and Matatiele. The Mgijimas, including Enoch Mgijima's grandfather, Mgijima, and his father, Jonas Mayekiso, were part of a fourth group under the leadership of Matomela and one of the sons of Mthimkulu II, Mhlambiso, who also trekked to the southwest, passing through Griqualand East and Thembuland before finding sanctuary among the Gcaleka Xhosa.

During the 1820s many emigrants, including Hlubi groups, settled among the Gcaleka kingdom. Because many of the groups were impoverished, the Gcaleka began calling them by a collective name, "Mfengu," a word derived from *siyamfenguza*, meaning "we are hungry and seeking shelter." The Gcaleka and Mfengu and European missionaries and colonial administrators put forward two very different explanations about how the Gcaleka treated them. The Gcaleka/Mfengu version casts the Gcaleka in a favorable light, maintaining that their chief Hintsa received them as he would have any newcomers by giving them the opportunity to incorporate themselves into Gcaleka society.[5] Through a customary practice of client-ship called *busa,* "strangers" attached themselves to Gcaleka households as clients, which provided them with enough milk and grain to support their families and the means to replenish their cattle herds. Eventually, they aimed to put themselves on an independent footing. Even though they had full rights and responsibilities during the early stages of assimilation, the Mfengu clearly played a subordinate role. On the other hand, British missionaries and colonial administrators depicted the Mfengu as a class of oppressed slaves who seized the opportunity to escape Gcaleka over-lordship and move into British-controlled territory across the Kei River.

Leaving aside the two different interpretations, it is clear that many Mfengu did not assimilate smoothly into Gcaleka society. During their wanderings the multiple shocks that Hlubi and other emigrant groups experienced left a deep-rooted distrust of outsiders and made them wary of extending loyalty to any host group, however generous they might be. They concealed who their chiefs were, fearing that they would be killed if their identities were exposed.[6] Richard Moyer has argued that the trauma and insecurities they experienced during their migrations and settling among Xhosa groups were critical in developing a suspicion of both whites and other Africans and their lack of "faith in their capacity to protect themselves" and "in their leaders and ancestral spirits."[7]

If external forces had not disrupted the developing relationship between Mfengu and Gcaleka, perhaps the assimilation process ultimately might have been successful, but the Mfengu arrived as the Gcaleka were starting to resist colonial conquest. Many Mfengu did not automatically identify with the Xhosa cause and instead transferred their loyalty to the British, whom they did not initially perceive as enemies and who also appeared to have the military advantage and lands to offer them. In the 1834–35 war between the Gcaleka and the British, many Mfengu either remained neu-tral or openly worked for the British as intelligence gatherers, messengers, and soldiers.[8] Shortly after the British forces crossed the Kei River into Hintsa's territory, they were joined by Mfengu chiefs and herdsmen who brought along their own cattle or seized them from their employers. The British settled them between the Fish and Keiskamma Rivers. By ceding this land to the Mfengu, the British thought that the Mfengu would be bound to them for protection and would remain faithful allies.

On the British side was the Wesleyan Methodist missionary John Ayliff, who oversaw the mission station at Butterworth in the Gcaleka chiefdom. The Wesleyans had commenced their work in the eastern Cape with the thirty-five hundred English colonists who settled in the Albany district in 1820. One of them was Ayliff, an unapologetic defender of British imperial rule. He saw God's hand at work in human history in both the allocation of land to the Old Testament Israelites and the expansion of the British Empire. "Hence it is that GOD has given to Britain more colonial territory than to all Europe; she is marked out by Providence to be the great mother of Empires."[9] He did, however, draw an interesting comparison between the fate of the Israelites and the Xhosa people. Just as the Israelites lost their "original inheritance," so, too, did the Xhosa because they failed to adequately develop the land: "The former inhabitants of this part of the world has [sic] not answered the purpose for which infinite Goodness and Wisdom had given them this land as their habitation. He appointed another people, speaking another language, to succeed them, planting them in this land, and giving them Albany for a possession."[10]

Determined to spread the Gospel to the "unblessed" and to develop the "vast natural and moral [African] wilderness," Ayliff became a Wesleyan missionary assistant in 1825 among slaves, Khoikhoi, and Xhosas. Six years later he took up residence at Butterworth, one of a chain of Wesleyan mission stations stretching from the eastern Cape to Natal. In 1835, he put another spin on providential design by describing the Mfengu migrations and what he called their delivery from Gcaleka bondage as another manifestation of God's will: "They were ignorant of Isreal's [sic] God, they knew nothing of his Providence, but were a host of desolate, destitute, wandering savages, wandering they knew not where—though in subsequent days a change from darkness to light, and from the power of Satan to God, has made them acquainted with that hand, which though unknown and unacknowledged, was leading their weary steps to a land of liberty and peace."[11]

Successive generations of Wesleyan clergy and many Mfengu converts accepted as gospel Ayliff's portrayal of the Mfengu as abject slaves longing to be freed from their cruel Gcaleka masters. According to Ayliff's narrative, Gcaleka overlords held the Mfengu in a state of bondage, treating them like "dogs." They tended Gcaleka cattle, milked their cows, cultivated and harvested their crops, and constructed their houses; in return, the Mfengu received only a pittance, milk and a few skins. Whenever any Mfengu were successful at growing their own crops, acquiring cattle, or selling skins, the Gcaleka would confiscate a sizable portion. This led the Mfengu to develop a "defensive armour of deception," to carry on trading in secret and hiding their cattle in remote glens and kloofs or to mixing them with the herds of sympathetic neighbors.[12]

As some Mfengu began settling at Ayliff's mission station and attending services, Hintsa began to feel that the missionaries were destabilizing his kingdom. On one occasion when he attended a church service with Mfengu in attendance, Ayliff claimed that Hintsa said: "This word may suit my dogs, the Fingos, but I and my people will not have it."[13] Relations between Hintsa and Ayliff continued to deteriorate until war broke out in December 1834 after warriors of two rival Xhosa chiefdoms, the Ndlambe and Ngqika, invaded white territory in the eastern Cape. During the war many more Mfengu began to settle at Butterworth and protected Ayliff's home even after he was forced to leave the area in February 1835.

Mission societies were not of a single mind about the war. Missionaries of the London Missionary Society generally opposed it, while Wesleyan missionaries, along with British settlers, were vocal proponents. Ayliff, whose advocacy of British imperialism was both well established and doctrinally blessed, gathered intelligence on the movement of Gcaleka forces for the British. He actively lobbied British officials about the plight of Mfengu in the Gcaleka kingdom and the necessity for British support in their escape from bondage. When the British commander, Col. Harry Smith, promised that the British would help the Mfengu "at a befitting time," Ayliff told his Mfengu supporters "that before long they would be under the shield of British protection and most probably removed from Kaffirland to the Colony."[14]

At the time the British were on the verge of invading Hintsa's Gcaleka kingdom and the Cape Colony's governor, Benjamin D'Urban, was looking for justifications to prosecute the war across the Kei. Since slaves were being freed in the Cape Colony as well as throughout the British Empire on 1 December 1834, he seized the opportunity to proclaim that he was also liberating the Mfengu "from the very lowest and worst state of slavery." As D'Urban phrased it, Mfengu emancipation conformed to "the true spirit of the sweeping emancipation so recently made by the Mother Country."[15] In keeping with the abolitionist argument that freed slaves would eventually be transformed into "free labor," D'Urban anticipated that the Mfengu would become a reliable source of workers for white farmers who chronically complained about a shortage of black labor. The governor was able to cloak practical ends with humanitarian zeal.

After declaring war on the Gcaleka on 24 April 1835, D'Urban agreed to meet with members of a Mfengu delegation near Butterworth. They had come to ask for the king of England's protection. On 3 May he issued Government Notice no. 14, which granted settlement rights to Mfengu refugees in an "uninhabited and worse than useless district" between the Fish and Lower Keiskamma Rivers and, to add to that magnanimous gesture, declared them British subjects. He described them as an "industrious, gentle, and well disposed tribe, good herdsman, good agriculturalists" and in an interesting turn of phrase, "useful servants."[16] For the Mfengu the offer amounted to trading one servitude for another. But for the governor it was a move to use the Mfengu not only as a buffer between European colonists and Xhosa groups but also as guides and fighters for the British in future wars of Xhosa dispossession.[17]

According to Ayliff's account, when Hintsa heard his "dogs" had sought protection from the British, he ordered retribution against them. But Hintsa rescinded his order after D'Urban bluntly told him he would execute two of Hintsa's entourage for every Mfengu he killed. D'Urban then offered sanctuary to the Mfengu and called on Ayliff to accompany refugees to land allocated for them near Fort Peddie.

The Exodus

Taking advantage of the offer, on 6 May 1835, Jonas Mayekiso Mgijima and his family joined the nearly seventeen thousand men, women, and children who took their belongings and over twenty thousand head of cattle (including cattle Gcaleka claimed were stolen from them) and flocks of goats and sheep on a trek across the Kei River. While a number of Mfengu stayed among the Xhosa, the majority accompanied Ayliff and his family and other missionaries and traders in wagons and formed a massive column with an escort of British troops in the rear. The column—described as eight miles in length and one and a half miles in breadth—took ten days to traverse the one hundred miles to a site near Fort Peddie. Even without the drama of pharaoh's chariots in hot pursuit and the parting of the Red Sea, the parallel of the Mfengu exodus with that of the biblical Israelites was not lost on James Alexander, an aide to Harry Smith. "Nothing like this flight had been seen, perhaps, since the days of Moses, and it was a just retribution on Hintza [*sic*], and on his people, who exercised the power of life and death over the Fingoes at will, and without appeal; and regarded them in little higher estimation than beasts." Pleased to witness an escape of such biblical proportions, Alexander also took pleasure in the fact that the Mfengu would benefit the white settlers by serving both as allies in defending the Cape Colony and as laborers, herdsmen, and shepherds on white farms.[18]

When the Mfengu arrived at Fort Peddie, Ayliff marked the occasion by convening a mass meeting near an *umqwashu* (milkwood) tree at Mqwashini. He reminded them of what the Wesleyans and the British government had done for them and appealed to them to enter into a triple covenant with the British government and the Wesleyan church. Raising their right hands, the Mfengu pledged "to be faithful to God, to be loyal to the British Government, and to do all in their power to support the missionaries and educate their children."[19] In exchange, they expected the British to reward their loyal service with land grants.

Despite Ayliff's portrayal of himself as both the defender and liberator of the Mfengu, one has to wonder how devoted he was to their cause. The entries in his personal diary began in the early 1830s and ended in March 1835 when the war broke out and he had to flee Butterworth for the safety of Clarkebury mission station. He curiously characterized the Mfengu as "poor" and "oppressed" only once, in July 1834.[20] Instead, his entries concentrated on other pressing concerns such as witchcraft and circumcision, Christian conversions, baptisms, and confirmation classes. He had regular exchanges with Hintsa, which were often frank but rarely cordial. But at no point did he question him about his treatment of the Mfengu. For instance, on 3 September 1834, Hintsa and his counselors approached Ayliff about vacating his mission and joining them because they were considering relocating to vacant land to the north. Ayliff resisted the idea, maintaining that he had to stay with his flock rather than moving to an area of potential danger.[21] Several days later, Hintsa sent Ayliff a gift of an ox as an "expression of good will" and expressed his desire to have a missionary accompany him to his new home.[22] Nevertheless, toward the end of the year, relations between the two badly deteriorated.

However one assesses Ayliff's dedication to the Mfengu cause, his rendering of the story became an article of faith to Wesleyan missionaries.[23]

Mfengu converts were one reason why the Wesleyans became the most popular mission denomination in the Cape. By 1891 the Wesleyans could boast of 91,000 African members, while the Anglicans, the second most popular denomination, lagged far behind with 13,100.

Mission Accomplished?

As European colonizers and African rulers fiercely contested political and economic sovereignty, devotees of mission Christianity and believers in indigenous cosmologies also engaged in a "battle for sacred power." Both sides questioned the foundation and authority of each other's spiritual truths. Janet Hodgson has divided this duel into three phases, the first being an "open frontier" in which neither side dominated.[24] Even though colonial rule ultimately triumphed, at no point did Africans, whether Christian converts or not, stop raising challenging questions about what Christianity meant for them personally and collectively.

In the phase of the "open frontier," European missionaries by and large did not believe that Xhosa societies had developed religious and moral concepts of their own. Dr. J. T. Van der Kemp, a London Missionary Society stalwart and an advocate of rights for indigenous peoples, argued that because Xhosa had not created a rigorous systematic theology, they could not have any sense of religious beliefs until they came into contact with external influences. "I never could perceive," he asserted, "that they had any religion, nor any idea of the existence of a God."[25] This became the prevalent notion, uncritically accepted, among most European missionaries in the eastern Cape. A Wesleyan Methodist historian William Moister summed up their view when he called African societies "degraded tribes" and contended that, except for the veneration of the ancestors and a belief in witchcraft, "the Kaffirs have, properly speaking, no religious system of their own, and consequently no forms of worship."[26] Because they were a tabula rasa, the missionaries felt they had an obligation to fill it in with their version of Christianity. Eugene Casalis, a French missionary representing the Paris Evangelical Mission Society in Moshoeshoe's Basotho kingdom, asserted that Christianity builds "the everlasting columns of truth in the place of the feeble props it destroys."[27] Or as Mary Kingsley, an English critic of European missionaries who ventured to West Africa in the 1890s, put it, missionaries came to view "African minds as so many jugs, which had only to be emptied of the stuff that is in them and refilled with the particular form of doctrine they, the missionaries, are engaged in teaching."[28]

Not all Europeans shared the mind-set of these missionaries. Quite an opposite opinion was held by the Wesleyan missionary W. M. S. Shrewsbury, who wrote that the Xhosa were "an acute and inquisitive people, and peculiarly evidencing a natural tendency to skepticism, since they are more ready at raising objections against divine truth, than at receiving it with a meek and lowly mind."[29] In a similar vein, Dunbar Moodie, a British military officer who served in the eastern Cape in the 1820s, contended that the Xhosa did not receive Christianity uncritically. Instead they interrogated and probed its doctrines and beliefs. "The [Xhosa] are a reasoning and independent people, who have no prejudices in favour of Christianity, and have no immediate interest to serve by adopting our religion; and it is only by argument that they are to be convinced of its truths."[30] Moodie was not surprised that so few Africans converted to Christianity when missionaries harped on so much about "sinful behavior" that they drained the vitality and joyfulness from church services. He also observed that because the different denominations emphasized their distinctive doctrines and their differences from each other, they were unable to convince people of the universal qualities that are at the heart of Christianity.

Instead of looking for common spiritual ground, most white missionaries were more concerned with touting the benefits of their particular brand of Christianity. They rarely examined African religious beliefs seriously. Hildegarde Fast's study amply illustrates how Xhosa people challenged the contradictions they saw in the missionaries' lifestyles and messages. For instance, the Wesleyan missionary Samuel Young was peppered with a series of penetrating questions: "Some asked what had become of all the old people who died before the Gospel came into the country; others wanted to know where Adam and Eve now are, whether they were saved or lost; some asked where God stood when he made the world, for they thought he could not have made a world like this without a proper standing place; others wanted to know . . . why God did not destroy Satan for introducing sin into the world, and causing so much confusion." Others asked why missionaries, who were advocating universal brotherhood, lived separately from Africans and why they were so quick to condemn African cultural practices? Why was it that God had limited his message to Europeans for such a long time, neglecting most Africans until the nineteenth century? How could God have offered up his son to such a cruel death? To whom were missionaries ultimately loyal, and were they less concerned with saving souls than with recruiting black soldiers and spies to conquer more African land? Why did missionaries tell their listeners to seek and prepare for the afterlife rather than addressing how to cope with the here and now? [31]

Persistent questioning and a variety of other forces in the nineteenth century impeded the efforts of white missionaries to win converts. Even among Mfengu, they met with little success. And even after a trickle of Africans began converting to the new faith, the new Christians still questioned Christianity's tenets and how the church accommodated African cultural practices. Such skepticism and doubt were especially characteristic of the independent church and prophet leaders who began to appear in the late nineteenth and early twentieth centuries challenging the verities of mission Christianity.

Kamastone

Only a small fraction of the Mfengu in the Peddie area actually found land and remained there. The rest became part of a far-flung Mfengu diaspora scattered about the region and beyond. Although a few were allocated conquered land elsewhere, most were forced to become laborers on white farms or in towns. While it took the Mgijimas many years to find a permanent home, according to Mgijima family lore, Mgijima, Enoch's grandfather, and his family were among those who followed Ayliff to the Peddie area.

The Mgijimas subsequently joined a pocket of Hlubis under Chief Mhlambiso, who had been granted land along the Orange River in the Herschel district. During the wars of 1846 and 1850 they joined Mfengu levies fighting for the British against Ndlambe and Ngqika Xhosa and their allies. Following these wars, two successive colonial governors, George Cathcart and George Grey, created buffer zones between "hostile" Africans and Cape colonists. This approach had the dual virtue of protecting the Cape frontier from a new outbreak of war and ensuring that white farmers would have reliable supplies of labor, since the land grants were not adequate to support all the Africans living in the area. Following the 1850–53 war, the British seized land in the Queenstown area from Chief Mapasa's Thembu and divided it up in a checkerboard pattern among white settlers, British army veterans, and African allies. Mfengu loyalists had assumed their service to the British would be rewarded with generous land concessions, but of the 1,794 square miles of land distributed in the Queenstown region, the British parceled out a meager 214 to Africans.

Queenstown, named to commemorate the queen's victory, was established at a trading site on the Komani River in September 1853. Along with Aliwal North and Whittlesea, it was one link in the chain of towns in the European corridor between the African reserves known as the Ciskei and Transkei. Laid out in a hexagonal pattern, with six streets radiating from a central market area, Queenstown was designed with security in mind and planned so that white farmers could easily move into town in case of an African attack.

When Mgijima's son Jonas grew dissatisfied with his lot in Herschel district, he looked for a place to settle in the newly opened black reserves near Queenstown. At the time of the cattle killings in 1856, he journeyed on horseback, first to Hewu to speak with the Wesleyan minister William Shepstone and then to the Amatole Basin to ask the Hlubi chief, Mhlambiso, for a new residence. Jonas was granted permission to settle along the Black Kei River at Ntabelanga, located about fifteen miles southwest of Queenstown.[32] The land Mgijima was allocated was situated at Bulhoek, a sublocation at the northernmost tip of the Ciskei bracketed on three sides by white farms.

In 1846 the War of the Axe broke out between alliances of the British, Khoikhoi, Mfengu, and British and Afrikaner settlers and Ngqika, Thembu, and some Ndlambe groups. When the conflict ended the following year, the area had been designated for Chief Kama, a Wesleyan convert, and his Gqunukwebe Xhosa, as a reward for loyal service to the British. Following the war of 1850–53, the British allocated Kama and his people new lands further south in the Keiskamma area and settled new residents, predominantly Mfengu, in their place at Oxkraal and Kamastone.[33]

The Kamastone location, which encompassed Ntabelanga, had roughly three thousand inhabitants and was comparable to other predominantly Mfengu locations in the Ciskei and Transkei.[34] British and Cape officials as well as white missionaries created an idealized identity of what they hoped the Mfengu would aspire to become, that is, Christians who embraced Western culture and education, loyalists to the Crown who rejected chieftainship, and agriculturalists who produced for the market on individual plots of land. They were to serve as an example of "civilized" behavior for other Africans to emulate. In 1865 an agricultural society for Africans at Kamastone, Glen Grey, and Lesseyton was established to put on an annual show that would "raise blacks from the low depths of barbarism to which they are now, to the more genial influences of civilization" by encouraging black farmers to become "producers" rather than "consumers." At the first show at Kamastone in April 1865, C. D. Griffith, the civil commissioner, addressing the crowd in Dutch, stressed that the show's goal was "to teach you habits of honesty and industry" through improved agriculture and stock rearing. Judges handed out prizes in a range of categories for animals (horses, pigs, milk cows, oxen, rams, sheep) and agricultural products (mealies, pumpkins, tobacco, beans, barley, and linseed). John Dondolo ended the 1865 show by calling on the audience to join him in shouting: *Three cheers for the Queen, and we serve the English* (italics in original).[35]

But no matter how much some Mfengu tried to assume this identity and follow the missionaries' script, in reality, white policies and practices often made it extremely difficult for them to fulfill their prescribed roles. When there was a discussion in 1864 about blacks having to give up "certificates of citizenship" they now held, a Kamastone headman shrewdly raised the question that since the aim of the certificates was making them white men, why was the government making a distinction in which some "white men" would have total freedom to do what they liked, while other "white men" had to carry passes? If that were the case, he wondered, "What was the use of being *white men*" (italics in original).[36]

In fact a large number of Mfengu did not convert to Christianity, but in Kamastone many did join mission churches that were a prominent feature of the location. By the end of the nineteenth century, the Wesleyan Methodists and Presbyterians together claimed about thirteen hundred adherents, but of the two denominations, the Wesleyans had the stronger support. Their mission was allotted a four-hundred-acre site, and a chapel was opened in 1856. The featured speaker on that occasion was Rev. Henry Dugmore, pastor of Queenstown's Methodist church, who crafted his sermon around Deuteronomy 8:2. His message of providential design must have resonated with many in his audience. Just as God shielded the children of Israel as they wandered through the wilderness for forty years before bringing them into the promised land, he would surely do the same for Kamastone's Mfengu. Dugmore "dwelt on the providential dealings of

God with the Fingoe tribes in those wars which had caused their dispersion, their wanderings, and afflictions, until, by a chain of providence,
they had been brought into their present happy circumstances, under the
benign and paternal rule of British power."[37]

In mid-July 1867 a revival brought many more converts into the fold.
William Taylor, a renowned Methodist Episcopal evangelist from California on a circuit throughout the eastern Cape, preached for several days
to mixed but segregated black and white audiences at Shepstone's chapel
at Kamastone. Saving sinners was Taylor's mission. He stressed that the
only path to salvation was through accepting Christ as their savior. Taylor
claimed his efforts were responsible for the baptism of hundreds of converts and the repenting of sins by many more who were won for Christ.
And the ranks of the Methodist mission swelled in the coming months.

Taylor openly credited his successes at Kamastone and elsewhere to
his interpreter, Charles Pamla, whom he had met the previous month in
King William's Town.[38] Pamla's family was among the refugees who had
settled in Hintsa's kingdom; indeed Hintsa himself had dubbed his father
"a wanderer."[39] Charles was born in 1834, a few years before his family had
joined the Mfengu exodus and had relocated to Keiskammahoek. After
receiving a call to ministry, Charles served the Methodists for many years
as an unpaid lay preacher before finally being employed as an evangelist
and accepted as a candidate for the ministry in 1866.

Pamla's help was crucial to Taylor because he translated his sermons
into isiXhosa and his cultural references into terms Africans would understand. Taylor had learned from the experience of another missionary
who spoke "high English" to his interpreter, who, unfamiliar with his vocabulary, put his own spin on it that grabbed his listeners' rapt attention:
"By that time the eyes of the whole audience glistened, and they began
freely to show their ivory, and the speaker seemed to think he was doing
it, for he could not understand a word that the interpreter said, and he
waxed eloquent in the flow of his great words; and the interpreter went
on to the close, replying to each sentence, closing with, 'Friends, if you
have understood any of that you have done more than I have. It is a grand
discourse, no doubt.'"[40]

With experiences like that in mind, Taylor would prepare by discuss-
ing every word in his sermons with Pamla and asking how his audiences
would receive them. If he planned to use an English word that Pamla did
not understand, he would find one that fit. If he proposed an example

that would be unfamiliar to audiences, then Pamla would come up with a suitable alternative. For example, Taylor wanted to put across a point about the deceit of sinners by using the analogy of ivy "entwining itself" around the "trunk of a young tree" and eventually sapping it of its life. The analogy was that sin had the same impact on a person's life. He wanted to convey the thought that sin would have an impact on a person's life, but since he knew that Africans were not familiar with ivy, Pamla decided to use the example of a milkwood tree that enveloped another tree and choked it to death.[41]

The 1835 pledge between the Wesleyan and the Mfengu affirmed the value of education, and Kamastone's residents placed a premium on their children's schooling. By 1910, there were eight primary schools in the area, and schoolchildren who went on for further education attended the region's premier mission schools, Healdtown and Lovedale. Because so many Afrikaner farmers lived in the area, Dutch, not English, was the European language Africans most commonly spoke.

The 1835 pledge had also stressed loyalty to the Crown, and liberal notions enshrined in the Cape constitution of 1853 stressed a nonracial identity and equal opportunity for South African men who met standards of civilization. In theory black groups such as the Griqua and Mfengu enjoyed an elevated status and were to be treated as "civilized." The constitution provided for a nonracial franchise restricted to all males over the age of twenty-one who owned property worth at least twenty-five pounds or earned a salary of at least fifty pounds per year.

However, a major shift in official thinking toward Africans took place in the years after the British granted the Cape responsible government in 1872.[42] Officials began to treat Mfengu not as a privileged group but as just another bunch of "natives." Hence, even though many Mfengu served as troops in service to the Cape government in wars with the Ngqika, Gcaleka, and Thembu in 1877, white settlers in the eastern Cape, fearing another uprising and concerned about Africans buying guns with their earnings on the diamond fields, decided that their interests would best be served by withholding guns from all Africans without exception. They had no room for sentimentality. Even if the Mfengu were being done an injustice, they believed it was an acceptable price for ensuring order and stability for whites. Although Queenstown's representative in the Legislative Assembly, John Frost, had many Mfengu voters in his constituency, he took the side of white settlers when he testified before a defense commission: "I am not in favor of arming them [Mfengu] at present. I would rather see white men armed."[43]

With the backing of High Commissioner Bartle Frere, Prime Minister Gordon Sprigg, an East London politician who championed the interests of eastern Cape white settlers, drew on the experience of British rule in Ireland and introduced the Peace Preservation Act of 1878 requiring all Africans to hand in their arms to a magistrate in their district in exchange for compensation. Those who did not comply could be subject to seven years in prison or a £500 fine. Sprigg's goal for disarmament, as William Storey put it, was not subtle; it "was to become a theatre of paternalism, with government playing its properly fatherly role and Africans playing their proper childlike role."[44]

To many Mfengu, owning a gun was held with almost the same sanctity as owning land. Given their recent service in Cape militias, many Mfengu were not only angry but suspicious about the motive behind the legislation. "If we have been disloyal, say right out when and where we have so acted; but if we have served the Government faithfully, we ought to be allowed to keep our guns."[45] Since Kamastone residents had provided several hundred soldiers to the Cape, it was not surprising that the disarmament policy incensed them so much that more than four hundred adult male Kamastone and Oxkraal residents petitioned the speaker and members of the House of Assembly expressing their dissatisfaction with their treatment. They were angry that their loyalty to the "Queen's Government" and their expectation that blacks and whites would be treated equally under the law had gone for naught. "We trust you Honourable House will not regard it as a little thing that we should be deprived of our arms; to us it is a very great thing, because our pride and joy has been that we were honoured and trusted by the Queen's Government and anything that takes away our self-respect, is most likely to lead, sooner or later, to our ruin."[46]

The petition's tone is very revealing. The Peace Preservation Act was a major blow to Mfengu faith in the fairness of the system. They had been schooled in the nonracial policies of inclusion and had taken pride in serving as an example of "civilised" behavior to other Africans, but now the Cape government was telling them that they no longer enjoyed a special status. They would be treated the same as all other "natives." Despite this painful affront, they still managed to express their opposition to disarmament through the proper constitutional method of petition.

The Peace Preservation Act was primarily responsible for an upsurge in political activity in locations such as Kamastone and Oxkraal, where a number of men had the vote largely because they each held title to six-acre lots and access to eight acres of commonage.[47] A sex and class bias was embedded in the Cape franchise but not one of color, yet the underlying assumption of Europeans was that the franchise was restrictive enough that few Africans and Coloureds would ever qualify for the vote. And the few Africans who did were generally confined to the Ciskei and a few areas of the Transkei. Despite the higher voting qualifications, the number of black voters steadily increased. In half a dozen eastern Cape parliamentary constituencies black voters made up a substantial bloc of voters, and newly formed black political organizations began representing their interests in alliance with white political parties.[48] For instance, the number of African voters in the Queenstown area surged from 220 in 1882 to 1,700 in 1886, about 45 percent of voters overall.[49] In Kamastone there were about 800 voters in 1887, while in Oxkraal there were an estimated 450 voters in 1888.[50]

As more of the Transkei was annexed to the Cape, white politicians grew alarmed at the prospect that even more Africans would become voters and passed the Cape Parliamentary Registration Act in 1887 that excluded anyone who owned land under "tribal tenure" from qualifying for the vote. The names of over twenty thousand Africans were purged from the voter rolls. Six hundred residents of Kamastone and Oxkraal responded by signing a petition opposing the act while still expressing their faith that white liberals would take up their case in Parliament.[51] Aware that the British government was unlikely to intervene on their behalf, ten Oxkraal residents appealed directly to Queen Victoria, imploring her to "exercise your Royal Prerogative in our favour." They feared that they were "doomed and handed over and sacrificed to their old enemy the Dutch. This intelligence fills us with dismay. We therefore pray your Most Gracious Majesty that the brave and generous English nation and the British Legislature will not abandon us to the tender mercy of those that are stronger than we are."[52] Their fears were realized in 1892 when another bill raised the property qualifications even higher and introduced a literacy test. When the franchise issue came to a head, the support of most white liberals who had promised to protect African rights mysteriously evaporated.

Despite the new restrictions, more and more African men eventually qualified for the vote, and by the 1920s they were once again a critical factor in elections. In 1903 there were still some five hundred registered black voters in Kamastone, including Enoch and eight other Mgijimas.[53]

To protect their franchise rights and advance their interests, eastern Cape Africans formed organizations such as Imbumba yama Nyama (South African Aborigines' society), which catered to Mfengu interests, and Iliso Lomzi (Native vigilance society), which dealt with land issues and had chapters in and around the Queenstown area. John Alfred Sishuba, who dominated local politics for decades, led Iliso Lomzi's Kamastone's branch, and John Tengo Jabavu committed his newspaper, *Imvo Zabantsundu* (Native opinion), to mobilizing Mfengu support against the franchise laws. Jabavu was a regular visitor to the area and was influential in political affairs in the years before 1910.

While black landholding was communal, Cape officials wanted to introduce private land ownership in Kamastone and Oxkraal. Shortly after establishing the locations, they attempted to conduct a systematic survey of the land in part to head off the encroachments of neighboring white farmers who were already trying to slice off pieces of land owned by blacks.[54] Black landholding remained communal, but the survey attempted to ensure that each family would be allocated roughly ninety-six acres.

Those who lived on mission land were more likely to support the survey. In the late 1860s a small number of Kamastone and Oxkraal residents called on Cape officials to survey the land with the aim of establishing individual title to the land. Among those who backed the survey were residents of the London Missionary Society station at Hackney in Oxkraal. They wrote to the Cape governor, Philip Wodehouse, who was leaving his post, to thank him for his services to the Mfengu, including granting them parcels of land across the Kei River in the area known as "Fingoland." They expressed their approval of the Mfengu being called on to serve as a bulwark for European settlers against "Kaffirs" (Xhosa), who were being held "as you would an angry dog behind the neck with a stiff hand." They unequivocally supported British rule and were prepared to join with white colonists to take up arms to preserve it. "Our weapons will, if necessary, always be ready to turn against the enemies of our Queen and the Colony."[55] Their loyalty, they assumed, would eventually pay dividends and lead to representation in divisional and municipal councils and even Parliament.

European missionaries were also vocal advocates of individual title and used their own mission lands as beneficial examples of the system. William Shepstone implied that those who opposed individual title did so because they were lazy and unwilling to work their lands. The Cape surveyor Francis Orpen had concentrated his survey on the Kamastone mission station, creating a blend of individual title holdings and communal areas. In Shepstone's view, this would establish the core of a trading village, which would eventually win over opponents of the new setup. The trading village would be in "close proximity to the Natives, and you will thereby Civilise more rapidly without the danger of throwing them back into barbarism."[56] Shepstone accepted that those living outside the mission station would be divided into wards in which claimants would have shared titles.

The mood of Cape officials changed with the institution of responsible government in 1872, which gave more power over decision making in the colony to the Cape government. One of the new government's acts was to appoint a secretary for Native Affairs, and the first secretary, Charles Brownlee, made Kamastone and Oxkraal a priority, visiting them in 1872 and 1873 to argue the case for individual title to six-acre plots of land. Kamastone and Oxkraal residents were vocal about opposing Brownlee's plan, which led the local superintendent of locations, E. C. Jeffrey, to opine that "the people of Kamastone are a nuisance—a bad lot."[57] Brownlee was not prepared to compromise on individual title. To him it was part of a larger plan of social engineering for Africans. Individual title would enhance the authority of the Cape government while at the same time undermining chiefly authority. Moreover, white farmers who neighbored or were in the vicinity of black locations would be more likely to secure black labor for their own farms.

Cape officials were not hesitant to use threats to effect their policy. If African landholders, whatever their misgivings, did not accept individual title, then the Cape government would simply confiscate their land and expel them. This threat certainly resonated with Kamastone and Oxkraal residents who Jeffrey observed were almost as agitated by the land issue as they were by possessing guns.[58] However, at least in their public utterances Mfengu landholders acceded to the idea of individual title. By 1875, 1,680 individuals had registered as claimants.[59] In 1877, officials surveyed and subdivided Kamastone (Bulhoek was one of eight sublocations) and Oxkraal locations into residential lots of about half an acre apiece and garden plots of about six acres each some distance away from residences. However, from the outset, African tenants regarded the survey as impractical. For instance, many of the 688 Kamastone grantees did not occupy their plots, partly for health reasons, since the land was marshy, and partly because squatting on the commonage allowed them to get much closer to their garden plots. Moreover, the officials who conducted the 1877 survey did not erect substantial beacons demarcating individual plots. Confusion over individual land rights proved to be a vexing problem decades later in the final stages of Mgijima's confrontation with the South African government.

Whatever reservations residents had about individual title, they utilized every scrap of land for productive purposes. Merino sheep were ideally suited to the well-watered pastures of the upper Black Kei, and African farmers regularly sold wool to Queenstown's prosperous European merchants, who relied on trade with African locations for a good portion of their business. By the 1870s Queenstown had become a major wool center, and about a half dozen firms were devoted to washing wool before it was taken by ox wagon to the coast, where it was shipped to English textile mills.[60] Diverting mountain streams for irrigation and utilizing American ploughs, Kamastone farmers also profitably cultivated wheat, barley, oats, beans, pumpkins, maize, sorghum, and millet for the market. Jeffrey noted that in the best years the farmers were reaping upwards of ten thousand bags of wheat for sale.[61]

Because so many of Kamastone's children attended schools, these productive farmers employed herdboys from the Transkei to tend their cattle and sheep. Several dozen residents earned livings as transport riders, masons, carpenters, and thatchers, and the local economy supported a half dozen black-owned shops. Touring the Kamastone area in 1876, John Hemming, a civil commissioner, highlighted this picture of prosperity and "progressive" adaptation to Western culture.

Wherever I went I found substantial huts and brick or stone tenements. In many cases, substantial brick houses had been erected, and strange in my experience of natives, fruit trees had been planted; wherever a stream of water could be made available it had been left out and the soil cultivated as far as it could be irrigated; the slopes of the hills and even the summits of the mountains were cultivated wherever a plough could be introduced. The extent of the land turned over surprised me; I have not seen such a large area of cultivated land for years.[62]

Further testimony to the material successes of some of these farmers appeared in glowing *Cape Argus* accounts of several lavish weddings at Kamastone in 1875. The brides and their attendants were decked out in all their finery. At one wedding, "the bride was handsomely dressed in wreath and fall, and the four bridesmaids in white muslin, and wreathes." At another, presided over by Rev. Charles Pamla, "Brides and bridesmaids, white dresses, flowing veils, and flowery wreaths, have been flitting about, hither and thither, reminding one of angels' visits, and exciting the imagination of the youthful and the single." Although the hosts at one ceremony observed the mission's strict temperance rules and served no alcohol, they slaughtered twenty-seven sheep and a fat ox, and their guests feasted on "meat pies, roast beef, stews, tarts, and puddings . . . and ample justice was done to the viands." To the correspondents, these weddings were ample evidence of African advances in "civilization and material wealth." And some of the celebrants themselves were even moved to express their thanks for the blessings of "those who had brought God's Word into the land and introduced civilization."[63]

This rosy image of Kamastone life, however, is misleading. Although some black farmers flourished in this environment, many saw their fortunes decline and their living conditions worsen. Colin Bundy has documented how white agrarian and mining interests engineered specific economic and political devices and pressures to undercut black agricultural productivity during this era. Consequently a growing number of Africans were increasingly unable to sustain an independent living from their land and were forced to sell their labor to European farmers or leave home to work in the mines.[64]

In general most African farmers in the late nineteenth and early twentieth century could not compete. An occasional good year was sandwiched between a string of poor ones in which grain had to be bought from white-owned trading stores, and stock was sold to pay for food or sent to the Katberg and Transkei for pasturage. In addition, natural disasters such as locusts, droughts, hailstorms, and frost and human and animal diseases such as influenza, smallpox, cholera, rinderpest, hoof and mouth disease, and East Coast fever repeatedly ravaged the area and compounded economic stress. The rinderpest epidemic of 1896, which wiped out three-fourths of Kamastone's cattle, and the East Coast fever of 1912, which destroyed nearly a third of the cattle, inflicted the severest blows. In late 1901 a severe drought destroyed so many animals and crops that some Kamastone residents had to walk the twenty-five miles to Queenstown to obtain food.[65] These dire conditions are documented in a report of a meeting called by Queenstown area white officials and clergy with Kamastone and Oxkraal residents on 24 November 1884 to deal with the large number of people who were chronically in arrears with quitrent payments. One clergymen, Read, lectured residents on the obligations they had first to God and then to the state. "They were expected to do what they could to promote the spread of the gospel, at the same time that they should observe all other temporal obligations" and pay their rates punctually. He ended his homily by reminding his audience of Christ's injunction, "Render unto God what is God's, and render unto Caesar what is Caesar's." The Queenstown politician John Frost added that although he sympathized with the residents' plight, the amount of the rent was 'trifling' and could be paid if they exerted themselves.[66]

A local chief, Zulu, succinctly summed up the view of most residents of their condition. "The country is dried up. There is no veldt. The cattle are lean. The horses are thin and the sheep are infected with *brandrikte*."[67] At a meeting the next day with Magistrate Garcia residents expressed the same view: "We are poor. God's hand has been heavily laid upon us. We have no crops. The few cattle we have left can be sold only as a sacrifice. Why then should the government, which is our father, put pressure upon us at this inopportune time?" While Garcia empathized with residents who had legitimate reasons for not paying arrears, he was committed to continue to press them to pay their obligations on time.[68]

In the ensuing decades conditions continued to deteriorate in Kamastone and many other rural African locations. Residents increasingly sought employment elsewhere, and survival became the thin cushion provided by the remittances sent home from these migrant laborers. In the 1870s many laborers had found jobs constructing the railway line from the port city of East London through Queenstown to the diamond fields at Kimberley, but now they were using the same railway to search for employment.[69] Local officials shifted from recording quantities of wool and wheat produced to tracking the number of permits issued to laborers looking for work elsewhere. That number rose from three hundred

(25–30 percent of the adult male population) in prosperous years to six hundred in the worst. When the Native Land Commission was gathering evidence in 1914, A. C. Bain, the Queenstown magistrate, described Kamastone as an overcrowded location for both people and stock. Because of chronic droughts and soil erosion, its residents could not support themselves. The superintendent for African locations at Whittlesea, W. C. P. Jones, echoed his observations. He added that residents "could not live properly on the produce from their arable lands without the selling of their stock and the money brought down from the mines. If they lived as cattle farmers we could not give them the land that they would require." Ema Makalima, a representative of the SANNC and a Kamastone resident, succinctly summed up their plight: "The main thing is this: that the natives of Oxkraal and Kamastone are packed like sardines; they cannot move."[70]

Fingo Emancipation Day

By the early twentieth century Mfengu communities were rent by social divisions, and many began questioning whether their loyalty to the colonial state had paid any dividends. While Mfengu loyalists remained faithful, they were sufficiently concerned about maintaining their relatively privileged status under British colonial rule that they proposed establishing an annual "Fingo Day" on 14 May to commemorate the anniversary of the 1835 ceremony where the Mfengu met Ayliff under the milkwood tree at Mqwashwini.

They had not fared well in subsequent decades and, following the end of the South African war in 1902, Mfengu leaders feared losing further ground in the union of colonies the British were proposing. The South African Native Affairs Commission (1903–5), which was convened to ensure that South African mines had continued access to cheap, unskilled black labor, recommended that the new union's system of native administration be based on tribal leadership and identity.[71] Hence, Mfengu leaders lobbied for their headmen to be officially recognized as chiefs. Moreover, they were concerned that their influence as a voting bloc would wane as more Rharhabe Xhosas and Thembus were winning the franchise.[72]

"Fingo Days" were intended to remind the colonial government that the Mfengu had remained faithful to the 1835 covenant. They had embraced Christianity and mission education and had been consistently loyal to the

Crown. On the first Fingo Day, on 22 February 1907, Mfengu representatives, including several from Kamastone, met at Zazulwana and passed a resolution that Mfengu "should tender our heartfelt thanks to His Majesty's Government for our emancipation."[73] Four months later a Mfengu delegation presented a petition for official recognition of Fingo Day to Walter Hely-Hutchinson, the British colonial governor in Cape Town.

The delegation's leader and Fingo Day's most vocal advocate was Capt. Veldtman Bikitsha, whose life had been a testament of devotion to the colonial order. As a young boy, he participated in the Mfengu exodus from Gcalekaland. In the wars of 1846 and 1850 he served the British with the rank of sergeant and, during the cattle-killing episode, as a policeman for Walter Currie. In the war of 1877–78, as a government headman in Fingoland, he received a commission as captain, a title that was passed on to his successors.[74] However, after losing his vote as a result of the 1887 legislation, he turned to lawyers to regain it. Bikitsha's crowning moment came in 1889 when he visited England and received an audience with Queen Victoria. He presented her with a gift of a shield and spears to show "that we have never feared a white man, and have never lifted our hand against any of your people."[75] Queen Victoria herself gave him an autographed photo of herself and a uniform for him to wear on official occasions.

Worried about resurrecting animosities and fanning ethnic rivalries, Hely-Hutchinson tested the climate among other ethnic groups before agreeing to declare a Fingo Day. Claiming the Thembu never participated in oppressing Mfengu, Thembu chief Dalindyebo objected to Fingo Day, arguing instead that his people had welcomed the Mfengu as they had many other refugee groups. A letter writer to the *Journal* expressed his concern that the day would prove to be a needless irritant between Xhosa and Mfengu, who had been striving for peaceful relations for many years. He warned: "I think to allow this is the causing of bitterness and that bitterness will lead to war. This Fingo Commemoration Day will never do good at all."[76]

Although the governor's compromise was that the celebration should be confined to Fingoland and places where Mfengu were concentrated, this did not deter rival Xhosa groups from establishing their own celebration, Ntsikana Day, on 10 April 1909, which highlighted the fact that the Ngqika prophet Ntsikana had embraced Christianity several decades before the Mfengu did.

Subsequent Fingo Day proclamations followed a ritualistic formula of reciting the 1835 pledges and expressing loyalty to the British Crown as well as registering some relevant comment about pressing issues. A 1911 proclamation noted: "Education is gaining its way as is shown that some of our children are in England and America. Darkness has fled before the Gospel. We adhere to the same principles as our forefathers, we wish to show our loyalty to our King George V on this year of his Coronation and say 'GOD SAVE THE KING.' Long may he reign over us."[77] At the 1910 Fingo Day celebration at Kamastone, the featured speaker pointedly drew a comparison between the Mfengu and the biblical Israelites, who had been brought "out of captivity to a fruitful land where they were dwelling in safety, peace and prosperity."[78]

To buttress their case for government recognition as a tribal group, some Mfengu leaders established a Fingo History Fund to which subscribers pledged a guinea each. Isiaih Bud-M'belle, an interpreter for the High Court in Kimberley, took the lead, and other contributors included such prominent figures as Solomon and Elizabeth Plaatje, Elijah Makiwane, Thomas Mapikela, P. Z. Mzimba, Enoch Mamba, John Alf Sishuba, Joseph Mbeki, and Queen Victoria's visitor, Veldtman Bikitsha. They commissioned Methodist minister Joseph Whiteside, author of several South African history textbooks, to write a history of the Mfengu that would give them an identity on par with other ethnic groups.[79] Their goal was to shift the perception of the Mfengu as a hodgepodge of rootless refugees to one of a shared ethnic identity based on a common ancestry as Abambo. Hence the book's opening chapters established how the Abambo had migrated from central Africa several centuries in the past and had established a chiefdom in the Buffalo River valley. The Abambo were made up of nine clans, which splintered under the onslaught of Matiwane's Ngwane. The rest of the book was largely taken from an Ayliff manuscript that his daughter had given to Whiteside, and he restated Ayliff's view that Mfengu refugees became Hintsa's abject slaves after settling in the Gcaleka kingdom. Whiteside reiterated how Ayliff had delivered the Mfengu from Hintsa's oppressive rule, how they sided with the British and prospered under their rule, and how Christianity had been an essential component of their progress. "But the elevation of the Fingos," Whiteside insisted, "depends largely if not wholly on their acceptance of Christianity. The Gospel has placed them in the van of the Native races, and it is the Gospel alone that will enable them to maintain their position."[80]

Nevertheless, advocates of Fingo Day found it difficult to generate widespread support because a growing number of Mfengu no longer subscribed to the belief that they were living in a land of milk and honey. So while loyalists were trying to resuscitate and breathe new life into their colonial pact, Enoch Mgijima was among those moving in a very different direction as he entered into his own chiliastic covenant with the Lord.

Ambassador of the Last Days

We know that from the time of the 1835 Mfengu covenant at Peddie the Mgijima family embraced Christianity, mission education, progressive agriculture, and loyalty to the Cape political system. After settling in the Peddie area, Mgijima converted to Christianity and joined the Wesleyan Methodist church. He narrated his conversion this way. While tending his sheep he watched some wolves tracking down prey. This reminded him of the Methodist hymn lyrics "God, my Lord, you loved me when lost, but you followed my trail and I am caught, my Lord."[81]

His son, Jonas, settled at Ntabelanga, and he prospered there, acquiring many sheep, cattle, goats, and horses. As a progressive farmer, he was receptive to the newest farming methods: he avidly participated in the Kamastone agricultural show and won prizes in 1865 and 1866 for washed wool, *kapaters* (a castrated male goat), and *hamels* (a castrated male sheep).[82]

Jonas and his wife, Makeswa, had five daughters, but he was not satisfied until he had a male heir. One day he climbed to a mountaintop and prayed, "God, you have given me these sheep, cattle, goats and horses, but I have no boy amongst my children."[83] His prayer was answered, for his next four children were sons: Timothy, Charles, Josiah, and Enoch, born in 1868.

Enoch's parents believed that mission education was the avenue to advancement. They raised their children in the Wesleyan church and encouraged their sons to seek education beyond the Standard III levels offered at Kamastone schools. Timothy, Josiah, and Charles proceeded to one of the most celebrated institutions in the region, Lovedale Institution, in Alice, and Josiah and Charles went even further to Zonnebloem College in Cape Town. Timothy and Josiah eventually became interpreters in Rhodesia, while Charles, who later became Enoch's right-hand man during the Israelite confrontation with the government, worked as a court interpreter and teacher.[84]

The family expected that their last-born son, Enoch, would follow his brothers' path, but he never advanced beyond Standard III. Each time he left for Lovedale, severe headaches forced him to turn back. Later his followers suggested that his headaches were a sign that God had other plans for him. So Enoch remained at Ntabelanga, where he became a landowner and small game hunter. He and his wife, Mamtembu, raised six sons, Innes, Zansi, Bumba, Mzanywa, Soni, and Mlaule, and one daughter, Tobi.[85]

We have no tangible indications that Enoch was preparing to make a break with the Mfengu covenant, but as he was nearing forty, his life and those of many around him were turned upside down when the spirit of God touched him on 9 April 1907. While hunting for small game, he had a vision in which he saw three mountains of varying heights in the distance.[86] "He wept without knowing why, but God told him that these mountains represented the different peoples whom he was going to preach to." God cautioned him that even though some would grasp his message immediately, he should not be discouraged if others received him reluctantly or rejected him altogether. Later in his vision, an angel snatched him up. He grew wings and flew into the heavens where he saw a blackboard, which a light from high up illuminated. Then the light went out and Mgijima could not see anything in front of him. The angel instructed him: "I'm sending you to people who see clearly today but nothing tomorrow. If you do not carry out this mission, I will take all the sins of the people and hold you accountable. I have sent you to these people because I am worried that although they worship me they are not honest in their worship of me. I want you to worship me according to your old traditions."[87]

The angel next took him across the sky and asked him, "Do you hear the sound in the distance?" Mgijima replied, "Yes." But when the angel asked, "Do you know the cause of this sound?" he admitted he did not. The angel explained, "There are rumors of war in the North. Look to the East instead. That war will not come from the North, but from the East." When the final cataclysm came, nothing would be spared—the birds in the air, the fish in the sea, or the meerkats in their holes. Only those who followed the name of God would escape His wrath.[88]

Following these revelations, Mgijima returned home, but like many prophets, he resisted the Lord's calling and wrestled with his self-doubt. He wondered how he, an unworthy sinner and a drunkard, could be capable of carrying out God's mission. But the Lord commanded him: "If you refuse to talk to my people, the blood of the punishment of these people will be called upon you." He gave in to the Lord's direction and accepted his calling as an independent evangelist.[89] Although he remained in the Wesleyan fold, he attracted a large personal following, who likened him to John the Baptist and gave him a variety of appellations: *inkintsela* (a resourceful person who accomplishes remarkable things), *ilunga lase mpumalanga* (good man of the east), *mlindi woSirayeli* (watchman of Israel), *lilungu lama lungu* (a man among men), and *unozakuzaku wokugqibela* (ambassador of the last days). He also garnered a reputation as a faith healer who treated barren women and those who were having problems in childbirth by laying his stick on them.

The Schism with the Moravians

Despite Mgijima's independent stature, the two established denominations in the area, the Wesleyans and the Moravians, were far more concerned with Catholic inroads than with his preaching. Hearing that Mgijima was responsible for a religious awakening at nearby Oxkraal and Kamastone, Moravian missionaries at Shiloh invited him to hold a revival in March 1912.[90] His services featured communal prayers and rhythmic hymn singing and were highlighted by his intense, fire-and-brimstone preaching.

The missionaries regarded him like other "prophets" who were roaming the area. "They profess to be able by prayer and the laying on of hands, to heal all kinds of sicknesses. Followed by a great retinue, they move about from one country to another, and cause a great commotion everywhere, which, however, only lasts for a short time."[91] Hoping that Mgijima would rejuvenate their congregations, they did not expect his presence would lead to a schism. Although they were clearly concerned that Mgijima brought along a large group of Wesleyans from Kamastone to participate in his services, they initially had no reason for alarm, since he admonished his congregants to adhere to the word of God and to remain faithful members of the mission churches. "Mgijima said he had come for the sole purpose of preaching repentance, for which he had been specifically called of God. Whoever, therefore, was convinced of sins was to go to his missionary and make confession of his sins."[92]

As the missionaries hoped, he attracted enthusiastic audiences wherever he appeared. Missionaries were bombarded with requests for baptisms, confirmations, and communion services and were gratified by the decline in immoral behavior, drinking, and fights. Despite Mgijima's success in rejuvenating their congregations, the Moravians began privately expressing misgivings about him. Although they had no objections to his dynamic preaching, they sensed he offered an alternative to their own leadership that would eventually pose a problem. Nevertheless, they still allowed him to visit Shiloh periodically.

As Mgijima and his assistants made repeated visits in the coming months, the missionaries began seeing evidence that many of their members at Shiloh were becoming estranged from them. Fewer people were showing up at their services. Some were making pilgrimages to Mgijima's home at Ntabelanga, where at sunset he was leading processions into the fields of people "going to meet the Lord"; at night, he was holding services in people's homes.[93]

The conflict came to a head because of the activities of one of Mgijima's zealous disciples, Jonathan Mdudu, a schoolteacher and lay preacher whose services often conflicted with Moravian services. His preaching disregarded a mission regulation that only evangelists, not young people, could lead meetings. When Mgijima visited Shiloh in October, he refused to rebuke Mdudu, claiming the spirit of God was acting through him. That same month, the mission council prohibited Mdudu from holding services at the mission church.[94]

The Moravian missionaries contended that their disagreement with Mdudu served as a convenient pretext for rallying dissidents who were resurrecting a recurring land controversy that dated back many decades. The Moravian Church had originated in Moravia and Bohemia (now part of the Czech Republic) in the fifteenth century. The Moravians had originated in the 1720s when Count Nikolaus Ludwig founded the first Moravian settlement ,called Herrnhut, in Saxony in what is now Germany. His aim was to establish a place where people of all denominations who were feeling persecuted could practice freedom of worship, a self-sufficient community where Christians could live in a "spiritual brotherhood" in which they would "be at the disposal of the Saviour for his plan in the world under the leadership of the Holy Spirit."[95] In 1737 Georg Schmidt transplanted the Moravian model to the western Cape, where a series of Christian communities such as Genadendal and Elim were founded among the Khoisan people. In the early nineteenth century the Moravians extended their network of missions to the eastern Cape.

Shiloh mission was established in 1828 when local chiefs granted the Moravians extensive lands along the Klippplaats River. In 1858, the Cape government issued communal titles to Moravian lands (each station had acreages of six thousand to thirteen thousand) and granted mission superintendents the right to administer the land as they saw fit. They were the proprietors and magistrates of their fiefdoms, screening individuals who wanted to live on their stations, levying taxes on residents (4s. per annum) and stock, and allocating land and building sites to Coloured and African residents.[96] Residents developed a perception that the missionaries were reaping considerable revenues from the taxes, church dues, and proceeds from the land.

Coming at a time when Coloureds and Africans were being stripped of their landholdings throughout the region, it was inevitable that mission stations, with their abundant lands and patriarchal missionaries supervising all secular affairs, would become sites of struggle.[97] On several occasions, Shiloh's Coloured residents pressed lawsuits seeking more rights and half the mission's land. None of their attempts was successful. In 1891, after a dissident group led by Gustaff Stoffels refused to pay church dues, claiming that whites wanted them to go deep into debt so that whites could buy up their land, the mission took them to court and had all but two Coloured families evicted. That action did not prevent a later protest by Stoffels and others who wanted to reclaim their land and an African group at Shiloh who styled themselves "The Fourteen." They agitated for more land for residents, especially direct access to the Klippplaats. The missionaries believed the heart of the conflict was more than the land issue. "The real cause lies far more in a conflict between darkness and light" as the dissenters sought "to free themselves from the law and the restraint of the Word of God."[98]

The Moravians were acutely aware of their predicament and supported a reform of the system that separated religious from secular matters. The Cape Parliament had introduced a Mission Stations Bill in 1902, but it was not until John X. Merriman became prime minister of the Cape Colony that the Mission Stations and Communal Reserves Act was enacted in 1909, giving a greater voice to their residents in the governance of mission stations and reallocating land holdings. The act required boards of management to have nine members elected by residents and three appointed by the governor.

Shiloh's mission land was surveyed and redistributed, with roughly 90 percent of the ten thousand acres going to its 770 residents (roughly three-quarters of them were African and the rest Coloured).[99] However, that did not lessen the tensions between the Moravians and disgruntled residents, who argued that the missionaries should not possess any more than their houses and a few small gardens. Despite hiring two lawyers to take the mission to court, the residents lost their case.[100] On 1 April 1912, when Rev. Walter Rubusana, a prominent eastern Cape politician and the only African member of the Cape provincial assembly, met with the minister of native affairs to discuss the Shiloh land question, he voiced the feeling of Shiloh residents that the Moravians had cheated them out of their land and water rights. They queried why the mission should get more than the forty acres on which the church and school stood and why the mission was allocated Lot B, the best land on the station.[101] Although the missionaries offered no direct evidence, they believed that the core of Mgijima's following was drawn from this disaffected group.[102] Indeed, Mdudu, a former Moravian and Shiloh landowner, had been a leading dissident.[103]

The event that triggered a schism at Shiloh came shortly after the disciplining of Mdudu. On 24 October 1912, Mgijima's supporters petitioned the mission council for permission to erect their own church, but by a five-to-four vote, the council turned them down. Mgijima's followers ignored the decision and began making bricks for their own church. The missionaries later conceded that Mgijima's movement might have collapsed if the board had not turned down the petitioners.[104]

Shiloh's missionaries launched an attack on Mgijima's movement, labeling it "a sect of Adventists, with . . . a dash of Mormonism in it"[105] and made a concerted effort to win back his converts to their fold. Walther Bourquin appealed to Emma Madolo, "Why not be with us?" When she explained that she could not "obey 2 gods," he insisted, "But we do have the same god."[106] On another occasion, Bourquin engaged John Gabela in an amicable discussion about why he was leaving the Moravians now that the mission station land had been reallocated. Bourquin was certain that Mgijima was misleading the people. "Mgijima is not wrong in every aspect, but he is wrong to take words from the Bible and using them out of context and turning them into laws. To be a believer does not mean that one has to be baptized in a river the way he [Gabela] was, but to offer Jesus one's heart and obey his will." Bourquin and Gabela also exchanged views on Mgijima's identification with the biblical Israelites. Gabela admitted he was not so much opposed to Bourquin as he was attracted to Mgijima.

"It is time for healing. Secrets are being revealed to and comprehended by dim-witted people such as myself, whereas the truth is shrouded in secrecy for small people such as yourself. Furthermore, you know Mgijima is one of us. We follow him even if all of us get lost, even if we go to hell. We follow him like sheep." Bourquin appealed to Gabela to show the courage to reverse course if he realized he was moving down the wrong path.[107]

In November 1912, as Mgijima commenced baptizing converts in the Black Kei River at Ntabelanga, he informed Shiloh residents that he had broken with the Wesleyans and joined an African American body, the Church of God and Saints of Christ (CGSC).[108] Many of his followers either proceeded to Ntabelanga or stayed at Shiloh for baptism. Bourquin described an affair at Shiloh in January 1913 at which Mgijima and a newcomer, the American-educated John Msikinya, who was proselytizing for the CGSC, presided over the mass baptism of several hundred people in a river. "The bishop ran up and down totally rapt making all sorts of gestures. The general picture was: Jesus was baptized in the river. We have to do as Jesus did. Not a soul can go to heaven if he is not baptized in the river and that includes the missionary. One God / one faith / one baptism / there is one heaven for whites, and there is another heaven for blacks."[109]

Most of Mgijima's initial converts were Christians breaking away from European-led denominations. Three hundred of the eight hundred Africans residing at Shiloh joined him, while another two hundred split from the Wesleyans in the Kamastone area.[110]

Although one can speculate about their reasons for turning to Mgijima's church, they very likely were similar to those of others who severed their ties with European missions. Their grievances included European missionaries practicing racial discrimination and attacking African culture, disagreements over church doctrine, the confusing multiplicity of European denominations, African desires to control church affairs, property and finance, and the obstacles placed in the way of Africans aspiring to leadership roles.[111]

A likely influence on Mgijima's secession was the Wesleyan Methodist church, which defined many African cultural practices—bridewealth payments, beer drinking, and polygyny—as "ungodly practices." Edward Barrett, the Wesleyans' resident missionary at Kamastone in the 1880s, delivered a broadside against African customs: "As our work is to reclaim the people from heathenism our helpers should be those who are thoroughly staunch in their opposition to all superstitious customs, barbarous and filthy practice, and I would add beer drinking. They should be men who having been set free by Christ detest the heathen rite of circumcision and who believe that women having been redeemed with the precious blood of Christ are not any longer to be bought and sold."[112]

Moreover, the Wesleyans erected barriers to Africans rising to higher positions in the church hierarchy—the first Africans were only ordained in 1910.[113] In the Queenstown area three decades earlier, white Wesleyan clergy had begun to segregate their district conference so that black ministers would have limited influence over decisions affecting all of them.[114] Thus it is not surprising that the majority of schisms from Protestant missions involved the Wesleyans. Mgijima's dilemma was painfully clear. Although he had proved himself as an evangelist, his race and limited education prevented him from aspiring to a higher status in the church.

White missionaries generally received the Ethiopian movement (as it was known) with hostility. Although most acknowledged that secessions were the result of the color bar in churches, they still took them personally as "betrayal, personal rejection, and 'ingratitude.'"[115] They contended that the motivations for breakaways were not of the highest order. "The restless, the discontented and the worthless," asserted Frederick Bridgman, were the ones who were most likely to be drawn into the Ethiopian churches. Those churches, he stated, were not imbued with a genuine missionary spirit. They took advantage of other people's hard work and attracted dissidents from white churches rather than proselytizing the unevangelized or enforcing strict discipline. Those who joined did not have to repent their sins but merely profess their faith. They sought privilege but not responsibility. These criticisms did not obviate the genuine feeling many Africans held that they had to gain control of their own churches. But the advice European missionaries offered betrayed their pervasive paternalism: "Is it not true of the native Christian, as of the headstrong lad," Bridgman observed, "that the disposition to throw off restraint only emphasizes his need of parental guidance?"[116]

To many whites, the Ethiopian movement also had more ominous overtones. Since independent churches were widely believed to be a cover for more insidious political ideas, they reasoned that as Africans moved from one stage of development to another, it would no longer be a question of independence only in religious matters but in political affairs as well. A Moravian missionary at Shiloh predicted that "in time . . . it will lead to a native rising. The Ethiopians say that we ought to have no white missionaries. When they have got rid of them, the next step will be to get rid of the magistrates, and there will be a war of races."[117]

Government officials throughout South Africa were anxious to prevent Ethiopianism from catching hold, but in the absence of concrete evidence that the movement was seditious, they were not prepared to suppress the movement because that might have increased its popularity. However, they had the latent suspicion that at heart the movement was politically motivated. The South African Native Affairs Commission conducted the most publicized official investigation of Ethiopianism in 1905. The commissioners had little sympathy for independent churches or faith in the moral qualities of its leaders. They were "men lacking in the breadth of view, wisdom and forethought necessary properly to foster and direct the fledgling ideals of a people just emerging from ignorance and barbarism into a state of enlightenment."[118] But they still concluded that the Ethiopians did not have political ambitions.

Disparaging this view, one missionary argued that the evidence presented to the commission suggested otherwise: "Wherever the apostles of Ethiopianism have appeared . . . they have caused unrest amongst the natives and have been condemned by the authorities. . . . When Ethiopian missionaries, saturated with American democratic ideas, go up and down the land telling the Kaffirs that South Africa is a black man's country, and that the blacks must 'stand up for their rights,' it is impossible to ignore the political aspect of the propagandism."[119]

This reference to Americans was also directed at linking Ethiopianism to the African American African Methodist Episcopal (AME) Church that had begun establishing a presence in South Africa at the end of the nineteenth century. Although AME clergy went out of their way to stress how well they accommodated British rule, a vocal group of white missionaries regularly attacked them for poisoning the minds of impressionable Africans with their pernicious ideas of freedom and equality and instilling a spirit of revolt. By encroaching on territory marked out by European missions, the AME was encouraging Africans to secede and "working injury to the cause of Christ" and inflaming European prejudice unnecessarily.[120] Moreover, the AME Church was stealing converts from mission churches rather than "reaching heathens" and was substituting African American for European domination.[121]

To whites, linking Ethiopianism with the Haitian revolution was even more sinister than African American influences because it raised the frightening specter that Ethiopianism could lead to the overthrow of white political control. The *Rand Daily Mail's* editor, Edwin Neame, observed that "the rapidity with which a native church may descend, when free from white control, is shown by the horrors of Hayti."[122]

Mgijima and his followers were not concerned with the fears of white missionaries but with the doctrines and practices associated with western Christianity and the identification of mission churches with white domination. Walter Dinca, defending his group's presence at Ntabelanga in 1920 from an accusation that they were "religious maniacs," articulated the Israelites' disenchantment with mission Christianity. Africans were staking their own claim on Christianity because, as a columnist in the SANNC newspaper, *Abantu Batho,* put it, whites had crudely appropriated religion as "an instrument of power for the establishment of white supremacy and domination in the world."[123] The writer pointed to the hypocrisy of how whites preached and practiced Christianity. How could they hate Africans so much when Christianity taught love for one's neighbors and exploit Africans in the face of the biblical injunction "Do unto others as they wouldst they unto you?" "Can any sane black man," he argued, "follow this religion which is out to extirminate the Natives of this country? I submit not. Why is your Government legislation so anti-native? Why all these colour bars and not equal opportunities? If you are Christians why act vice versa?"[124] One way Mgijima addressed these questions was by joining an African American denomination, the Church of God and Saints of Christ.

2 The Prophet's Call

And he said, "Hear my words. If there is a prophet among you, I the Lord make myself known to him in a vision. I speak with him in a dream."

—Numbers 12:6

Mgijima's decision to establish a direct connection with a little-known African American church, the Church of God and Saints of Christ, led by prophet William Saunders Crowdy, is striking because he could have chosen to join one of many other breakaway church groups in his area for expressing his spiritual leadership and his disillusionment with Western Christianity. One of the earliest independent churches, the Ethiopian Church, founded in 1892 by former Wesleyan clergymen such as Mangena Mokone and James Dwane, had a branch in Queenstown.[1] Several other independent churches, the African Presbyterian Church and the African Native Mission Church (Nehemiah Tile's church), as well as the African Methodist Episcopal Church had taken root with some success in the Kamastone area. If Mgijima had been interested in transferring his allegiance to a Wesleyan offshoot, he could have joined Tile's church.

If he had desired affiliation with an African American church, he could have embraced the AME, which had been creating a mission network throughout the region since the late 1890s and offered autonomy from European missions and a decentralized structure that gave ample freedom to local ministers, an international presence, and a modernizing message with an emphasis on establishing its own schools. Mgijima was personally familiar with his contemporary, Rev. Isaiah Sishuba, an AME minister in Queenstown who had spent part of his youth in the home of his uncle Charles Pamla at Kamastone. Instead Mgijima threw his lot with the Church of God and Saints of Christ.

Mgijima's choice of an African American church is understandable because of the rich diasporic connections between African Americans and black South Africans that developed over their shared experiences with white domination and discrimination and racial segregation.[2] They are fascinating because most African Americans are descended from peoples brought to the Americas during the transatlantic slave trade from western and central Africa, and the African Americans and black South Africans who crossed the Atlantic to each other's countries numbered in the hundreds, not the hundreds of thousands.

The interchanges started in the late eighteenth century as African Americans began making their way to southern Africa, mostly as sailors on whaling ships who docked in Cape Town, Port Elizabeth, and Durban. Some settled permanently, while others filtered into the interior as entrepreneurs and adventurers on the diamond and gold fields. Yankee Wood, for example, ran a hotel in Queenstown in the 1870s. In the 1890s the Jubilee Singers toured South Africa on three occasions, leaving an enduring mark on black South African choral and performance styles, and missionaries from the Negro Baptists and the AME founded churches all over the region. African American control of the church, an institution that had become central in their community life, was a source of inspiration to many black South Africans, who were also creating their own institutions in a white-dominated segregated environment.

Largely because of the missionary ties, several hundred black South Africans, prohibited from attending college in their own country, journeyed to the United States for higher education and enrolled at black campuses such as Wilberforce, Fisk, Lincoln, Hampton, and Tuskegee. There many of them imbibed Tuskegee principal Booker T. Washington's educational philosophy of self-reliance and industrial education, which they transplanted to their own schools back home.

A Black Elijah from America

Mgijima chose to join the CGSC and not the AME Church or any of the other independent churches because they did not offer the same creative outlet as the CGSC for institutionalizing his charismatic leadership and prophetic gifts and providing a liberatory theology inspired by the book of Exodus. Unlike most other Ethiopian churches, which did not secede from European denominations because of doctrinal differences, Mgijima was making a dramatic break on both an institutional and theological level.

Like Mgijima, William Crowdy's search for the promised land animated his life.[3] He was named Wilson when he was born into a slave family on

11 August 1847 on the Chesley Hill farm of Col. John Sothoron (1807–93) in Saint Mary's County in southern Maryland. A stalwart of the planter aristocracy, Sothoron, according to the 1860 U.S. Slave Census, owned fifty-seven slaves who labored on his two farms, Chesley Hill and the Plains, on the Patuxent River, producing 120,000 pounds of tobacco annually.[4] Wilson's parents were not field hands. His father, Basil, was responsible for overseeing the drying of bricks at the farm's kiln, while his mother, Sarah Ann, was a cook.

On 1 January 1863 President Abraham Lincoln issued the Emancipation Proclamation, which freed slaves in the Confederacy but exempted border states such as Maryland to keep them from seceding from the Union. However, in October 1863, the U.S. government issued an order allowing the Union army to recruit slaves into black regiments. The U.S. government promised it would eventually compensate slave owners who remained "loyal" to Union for the loss of any of their slaves to the army.[5] However, some recruiters aggressively sought out slaves, rankling their owners. Recruiting squads were sent to six farms on the Patuxent River, and on 20 October two black soldiers and a white officer of the Seventh U.S. Colored Regiment, Lt. Eben White, arrived in a rowboat at the Plains to sign up Sothoron's slaves into the Union army. John and his son Webster confronted them as they went to the fields to recruit among the laborers, and in the ensuring altercation, John shot and killed White. The pair immediately fled to Virginia. Union troops occupied the farm and placed Sothoron's wife and their other seven children under house arrest. The following January the government not only freed and relocated the remaining slaves on the Sothoron farms but also confiscated the farms and used them to produce food for Union troops.[6]

In December 1863, sixteen-year-old Wilson and his twenty-one-year-old brother Daniel took advantage of their slave master's absence to journey several miles to Camp Stanton to enroll in the Union army's Nineteenth Colored Regiment, which was largely made up of runaway slaves from southern Maryland.[7] Daniel joined as a private, while the underage Wilson served as a laborer and supply storesman. They joined some ten thousand freedmen and slaves who bolstered Union regiments during the Civil War.

Even though the Crowdy family was freed, they could not escape vestiges of the system even at the end of the war. As slavery was collapsing in Maryland, slave owners, using old laws, took steps to bind the children of slaves as apprentices if they could get their parents' consent. They could also bind the children if the parents were regarded as vagrants. So an estimated ten thousand children found themselves bound to their former owners. White judges were rarely sympathetic to parents who sought to protect their children. Hence, when Basil and Sarah Ann, who had moved their family to neighboring Calvert County, brought a complaint before a court that three of their children had been illegally bound as apprentices to a white farmer, the police and judges treated them with contempt. At the hearing "Constable A. O. Buckmunslin finding the mother obdurate struck her in the face with his fist in the presence of the judges."[8] The Crowdys eventually made their way to Baltimore.

Crowdy changed his name from Wilson to William, and he and the Nineteenth Regiment saw action at the Battle of the Wilderness in May 1864 and in the capture of the Confederate capitol, Richmond, in April 1865. After their unit was mustered out in Brownsville, Texas, in January 1867, William joined a Buffalo Soldier unit, the Tenth Regular Cavalry, serving for five years as a quartermaster sergeant in a unit that waged campaigns against Indian tribes in Wyoming and New Mexico.[9] After leaving the army Crowdy found employment as a cook for the Atchison, Topeka, and Santa Fe Railway and joined some twenty thousand African Americans, driven from southern states such as Mississippi, Louisiana, and Texas because of the failure of Reconstruction and escalating white violence against blacks, who were settling in Kansas, which they saw as a "modern Canaan and the God-appointed home of the negro race."[10] He worked as a cook at a railway hotel in Kansas City, Missouri. In 1886 or 1887 he married Lovey Yates Higgins, who cooked in the homes of white families in Hannibal, Missouri. They had three children.[11]

On 22 April 1889, fifty thousand settlers poured into the neighboring Indian territory of Oklahoma to stake out land claims. Among them were nearly three thousand African Americans who bought into the idea black newspapers promoted that Oklahoma might be a refuge from racial discrimination. Crowdy joined them during a second land run in 1891, purchasing a 160-acre farm near Guthrie, a town on the Santa Fe railroad with an energetic African American community. To augment his income, he worked as a cook in Guthrie's English Kitchen restaurant. He was also an active figure in the Baptist church, a captain in a black militia force, and devoted to Prince Hall Masonry, which specifically offered membership to African Americans who were drawn to its promotion of black self-determination and autonomy and its social welfare programs such as burial societies.[12] By the turn of the twentieth century, about fifty thousand African Americans had become Prince Hall Masons.[13]

In 1893 Crowdy's spiritual convictions were profoundly shaken after he began receiving personal visitations from the Lord. One spring morning he was clearing trees and stumps for planting a new field.

> Suddenly, he said something flew up with a great rushing sound as though a great flock of birds had flown over his head and he heard a voice speaking to him saying, "Run for your life!" He said that he dropped his ax, but took his mattock and started running down through the woods as fast as he could go blazing the trees as he went, for he was sure he was going away into the woods to die and he wanted the people to find him before the buzzards should eat his body, the blazed trees were to serve as a mark that someone had gone that way. He stopped to rest and while there fell into a deep sleep.[14]

He dreamed that he was in a large room in which tables were "coming down from the ceiling." As he inspected each table more closely, he noted that all of them were covered with "filthy vomit" and that on each one of them was written the name of a church.[15] The largest and "filthiest" table was the one with the name Baptist on it. Although he had been a deacon in the Baptist church in Guthrie, he took it as a sign that he should never attend the Baptist church again. Then a small table descended before him that was "clean and white." The name "Church of God and Saints of Christ" was inscribed on it, and it grew until it filled the room and squeezed out the other tables. Then he was shown seven keys, each with a set of scriptural references attached to them. In the last part of his vision, he saw a Bible and was instructed to eat it (Rev. 10:2–10). In that way the whole Bible and every chapter and verse became part of him.[16]

Crowdy likened his vision to what was recorded in Jeremiah 1:5: "Before I formed thee, in the belly I knew thee; and before thou camest forth out of the womb I sanctified thee; and I ordained thee a prophet unto the nations."[17]

He returned home a changed man. After losing considerable weight, he wrote on a "tablet" the seven keys revealed to him and claimed that he had been called to preach in the tradition of a long line of Old Testament prophets from Abraham to Moses to Jeremiah and Elijah. This inspired him to begin evangelizing, converting, and baptizing, first in the streets of Guthrie and then in nearby villages and towns as well as neighboring states. Although he was initially unsure about how far he should extend his ministry, he was given clarity when a voice told him: "As he [God] said to Ezekiel, Son of Man, I send thee to the children of Israel, and to all the nations of the earth that hath rebelled against me."[18] A powerful singer and orator, he dubbed himself the "World's Evangelist."

Realizing that he had to take care of his family before expanding his ministry, he asked the Lord for a bountiful season. After an abundant crop, he asked the Lord for another good year, and he had an even better harvest. Again he appealed to the Lord for a prosperous growing season, but this time, his crops failed and he was left penniless. This setback inspired him to extend his circuit and evangelize in Texas. But because his wife suspected that he was running off with another woman, she sent their eldest son, Isaac, with him.[19]

In Texas and Arkansas he suffered persecution everywhere he preached. He related that hostile officials in Arkansas arrested him twenty-one times in one day for asserting that Christ was black.[20] Vindictive cowboys in Texas hounded him. "In one place the cowboys captured him and asked him if he could dance. He told them 'No.' . . . 'When they began to shoot hot lead at my feet I danced all right to keep a bullet from going through my feet!'"[21] On another occasion cowboys abducted and stranded him with nothing but a buffalo hide wrapped around him and buzzards circling overhead. His son brought help and providentially saved him.

After leaving Texas, he sent his son home and set off for the North on his own, baptizing and converting people along the way. In 1896, claiming that he was the reincarnation of the prophet Elijah, he acquired a reputation as the "black Elijah" as he preached to black and white audiences on Chicago's State Street. His meetings had the religious fervor of a southern camp meeting, with his audiences clapping their hands and stomping their feet and converts being led into a nearby stream for baptism.

The following year he headed to Lawrence, Kansas, a popular destination for ex-slaves after the Civil War. A quarter of the town's nearly ten thousand people were black. He spread his ministry to other towns around the state and, in October 1898, he decided to institutionalize his beliefs and convened his church's first General Assembly in Emporia, where he baptized followers in the Cottonwood River.[22] His followers consecrated him as bishop. In subsequent years Crowdy toured the Midwest and the East and eastern Canada, founding congregations in Michigan, New York, Connecticut, New Jersey, Massachusetts, and Pennsylvania. When a woman invited him to preach in Oneida, New York, in 1898, a center of Seventh-Day Adventism, Crowdy seized the occasion to denounce the denomination. At other times he claimed to have visited the nation's capital, where he requested an audience with President McKinley to give him a sealed message from God[23] and said that God instructed him to convert the prominent Republican politician, "the great agnostic," Robert Ingersoll.[24]

Crowdy stood out in American religious circles for ignoring the color line in his appeal for converts. For instance, most of his converts in Oneida were white, as were a significant number of his followers at his death. One newspaper account highlighted the broad racial appeal of his ministry.

> The color line is totally obliterated. Whites and blacks, males and females, Germans and Irish, Scandinavians and Welsh, fraternize and meet in a perfect equality and sociability such as certainly never before been witnessed in the United States. The most delicate and refined Caucasian girl or woman, when she becomes a convert to this church, or belief, thinks nothing out of the way, and displays not the least hesitation to receive the 'holy kiss' from the lips of the blackest negro in the congregation. On this point do the followers of Crowdy especially pride themselves, and claim that they are doing more than any other force being brought to bear in eradication of the color line.[25]

Speaking to an audience in Boston six years later, he noted how some white people could not accept the idea that God sent an angel in the form of a black man to do his work on earth.[26]

The headquarters for his ministry eventually became Philadelphia, his primary residence from 1899 to 1902. Crowdy's church stressed self-sufficiency and entrepreneurship and set up businesses on Fitzwater Street between Fifteenth and Broad Streets that bore the church's name: a Saints of Christ grocery store, a Daughters of Jerusalem / Noah's Ark store that provided furnishings for members, a Church of God café, a barbershop, and a printing shop that produced the church newspaper, the *Weekly Prophet*. Members were expected to tithe a tenth of their wages to the church, and their businesses also paid a tax to the church.[27]

Crowdy's preaching in the streets and at O'Neill Hall at Lombard and Broad Streets provoked a harsh response from rival black ministers linked to the Negro Ministerial Alliance. They branded his doctrines pernicious and petitioned city officials to investigate his teachings. One minister charged: "This false Negro prophet assails not only the moral law but seeks to destroy our civil law as well by teaching that it is not necessary for any member of his congregation to respect or regard the mandates of the civil Government, and insists that every man be a Socialist, Anarchist, or whatever he pleases." Their attacks did not deter Crowdy. "The more they denounce me," he boasted, "the more they'll pack my services."[28] Preaching in Boston several years later, he took pride in the fact that he had stirred up other black ministers who attacked him wherever he showed up. He compared himself to a hawk who sets upon a bunch of crows perched on a tree limb.[29]

In December 1903 when a smallpox epidemic struck Philadelphia and several cases were identified among Crowdy's followers in church stores, black clergy representing twenty congregations lobbied the city's health department to shut down his stores "on the ground that they spread disease, and are therefore a menace to the community in which they are situated."[30] This time Crowdy decided to move his main tabernacle to Washington, D.C., the city he considered his Jerusalem, the center of the world's power. Following the pattern set in Philadelphia, he encouraged his members to establish small business ventures such as a warehouse, a coal and wood yard, a shaving parlor, a grocery store, and a grocery store that took only cash. The church's newspaper, the Weekly Prophet, also founded about this time, set down strict rules to guide grocery store clerks. "If the Clerk let any thing out from the Store without the Manager's consent, he must pay for it; and if they can't pay in one week they can't get nothing. You must pay as you go. This is a general rule to all the people. You must work while you are playing so much, do not let nothing go from any of the employments."[31] Crowdy also enjoined church members not to grow cotton for sale because "we picked enough in slavery."[32]

By 1906, his church claimed a membership of nearly two thousand (of which about 70 percent were women) and operated almost fifty tabernacles in fourteen American states, several in Canada and the West Indies, and a dozen in South Africa.[33]

Crowdy presided over the church by virtue of his prophetic role, since he was believed to be in direct communication with God and prophesied according to God's will. Among his predictions were the assassination of President McKinley, the death of Queen Victoria, and the Spanish-

American War, which he saw as a prelude to a global conflagration in which the United States and Britain would "represent the second beast spoken of in the Revelations, which had two horns which prevailed against all others. Blood, he claims will run like water in the streets during the second war, but that in the end righteousness will triumph and the kingdom of God will prevail."[34] He also acquired a reputation for performing miracles.

The cornerstone of Crowdy's beliefs was the revelations in which he discovered the "stone of truth" (1 Cor 1:1–2), which shed light on how scripture originated and how to use it and ancestral data about the origins of the "Negro" race. God, he maintained, revealed to him that blacks were Jews descended from the lost tribes of Israel and the chosen people. Biblical personages, prophets, judges, apostles, and kings such as Adam, Moses, Solomon, and Christ were black men. Contemporary Jews were the descendants of blacks whose skin had become lighter through mixing with whites after the death of Christ. Crowdy's belief was based on his rendering of the opening of the book of Genesis. When God created heaven and earth, "darkness was upon the face of the deep, and the spirit of God moved upon the face of the waters." He interpreted "the waters" as referring to humans who were black.[35]

Crowdy was certainly not unique among African American religious leaders in referencing histories of dispersion, bondage, persecution, and emancipation.[36] The stories of the Hebrews in the book of Exodus and the figures of Moses and Joshua were woven into their sermons, hymns, and prayers and were a guiding moral and political compass during and after the years of slavery. Their example challenged the idea that blacks were consigned to slavery and subservience and served as a critique of the injustices inflicted on African Americans that ran counter to American ideals. "Is America Israel," they asked, "or is she Egypt?"[37] So Crowdy likened the American Civil War to the Exodus story—because the children of Israel (African Americans) had been freed from their bondage and were beginning anew.[38]

Crowdy's theology was based on a literal reading of Old Testament doctrine and ritual. He declared, "I haven't got a new doctrine. It's been noised about that I have, but I haven't. Everything I tell you is right there in the Bible."[39] Hence the church's statement of faith simply stated: "We, the Church of God and Saints of Christ, believe the Bible as it is; repentance, faith and baptism by burial into the water."[40] Adopting the Gregorian calendar that featured Hebrew names for months (and honored Christian saints), the CGSC observed Jewish feast days and a Sabbath that began on Friday at sunset and ended at the same time on Saturday.

Crowdy based the Seven Keys, the central pillars of his church's beliefs, on both Old and New Testament teachings. A litany of Bible verses amplified the meaning of each key. The first key was that the CGSC was God's representative on earth (1 Corinthians 1:1–2). Crowdy was a strong supporter of temperance, so the second key prohibited wine (and all products derived from grapes) in the sacrament of the Lord's Supper (Leviticus 10:9–10). The third was that unleavened bread and water symbolized Christ's body and blood. The fourth and fifth strictly honored the Lord's or Disciples' Prayer (Matthew 6:9–13) and the Ten Commandments (Exodus 20:1–17). The sixth required members to greet each other with a holy kiss, a symbol of accepting the Holy Spirit (Romans 16:16 and John 20:22). The final key commanded members to follow the example of Jesus with his disciples and perform foot washing when receiving new members or members from another place (John 13:1–23). Because of this ritual, church members became popularly known as the "foot washers."

The church believes that Christ was a Jewish prophet and that his teachings were in line with Judaism. Christ was neither the Son of God nor the savior and was not born on 25 December. Hence, Christmas and Easter are not celebrated. Instead, the church's main religious festival is Passover, observed annually, which all members are expected to attend. The first Passovers were held in 1899 in Lawrence and Emporia, Kansas.[41] The *Emporia Daily Gazette* described the Passover feast on the first day.

> After the feast had been spread, the "saints" repeated together the Lord's Prayer. Then ranging themselves about a long dining table the pastor said grace in a few words, a "saint" thrust the carving knife home, there was a crackling of crusts and the feast was on. After passing up the plates several times, the cup went round. It contained only water, supposedly taking the place of wine. Then the usual form of the sacrament was gone through, with water taking the place of grape-juice. To close with, the saints sang heartily several stanzas of "At the Cross."[42]

Seven years later, when western and eastern tabernacles attended a Passover for the first time together, thousands of church members converged on Reform Hall in Plainfield, a New Jersey town near New York

City. The afternoon before Passover commenced, they paraded through the streets singing hymns, with a bugler "blowing mighty blasts on a silver trumpet, shaped like a ram's horn."[43]

Crowdy, whose right arm lay limp at his side because of a recent stroke, presided over the festivities. A *New York Times* journalist described him: "Elijah was attired in a loose fitting brown suit. His feet were adorned with brown spats and he wore a beautiful crown of vari-colored silk. The shape is mortar board. On his hands he wore a pair of long, loose fitting white cotton gloves, and after getting upon his throne he looked very impressive."[44] A *New York Tribune* correspondent remarked on the vibrant singing and marching that were an essential part of services.

> One hundred prancing young daughters of Zion in blue waists but cardinal crowns, echoed the contralto: Why harden your heart? The sopranos repeated, this time answered by a score of tenors and basses in long brown suits. Thereupon the entire choir, in response to the baton of the buxom, joyous and ever smiling leader, Sister Mercy of a canary yellow crown, thundered forth: Let my people go! Other hymns and melodies were sung on the march, while the male saints double-shuffled and slapped their legs and the sisters exercised their shoulders and hips as much as they did their tuneful throats.[45]

After a lengthy evening service that lasted till midnight, the whole gathering, as called for in scripture, consumed unleavened bread and roasted paschal lambs (slaughtered by a kosher butcher) and drank water.

The church's group identity was reinforced through its rituals as well as its member's distinctive uniforms and the music and marching drills they performed during services. Sara Stone argues that Crowdy, who attained the rank of thirty-third degree Mason, very likely adopted these features from the Masons.[46] For instance, the dress of officers of both Masons and the CGSC featured shoulder sashes, ribbon rosettes, and belts. Like Masons, church stewards and elders carried rods and swords. Members wore different styles and colors of dress depending on the occasion. The symbols of an all-seeing eye representing God's omnipotence and constant watching over his people and the Stone of Truth as well as keys were important to the CGSC and Masons.[47]

At Masonic meetings and CGSC services members perform intricate marches in formation while singing hymns. Observed at every Sabbath service and on specified days of the Passover festival, these demonstration marches, as CGSC members call them, give the appearance of an army drilling in cadence.

Crowdy lived a few years after his stroke. He spent the last three weeks of his life in Newark, New Jersey, where he died on 4 August 1908. In the years after his death church factions began quarreling, partly over race and the succession of Bishop J. M. Grove, a white man from Emporia, Kansas, as leader of the church. The church split into eastern, western, and southern districts, with Crowdy's nephew Joseph Crowdy heading the eastern district and Grove the western district.[48] The eastern district's headquarters moved to Bellville, Virginia, a hundred miles south of where Crowdy had been a slave, where the church purchased land for a home for widows and orphans and aimed to create a self-sufficient communal society.[49]

Birds of the Air: John Msikinya and the Church of God and Saints of Christ in South Africa

Although Crowdy expressed interest in visiting South Africa in 1902, he was denied permission to enter. He sent in his place Albert Christian, a Jamaican sailor who had visited South Africa in 1899 as a member of Orpheus McAdoo's Jubilee Singers on its third tour around the country.[50] He had stayed on as a Baptist missionary in Port Elizabeth until 1902, when he began having serious doubts about his mission in life. He dreamed "of a Prophet a man he had never seen but who always calling him in his sleep telling him that God had a work for him to do." Christian left to search for this prophet, first in England and then, after the dream recurred, in New York. His search eventually led him to Philadelphia, where he came face to face with Crowdy walking down a street. "The man from Africa ran across the street and fell down on his knees at the Prophet's feet. The Prophet quickly kneeled down and said, 'See thou do it not. I am thy fellow servant of thy brethren that have the testimony of Jesus. Worship God for the testimony of Jesus is the Spirit of Prophecy.'" After Crowdy stood up, they embraced each other.[51]

Crowdy delegated Christian to carry the CGSC message to Africa. He was baptized in the CGSC, ordained a minister, and sent to the Cape Colony as an evangelist. After an unsuccessful start in Cape Town he founded branches in Uitenhage, New Brighton, and Port Elizabeth, where he won converts in both the Coloured and African communities. By the time illness forced him to leave South Africa in 1905, he had spread the church throughout the eastern Cape and as far away as Potgietersrus in the northern Transvaal. Returning to the United States, he stayed in Crowdy's home in Washington, D.C., until his death in spring 1906. He was buried in Washington[52]

Mgijima learned about the CGSC through Christian's successor as evangelist in charge, Charles Motlabane; the Matshaka brothers, Samuel, Peter, and Andrew; and the CGSC bishop for South Africa, John I. Msikinya. Born about 1877 to an Mfengu family in the Fort Beaufort area, Msikinya qualified for a teacher's certificate at nearby Healdtown Institution and then taught at Aliwal North and Kimberley.[53] Although his family had been Wesleyan Methodists for three generations, he and his brother, Henry, joined the AME Church.

With no possibility for a university education for Africans in South Africa, the Msikinyas joined several hundred other African students who journeyed to the United States for higher education in the late nineteenth and early twentieth centuries. The brothers took advantage of AME support and enrolled at African American colleges. After receiving a B.A. from Wilberforce, an AME college in Ohio, Henry later served as principal of the AME's Wilberforce Institute, at Evaton, Transvaal.

John, however, took a different path. While attending Lincoln College on the outskirts of Philadelphia for a year in 1903–4, he wrote in Solomon Plaatje's newspaper, *Koranta ea Becoana* (baTswana Newspaper), a call for blacks in the diaspora to recognize their common identity and critique the attacks of "deceivers" in the white press in South Africa who decried African American influences on African independent churches in South Africa. Msikinya admired Booker T. Washington for concentrating his educational initiatives among black folk in the rural South and not in the urban areas of the North. He concluded his remarks with his poem "Africa's Tears."

> Come to me, oh, ye children,
> For I'm old and out of date;
> Bring with you the wisdom
> Whence it may be obtained;
> Tell me not of Socrates and Plato
> For their words are old and gray,
> But your youngest infant state.

I have worried long without you,
For a thousand years or so
Come and put us "in the know";
I have sat in the quiet cloister,
My light behind a bush
And I need your kind assistance
In the modern game of push.[54]

At Lincoln, Msikinya learned of Crowdy's ministry in nearby Philadelphia and began attending services. After attending his first Passover in 1905, the following year he was baptized and ordained, participated in the landmark Passover at Plainfield, and was appointed pastor in charge of a congregation in Jersey City, New Jersey. In 1909, he was elevated to bishop and sent to South Africa.[55]

A letter Msikinya penned for the CGSC newspaper, Weekly Prophet (15 November 1912), reveals much about his lack of respect for white missionaries in contrast to his new faith's beliefs. Msikinya was especially disturbed by the "sectarian faiths," the multiplicity of European denominations that sowed confusion in the minds of Africans and made it difficult for their leaders to govern effectively. European missionary teachings undermined the moral character of their followers by introducing them to drinking wine at Communion, a practice the CGSC shunned.

A sober man and woman who never tasted wine or any strong drink turned to drunkards, and the missionary is the first man to hand him a glass of wine, saying drink, this is the blood which was shed for you. Jesus says as often as ye drink of this cup, ye remember him. He tells not how often we would do this, but he says as often as we do so we remember him, and thus it will be seen that every man or woman remembered Christ as often as he or she laid their hand on a bottle of wine. . . . Such is the work accomplished by the missionaries, which made me to forsake my country.

Msikinya commenced his circuit in the eastern Cape as anti-Ethiopian sentiments among white officials and missionaries were reaching a fever pitch. His first port of call was Uitenhage, where city officials were already in an uproar over the "unrest and dissension" caused by independent churches such as the AME.[56] What one speaker at a CGSC service told his audience alarmed a white school board member. Jesus, the speaker revealed, was black, and Africans were his descendants. "The white people [claim] that he was a white man but they do not like to hear the truth about Jesus Christ." Certain people, he added, were made whites as punishment for their sins and were "looked down upon by our own people." Whites had to be put in their places; otherwise "they will drag you lower and lower until you are all slaves." The speaker concluded by predicting that bloodshed was inevitable.[57]

At Durban mission station near Peddie, government officials received reports of a new church with a Saturday Sabbath practicing a kiss of peace and holding Saturday night baptisms in the river. Walter Mafongosi witnessed Msikinya's preaching on 27 June 1910.

> He said the white people brought the Bible but they only showed us half and therefore they were liars—they called the English and Wesleyan Churches the gates of Hell—All those that take wine and call it the blood of Christ are going to Hell—He said King George was going to send out soldiers to kill the Black people and that the Natives were fools to be led astray by the white man—He said Christ was a black man, Moses was a black man and the Jews were black—He said the white man was the goat of the flock because he had long hair and the black man was the sheep of the flock because he had wooly hair and therefore they were the chosen people of God—He further said the Native Chiefs were not chiefs but the slaves of the white man.[58]

Officials had a problem with believers refusing to work on Saturdays and the kiss of peace, which they regarded as a sign of promiscuity. Reacting to these and other reports, officials in Uitenhage and Peddie turned down Msikinya's applications for a church and school site. Their decision had the blessing of the secretary for Native Affairs, Edward Dower, who advised on the Peddie case that because "the blood of martyrs is the seed of the church," they should refrain from taking any extreme measures against Msikinya or his followers and hope that his group would "peacefully dissolve . . . as has apparently been the case in other Districts."[59]

Msikinya and his disciples encountered an even more hostile environment in Grahamstown, where police detectives closely monitored their activities. When a detective challenged Adonis Matshaka and Charles Mhlabane to explain how they supported themselves, they proudly responded that they lived like "birds of the air," relying on money collected from people in the street.[60] They were willing to make sacrifices and endure persecution like the apostle Paul because God had ordained them to spread his word. Local officials could try all manner of tactics to suppress them. "They could hang us, shoot us. They say we are loafers . . . they say we pray in the street . . . they will preach in the streets and at the corners of the streets as they had been sent by God."[61]

In similar fashion, when a detective challenged Msikinya to justify his livelihood, he explained that the Gospel of Christ sustained him and his followers. They followed the example of Saul and Paul by relying on donations of food from the people "and if they did not get it they had to go without it as they did not earn any money."[62] To the authorities, however, this was not proof of devotion to the Lord but an admission that they had no visible means of support and was grounds for charging Msikinya and his followers with vagrancy—"wrongfully and unlawfully wandering abroad without any visible means of support." In two separate trials in August 1910, a magistrate found Mhlabane and Matshaka guilty and sentenced them to a month of hard labor and sentenced Msikinya and a number of women followers to three months' hard labor.[63]

Enoch Mgijima Joins the Church of God and Saints of Christ

Despite the adversity, Msikinya, assisted by the Matshaka brothers, established the church in a number of communities. The CGSC contacted Mgijima in the second half of 1912 when Joseph Tuso, a schoolmaster, invited Samuel Matshaka from Healdtown to Kamastone to discuss the church and its beliefs. After establishing a rapport with local residents, Matshaka stayed long enough to baptize a small group of converts—Mgijima, Tuso, Victor Ndlangisa, and John Ntlangweni.[64] The following year, the church held its first Passover from 14 to 21 April at Kamastone. It lasted seven days and attracted over a thousand people.

Soon after Mgijima joined his church, Msikinya was faced with the question of what role to give Mgijima, since he already commanded a sizable personal following. His solution was to appoint him as high evangelist, or evangelist in chief. But a short time later, Mgijima began to wield enormous influence over him and became the dominant personality in the church. Msikinya reportedly justified this reversal of roles by relating that Crowdy had told him that there was a man in Africa exactly like himself. He had instructed Msikinya that when he recognized this man, "you will have an experience like a pillow being turned inside out with its feathers spreading everywhere in the wind. That is how you are going to spread when you come into contact with him."[65] That man would be the same as Crowdy, who had been prevented from visiting Africa but claimed that after he died in America, he would "arise in Africa speaking the languages of the native people."[66]

However, when Msikinya met Mgijima for the first time, he did not immediately recognize him as Crowdy's messenger in Africa. They quarreled about that as well as doctrinal issues. Eventually, Msikinya recanted and, a short time later, Mgijima became head of the Kamastone branch. When Msikinya died around 1913, Mgijima assumed the mantle of bishop.[67] The CGSC, however, did not accept Mgijima's claim that he was Crowdy's messenger in Africa. It maintained that Crowdy never made such a prophecy and that Mgijima made up the tale to consolidate his leadership over the church.[68]

Establishing institutional links with the CGSC was vital for Mgijima because he elevated his status from an itinerant evangelist to leader of an established, if not mainstream, denomination. And it provided him with an organizational base for articulating his frequent prophetic visions. According to his followers, he predicted the appearance of the first automobile—"men are going to run sitting"—and the airplane. He foresaw the devastation wrought by the influenza pandemic of 1918, which he described as "O's" (umnqingo), round things that would encompass everyone. An ominous portent for the Israelites was his vision in 1920 of children lying on their backs kicking their feet up in the air.[69] Although his followers did not understand it then, they realized later that he was foretelling the massacre at Bulhoek.

Mgijima had launched his prophetic mission with his 1907 vision of an approaching cataclysm. In April 1910, he predicted that a star would appear from the East. When Halley's comet blazed across the sky soon after that, he interpreted it as a manifestation of God's will. "Jehovah is angry. . . . Unless men turn to their ancient religion, the earth will meet some great disaster. . . . We must . . . worship on the model of the Israelite patriarchs who in their day were liberated by Jehovah from the yoke of oppressive rulers."[70]

The passage of Halley's comet had a profound effect not only on Mgijima but also on many others throughout southern Africa. Bengt Sundkler relates the example of another prophet, Timothy Cekwana, of Himeville, Natal, who was holding a prayer meeting when "there appeared in the firmament a miraculous star with a long tail. Moreover it stood still ex-actly over the place where Timothy prayed upon the mountain. Wild with a joy of excitement, the group hailed Timothy as the Elect. The heavens, the stars, Halley's comet itself, yes, the whole cosmos, proclaimed the unique spiritual authority of their leader." Ian and Jane Linden report that in Nyasaland Halley's comet "brought hundreds of villagers fleeing into the bush to confess their sins and prepare for the end of the world."[71]

In the Transkei, Native Affairs officials advised Africans of the comet's approach, since they worried that the opportunity "may very likely be taken advantage of by clever imposters to exploit the ignorance of the Natives in the Transkeian Territories . . . and that apart from conscious fraud striking phenomena may occur such as will be likely to cause panic to the superstitious unless they have been forewarned."[72]

Mgijima refrained from pinpointing a date for the millennium until shortly after he joined the CGSC. In late 1912, as the region suffered through a severe drought and East Coast fever, he predicted that the mil-lennium would take place by Christmas Day. At Shiloh mission station, those loyal to the Moravians prayed for rain, while Mgijima's followers mocked them. "You are praying to Baal," they said. "The rain will not come." Although rain did come a few days later, Mgijima predicted an eighty-day deluge that would sweep away all those whom he had not bap-tized. When the "time was over," he said, "the door of grace would be closed to non-believers and by Christmas the believers would be taken away by the Lord" in a saloon car.[73] Anticipating the appointed day, his followers did not plough their fields or harvest their crops. To prepare for the end of time, girls had to be properly attired, donning white silken dresses and putting white ribbons in their hair. Although the millennium did not materialize, his followers apparently did not lose their faith, and his following did not diminish.

In subsequent years he did not stake his credibility on predicting a precise date for the millennium, but he continued to elaborate on it. On the eve of World War I, he related that God had asked him if he had heard a thunderous sound, a sign that there was going to be a "big war on earth, which will cause the destruction of all sinners, and he will only save those who obey His commandments. The Lord informed me that the war will begin in 1914 and from thence there shall be no peace on earth."[74] When the final judgment came, Mgijima believed his followers would be the elect who would achieve salvation and redemption.

Mgijima's interpretation of the millennium eventually led to a rupture with the CGSC. His vision of a violent and turbulent cataclysm did not square with Crowdy's pacific prophecies. In particular, a series of Mgijima's visions that appeared to be directed against whites disturbed the CGSC. At one Passover, Mgijima spoke of a vision in which two goats fought a baboon three times, with the baboon coming out victorious. At first, Mgijima refused to reveal what the vision meant, but later he explained that he had "seen a vision of a great war, in which the whole of this country would be engaged, between the whites and the blacks but in which the members of their church would not be included."[75] The two goats, he disclosed, symbolized Europeans and the baboon Africans. Mgijima said that one of his visions and his reading of Jeremiah 4:19 revealed that there would be a great war in which armies would come from the East and the West and clash in Africa.

According to Samuel Matshaka, Mgijima's visions were apostasy, since the CGSC "taught implicit obedience to those in Authority" and did not envision a conflict or war. On the contrary, the first of the Seven Keys made reference to Isaiah 2:4: "And they shall beat their swords into plowshares, and their spears into pruning hooks; nation shall not lift up sword against nation, neither shall they learn war anymore."[76] On several occasions American church officials warned Mgijima to disavow his prophecies. When he did not recant, C. P. Mhlabane of Uitenhage wrote Mgijima on 8 August 1916 that his teachings "interfear [sic] with the Constitution of the Church of God and Saints of Christ" and that he had "to stop preaching or doing anything declaring that you are under the name Church of God and Saints of Christ."[77] The church's organ, the *Weekly Prophet*, reported in its 24 November 1916 edition that Mgijima had been "discommunicated" (excommunicated) from the church "for preaching false doctrine, claiming to be the founder of the Church of God and Saints of Christ."[78] A faction led by Peter Matshaka and centered at Uitenhage remained loyal to the parent church. Mgijima's branch, which retained the name Church of God and Saints of Christ, became more popularly known as the Israelites, a name taken from Genesis 32:38.

Israelite Liturgies of Liberation and Redemption

At the heart of the Israelite faith was their search for salvation and deliverance from tyrannical authority. They relied on God to bring about freedom. Their god, like Israel's god, was a god of transformation who stood for justice and who would topple wicked and unjust rulers and usher in his own reign of freedom. Surely good would inevitably triumph over evil and God would deliver Mgijima's Israelites from the yoke of an oppressive regime.

The Israelites embraced biblical culture as their own and closely identified with the Old Testament Israelites on several levels. Mgijima could draw parallels between the latter's historical experiences and culture and his own Hlubi ancestors. Both shared similar ritual practices and social structures. Like the Israelites, the Hlubi had been forced into exile and suffered many deprivations before finding a new home. They had endured bondage under pharonic rulers. But while the biblical Israelites had escaped pharaoh's persecution in Egypt and reached the promised land after many ordeals, Mgijima and his Israelites still had not found solace in South Africa.

Mgijima's Israelites drew on both Old and New Testament scripture as sources of inspiration and validation for the group's identity and its dress, code of conduct, and rituals.[79] Mgijima claimed his Israelites were direct descendants of two tribes, Judah and Benjamin. The men shaved their heads (Ezekiel 5:1), wore white tunics for their uniforms, and carried ceremonial swords (Luke 22:36). As a call to worship they blew bugles to invite the presence of God (Joshua 6:4–5). They greeted each other with the words "Bota [Hail], Israel" (Matthew 28:9).

They worshipped in a tabernacle and strictly followed the moral code of the Ten Commandments. The centerpiece of their worship was an Ark of the Covenant, on which the Ten Commandments were ornately written in isiXhosa on a large scroll that was brought to the Israelites around 1919. Just as the Ten Commandments were revealed to Moses as the Israelites were being led to the promised land, the same was happening to Mgijima and his followers.

By adopting the Hebrew calendar and measurement of time, the Israelites also reconstituted how Europeans calculated time. Israelite time became freedom time, in which the shackles of white oppression were loosed; they derisively referred to European time as "heathen time." Hence the first month of the Israelite calendar was April, the month the biblical Israelites were freed from the Egyptians.

Two ritual observances, the Passover festival of the book of Exodus and Esther's fast, reinforced this message by narrating tales of exile and captivity and the quest for freedom of the biblical Israelites in foreign lands. But there was an important historical difference between them. Mgijima's Israelites were not aiming to escape from South Africa. They were "inziles," people who had become strangers in their own land, a feeling expressed in the haunting lament of their hymn "By the River": "We cannot sing the Lord's song in a strange land."[80]

The compelling force of the Exodus story has been a particular source of inspiration for both religious and secular movements, galvanizing revolutionaries, social reformers, and nationalists alike who have identified with the Israelites' trials and tribulations as well as their dreams and triumphs. As Michael Walzer puts it, "Wherever people know the Bible, and experience oppression, the Exodus has sustained their spirits and (sometimes) inspired their resistance."[81] Hence, Exodus had a particular resonance for African and African American Christians living under white oppression in the United States and Africa as well as Afrikaner nationalists of the nineteenth century defining themselves as a chosen people.[82]

The Exodus narrative typically features a sequence of events, beginning with an experience of persecution and the cry of a people for freedom. It then progresses to a call for a prophet to lead them, a challenge to and breaking away from an oppressor, wandering in the wilderness, the forging of a covenant, and the vanquishing of an oppressor. Finally a new community of believers is built, which eventually crosses over into the promised land. Depending on the movement, that ultimate deliverance comes either through divine intervention or because of the oppressed's conscious efforts.

Mgijima's Israelites imagined their own history as a reenactment of the Exodus narrative. The Passover (*Pasika*) is a ritualistic affirmation that God is a god of salvation and that he is preparing the way for the liberation of his chosen people. Departing from European missionaries who preached an individual salvation, the Israelites envisioned a collective salvation for their Exodus community. The first of the seven days of Passover opens with evangelists and elders ritually slaughtering a lamb for a paschal meal.[83] Then Exodus 13 is read at a service, its message conveying the expectation that God will show mercy on the Israelites by forcing Pharaoh to free the Israelites from bondage. A highlight of day two is the recessional march, re-creating Pharaoh's chariots chasing after the Israelites and their horses getting stuck in mud before being swallowed up in the Red Sea. Pharaoh's symbols of power, his chariots and horses, are vanquished.

The Great Marches of days three and four feature the singing of Passover hymns and the performance of a paschal dance that symbolizes "the Lord passing over the Israelites" and traces their movement "from a people enslaved to a people freed." Performers carry ribbons with many colors that differentiate their rank, age, gender, and marital status. Their homilies typically narrate their escape from an oppressive ruler and their perilous journey of salvation to the promised land.

The other principal church festival is Esther's fast, which takes its inspiration from the book of Esther (*inzila ka Esteri*). Mgijima's selection of Esther is significant because he favored stories and prophets such as Ezekiel and Daniel set during the historical period of the late seventh and sixth century B.C.E. when the Chaldeans had conquered the kingdom of Judah, ending four centuries of independence, and capturing its aristocracy and priesthood and sending them into exile.[84]

Esther narrates how the Hebrews had been colonized and sent into Babylonian captivity. Although many Jews had eventually been freed and allowed to return to their homeland, a small remnant remained there after the Persians conquered it in 539 B.C.E.

Esther tells how the Persian king Ahasueros (probably Xerxes I, 486–465 B.C.E.) had selected Esther as his new queen after Queen Vashti refused to do the king's bidding and parade before him. The king was unaware that Esther was a Jew raised by her uncle Mordecai after her parents had passed away. Mordecai had offended Haman, the king's prime minister, who plotted to execute Mordecai and exterminate the Jewish community on the twelfth day of Adar. However, Esther exposed Haman's planned pogrom to the king, who instead had Haman hung on the gallows constructed for Mordecai and decreed that the Jews could not only protect themselves but could seek retribution against their enemies. On the same day that Haman had planned to eradicate the Jews, they set out for vengeance. The following two days they feasted to commemorate the Jews' deliverance from their enemies.

Like Exodus, the story of Esther reinforces the message that God is sovereign, but it differs in emphasizing human agency rather than God directly intervening to deliver the Jewish people from extermination.

Esther is best known as the basis for Purim, a Jewish observance that is highlighted by a feast, not a fast, and the giving of food to others and charity to the poor. Although religious movements rarely cite Esther as a liberatory text, Mgijima interpreted it to mean that "the dark cloud over the Israelites was still with us" in South Africa and that his Israelites had to rely totally on God to transform the world and replace secular rulers with his own order.[85]

The Israelite observance begins on 3 January and they read a chapter of Esther and discuss it each day of the seven-day period. Church services are held every day, with Holy Communion observed on the sixth day and a fast on the last day. After the observance is completed, the Israelites celebrate with a feast known as Tebeta.

The Summons to Ntabelanga

In early 1919, Enoch Mgijima stood outside the Israelite tabernacle at a midday church service. Holding two crossed sticks in front of him, he uttered the words "Juda, Efrayime, Josef, *nezalwane* [Judah, Ephraim, Joseph, and brethren]." Then he exclaimed, "*Bonke bevile* [They have all heard me]."[86]

Mgijima's dramatic pronouncement summoned his followers to gather together at their holy village of Ntabelanga. According to Israelite testimony, he made his invitation but once, and his followers heard and understood him and began journeying to his home. Eventually some three thousand followers, most of them from within a few hundred miles' radius but some from as far away as the eastern Transvaal, were to settle at Ntabelanga.

Mgijima's call rested on the assurance of scripture and drew on the prophecies of the visionary Ezekiel, one of the priests in the temple in Jerusalem who had been captured and taken to Nebuchadnezzar's Babylon. Ezekiel longed for a return to the time when Israel had been united and sovereign. God commanded him to hold up two sticks, one signifying Judah and the other all the other tribes of Israel. God held out the promise that he would unify them into one nation. "I will take the children of Israel from among the heathen . . . and will gather them on every side, and bring them into their own land."[87] Proclaiming that King David would rule for all generations, he promised that he would forge a covenant of peace with them that would last forever. "Yea, I will be their God, and they shall be my people, And the heathen shall know that I the Lord do sanctify Israel, when my sanctuary shall be in the midst of them for evermore."[88]

Like Ezekiel Mgijima called his followers of all nations to come together. And, like Ezekiel, who preached to the people of Israel of an impending catastrophe, he told them to prepare for an imminent judgment day.

One family who responded to Mgijima's call was the Ntlokos, who had been prosperous farmers in the Nqamakwe area until their fortunes began to decline. They had been staunch Methodists, but Dora Tamana, who was in her teens at the time, remembered the racism of white Wesleyan clergy. Her family had heard Samuel Masiza sound a trumpet and tell them that he had been sent by Mgijima to warn "that the whole world was going to be in trouble, the big war will affect everybody and this war will be followed by the battle of Armageddon."[89] That is when they joined the Church of God and Saints of Christ.

Her family had joined the Israelites and attended several Passovers at Kamastone. When they learned of Mgijima's call for all the Israelites to come together, they packed their belongings and moved to Ntabelanga. Tamana spoke of the hope that Mgijima offered: "We had a belief that the church would do something better than we are now. Because we had been struggling and I think it was a sort of change in the mind that the people must fight for themselves. But this was religious."[90]

Another Israelite who heeded Mgijima's call was Benjamin Duba at his Tsomo home. Elder Hezekiah Mgijima instructed him and his family to "closely study the teachings of the Old Testament, and that they should know that Jehovah had anointed him [Enoch] a Prophet to lead them from this part of the World to the land of Promise, just as the Israelites were led out of Egypt to the Land of Promise." Duba sold all his possessions and journeyed with his mother, wife, two children, two brothers, and two sisters to join the others flocking to Ntabelanga to prepare for "their long journey to the Land of Promise."[91]

Why Mgijima made his call at this particular time is not readily apparent. There is not enough evidence to speculate whether personal grievances or a personal crisis contributed to his decision. We know that he had a running dispute with local European officials over a boundary issue, but that was not an overwhelming complaint. Although it would be fascinating to establish this sort of linkage, what is more important is to understand why some people were so receptive to his call. One explanation is that many Africans in the region had experienced a long decline in their economic fortunes and suffered through a prolonged wave of diseases and both man-made and natural disasters that swept through the region. Around the time of World War I, these pressures intensified, and one major shock after another struck without any respite. First came the East Coast fever of 1912, which destroyed many hundreds of thousands of cattle, and then World War I with its attendant inflationary spiral and higher taxes, which were particularly burdensome to Africans.[92]

Food prices alone rose almost 100 percent between 1910 and 1920, with most of the increase coming during the postwar years. African wages, however, did not keep up with inflation. Africans frequently vented their feelings in letters to the editor of the Queenstown newspaper. For instance, "Africanus" wrote to the *Queensland Daily Representative* (6 November 1920) pointing out how challenging it was for many blacks to make ends meet in these stressful times. He asked:

> Is it just and fair to pay an upgrown person 2s per diem working 8 to 10 hours a day? Is that freedom or serfdom, justice or what? Such an upgrown man feeds and clothes his wife and children; and consequently educates the latter, and finally but not least pays his yearly taxes as there are laws in the country that regulate you—6d or 1s per day would be adequate and the employed would be very pleased, thankful and satisfied. Secondly, I see no reason why the natives are not highly paid, for the money they get here they spend in this country and nowhere else. . . . As for the skilled and unskilled labour—the unskilled being performed by the natives—the skilled labour cannot be done without the former. Hence the natives are indispensable tools in every department of labour. I unfeighnedly appeal to the sympathetic feelings of our masters. *Spero meliora.* Have sympathy with your black brethren.

The potent combination of drought and disease, which animated Mgijima's vision of an imminent millennium in 1912, was repeated six years later. Between September and November 1918 the cataclysmic Spanish influenza pandemic—known to the Xhosa as *umbathalala*, or the disaster—swept through South Africa, leaving an estimated quarter of a million dead in its wake. This epic disaster left few families or communities untouched. The death toll in the African reserves of the Ciskei and Transkei was especially high, with an estimated one thousand Africans dying in the Queenstown district alone. The first cases reported at Kamastone in early October were initially laughed off since they came a day after a marriage festival and the illnesses were attributed to too much drink. But then the deaths quickly mounted. The number of deaths in Kamastone was put at 150, or about 50 per thousand, almost twice as high as the national average.[93] Mgijima, who had foretold the pandemic by referring to a round thing that would envelop the world, leaving no place unaffected, instructed his followers to paint their houses white so the plague would not touch them.

A severe drought immediately followed the influenza. Rainfall in the region had been minimal for several years, but it was at its lowest in decades in 1919. The amounts for the following year were even lower, creating water shortages, destroying pasturage, wiping out crops and tens of thousands of animals, and raising the prospect of famine. The drought had a serious impact on lambing and kidding, and farmers had to destroy many animals to save their mothers.[94]

Africans were constantly reminded that the government would not provide any relief from their burdens. For instance, the 1913 Natives' Land Act freezing the unequal land division between whites and blacks dashed the hopes of many Africans of alleviating critical land shortages. The magistrate of Lady Frere, M. G. Apthorp, reported that among Africans, "The cry everywhere is 'land.'"[95]

During World War I and its aftermath, many Africans held high expectations that the government would reward them for their loyalty and service. Instead the government passed or proposed more legislation tightening controls on Africans. In 1919, a delegation of African political leaders from South Africa traveled to England and the Versailles Peace Conference to appeal for a redress of injustices and returned home empty-handed.[96]

To many Africans, it had become increasingly clear that something was radically wrong with the world and that they had lost control over their lives. Edward Barrett, the secretary for native affairs, did not remotely share their perception. In the midst of the 1919 drought, when a reporter asked him, "How does the native take these misfortunes?" he responded, "I can only say that he meets the prevalent distress with a quiet fortitude which one does not always find among other peoples."[97] But it is evident that many Africans were not placidly resigned to their fates and were desperately searching for immediate answers to their plight.

Mgijima's millennial vision offered an attractive alternative by providing a grand narrative that not only explained these disasters but also offered a radical solution. Had he not predicted that World War I would happen? Had he not prophesied that there would be a period of instability and chaos before the millennium unfolded? Could he not justify his visions by quoting scripture that spoke of the fire, war, and devastation that would accompany the millennium? And could he not guarantee his faithful followers redemption and salvation?

Mgijima's active engagement with the events of the times is reflected in correspondence with his nephew, Gilbert Matshoba, a clerk for a Queenstown lawyer, who kept him informed about the unsettled atmosphere of the postwar world. Matshoba wrote about African strikes on the Rand and in Aliwal North;[98] the calls by Queenstown Africans for higher wages and the abolition of the pass system; a food riot by Lovedale students in May 1920;[99] the worsening drought in the eastern Cape, which drove Afrikaner farmers around Cradock to fire their rifles in the air and to implore the Lord to send rain; and the August 1920 convention in New York City of Marcus Garvey's Universal Negro Improvement Association (UNIA), which was denouncing colonialism and advocating freedom for the African continent. News of the Garvey movement was filtering into South Africa and was responsible for creating a false expectation among Africans that African Americans were arriving soon to drive out whites.[100] Reporting on the UNIA meeting, which attracted several thousand people from the United States, the Caribbean, and Africa, Matshoba related Garvey's vow:

> We will not ask England, France, Italy or Belgium, or in other words we will not ask from them why are you . . . in this place [Africa]. We will only direct them to get out. We will only formulate a Bill of Rights embracing all the black natives and also law to administrate their welfare. The blood of all wars is about to arrive (its compensation is due). Then Europe puts her might against Asia. Then it will be time for the negroes to lift up their sword of the liberty of the Africans. Father, that is the news of our black countrymen. . . . Abide with me, Father, in the year when the babes are lying on their backs, affairs are topsy-turvy with the result that one does not know which is which.[101]

When taken collectively, Mgijima's interpretation of these events reinforced his belief that the world around him was collapsing and was a significant stimulus to his prediction that the millennium was drawing nigh. That many others shared his perception of turmoil is apparent, for his call to his followers to join him on a journey of redemption at Ntabelanga struck a responsive chord.

Mgijima's move to establish his own Exodus community was a logical step since that image was extraordinarily appealing to followers who had been waging a losing battle to retain their independence and identity in an unstable and hostile world. At Ntabelanga his elect could withdraw from the temptation and immorality of a corrupt world. There they could sever their ties with the past and be freed from external pressures. There they could find solace and comfort insulated from an antagonistic outside world. Mgijima expected tremendous sacrifice from his followers, but in return, he could promise them that God had ordained a special place for them in his divine plan.

However, by establishing their New Jerusalem on land they did not own, the Israelites threw down the gauntlet to the South African government.[102] Confronted by the Israelites' illegal occupation, their aggressively defiant stance, and their unwillingness to compromise or seriously negotiate with secular authorities, government officials, first at the local and then at the national level, came to interpret their actions as a prelude to an outright rebellion and ultimately resorted to force to evict them. The Israelites were not a revolutionary sect on the order of the medieval Taborites, who established their own New Jerusalems and physically warred against other groups.[103] The Taborites entered an aggressive phase partly because they believed their own initiatives were an essential precondition for bringing on and hastening the millennium. In contrast, the Israelites settled at Ntabelanga not because they desired to be pitted against the state but only to await peacefully the Lord's direction. But a confrontation may have been unavoidable, as Kenelm Burridge has observed of similar situations:

> Since all millenarian activities must be in some part challenging, rebellious or revolutionary, an administration must seek either to contain or insulate them, or it must suppress them. The result is that whether or not the activities in question are initially directed against the administration, they always end up by appearing to be so. And it is this feature which so often obscures the fact that millenarian activities tend to be "inner" rather than "outer" directed, are a protest or rebellion against a community's own condition first, only later identify, and set themselves against, those who appear to be preventing the shift into a new way of life.[104]

To use Burridge's terminology, Mgijima's millenarianism was "inner" directed, tailored to provide an explanatory framework and a radical solution for the rural crisis that was engulfing Africans. When seen against the backdrop of the steady decline in African economic and political fortunes and the repeated shock of disasters over the previous half century, the appeal of Mgijima's prophecies to some Africans makes sense. Ironically, at the same time as the Israelites were preparing to cushion themselves from further blows by withdrawing from society, their illegal occupation of Ntabelanga became an open challenge to the security and legitimacy of the South African state. Although it is unlikely Mgijima or any of his followers anticipated that their actions would lead to a major confrontation, they set in motion the events that culminated in the deaths of so many of their number on 24 May 1921.

3 The Making of a Massacre

I heard a sweet voice Calling
O Listen to the Sound
It is the voice of an Angel
That God through his promise has sent Down
And he will take me to the City
That shall come down from Above
And God, himself shall dwell with Us
And we shall sing redemption Song.

Chorus:
All: In the new Jerusalem
Bass: Won't you come go along with us
All: Where Christ has gone to prepare
Bass: To the Holy City
All: He then shall reign for-ever
*   In the bright Celestial Shone.*

—Israelite hymn, "The Holy City"

The arrival of the first pilgrims at Ntabelanga was tied to the Israelites' mid-April observance of Passover. The first of the Israelite Passovers had been held at Kamastone. Thereafter Shiloh Mission was the site until Moravian missionaries withdrew permission for the Israelites to gather there in 1916. For the next few years, government officials allowed the Israelites to observe the festival at Mceula and Kamastone.

The thousand or so followers who normally attended Passovers were usually housed in temporary shelters fashioned from harpuis bush and stayed for as long as six weeks before dismantling their abodes and dispersing. This arrangement worked well with the authorities until February 1920, when Mgijima, explaining that he required time to communicate with followers who lived far away, applied earlier than usual for permission to hold the Passover at his home at Ntabelanga. Since the inspector of locations, Geoffrey Nightingale, had heard that "strangers" were selling all their possessions and settling at Bulhoek with the intention of taking up permanent residence, he hesitated to grant the request.

However, Mgijima assured him the reports were false since the "strangers" were actually Israelites who had been unable to attend the last Passover and who had come to Ntabelanga solely for a special service. Mgijima thought it presumptuous for anyone to think he would allow outsiders to stay indefinitely. "I Enoch had no land here—no private farm here—the only land I have is that registered in my name. I have no right to put people on land which does not belong to me."[1] Because Nightingale was not aware of Mgijima's call for his followers to assemble at Ntabelanga, he granted permission for the Passover to take place and for the "strangers" to remain until the Israelites completed their services.

The crippling drought and the difficulty of securing firewood, water, and pasturage delayed the Passover until May. When Nightingale revisited the Israelite village in early June, he found it not only intact but with even more makeshift dwellings (such as green brick lean-tos) under construction. Mgijima informed him the new residences were for some of his newly married sons and for nonresidents who had stayed on for a variety of reasons—illnesses, the intense winter cold, the lack of railway fares or transportation to return home, and husbands not fetching wives. He promised the nonresidents were going to leave after the Israelites held a special service several weeks later. Nightingale specified that Mgijima could put up new dwellings for his own family but not for squatters, and he agreed to another extension of time.[2]

When the confrontation between the Israelites and the government later reached a boiling point, officials in Pretoria severely criticized Nightingale for temporizing with Mgijima and not immediately tearing down the temporary buildings. In fairness to Nightingale, he could not have foreseen where events were leading. Moreover, his reluctance to deal forcefully with the "strangers" was not surprising since the larger issue of squatters in rural African locations had vexed his predecessors for the previous half century.

As we have seen, an early attempt to address the problem came in the 1870s. Owing to the complaints of white farmers that African "strangers" were moving into African locations, a government commission recommended that the Cape Colony should give firm title to those it had already granted land.[3] Establishing private ownership and fixed tenure would wean Africans away from the "arbitrary and despotic will" of their chiefs and the principle of communal land ownership and inculcate "civilized" qualities such as "habits of industry and the desire to improve" in African farmers.[4] In 1877, officials had surveyed and subdivided Kamastone and Oxkraal locations into residential lots of about half an acre apiece and garden plots of about six acres each some distance away from residences. However, from the outset, African tenants regarded the survey as impractical. Many did not occupy their allotted plots of land, and squatting on the commonage became commonplace. The local Village Management Board (made up of local residents) often took the position that the commonage was not Crown land but its own property to allocate as it saw fit. In other cases, residents squatted on the commonage without the board's permission.[5]

In addition, the officials who conducted the 1877 survey did not erect substantial beacons demarcating individual plots. Thus, in 1911, when government surveyors attempted to resolve the boundary lines between residents in Kamastone and Oxkraal, they found that beacons had not been maintained and that since farmers did not respect the boundaries of lots, they usually selected the most suitable land for cultivation. Nor were they interested in resolving the issue. The native locations surveyor, L. M. Walton, generally found that land encroachments—in some cases by people who were not lot holders—were commonplace, that the original beacons were difficult to locate or badly preserved, and that residents were cordial but not really interested in helping Walton conduct his work. At Mceula, they pointed out their own beacons as the correct ones. When Walton showed one resident the correct place for a beacon, he told the surveyor that "he knew all the time where the correct position was, but wanted to see whether I could find it myself."[6]

This state of confusion inevitably led to many clashes, especially over rights to the commonage. A dispute over regulating grazing rights provoked an 1894 petition from almost sixty Bulhoek residents, including Enoch Mgijima.[7] In 1914, Kamastone's superintendent, Clement Gladwin, stirred up considerable ill will among residents when he unsuccessfully brought a legal case against Nodala Nkopo for building a dwelling on the commonage even though he had been residing there for forty years.[8] Indeed, W. F. Murray of the surveyor-general's office determined that some Bulhoek residents moved onto commonage without permission and the Village Management Board, believing it had the right to disperse commonage land, had in some cases supported encroachments on the commonage.[9]

Investigating the tangled web of conflicting land claims, the 1922 Native Locations Survey unsurprisingly found that since the commonage was extensive, residents would occupy a cattle post nearer their home at which a relative would live. But that complicated things because a resident might have legal title to three sections of land on which he was the rightful owner but no longer be residing on another section of land he was not occupying.[10]

Over the years local administrators made minimal efforts to ascertain whether rightful owners were still holding their plots. The 1922 survey determined that of 723 garden plots allocated in Kamastone, rightful owners only occupied 200. Because an earlier location survey made no effort to find out if the original owners still occupied the land, the commission concluded that it was nearly impossible to restrict Africans to their original lots.[11]

The chaotic nature of land grants and building sites was at the center of a dispute in 1917 between Mgijima and Gladwin. Mgijima had built a house on the commonage some eight years earlier and, in 1917, had erected some five or six more. He was not alone in encroaching on the commonage, for at least several dozen other Africans at Bulhoek had done likewise. The land originally allocated to Mgijima's family and the others was on swampy ground. Around 1879, they lodged an appeal with the superintendent, E. C. Jeffrey, who granted them spots on drier and higher ground in the commonage. Although they had lived on these plots for over a generation, the government had never surveyed and registered them.

Nevertheless, Gladwin still ordered Mgijima to demolish recently erected buildings. Following the advice of his attorney, Lamb Brinkman, that the original agreement with Jeffrey was still binding, Mgijima decided to let his buildings stand until officials satisfactorily resolved the issue.[12] Gladwin backed down a short time later, reasoning there was too much confusion as to who owned what and that there were twenty-three others who were encroaching on the Bulhoek commonage alone. He also recognized that if he prosecuted Mgijima, he would have to bring cases against more than two hundred other violators in Kamastone. He dropped the matter reluctantly since he believed white administration in the area was bound to suffer if he did not make an example of Mgijima. He lamented: "No punishment is meted out to the wrongdoers and so all may participate in the good luck."[13] When Nightingale took over in February 1918, he decided not "to stir up muddy water" and acted as if his predecessor had already settled the matter.[14]

While officials skirted around the question of illegal building on the commonage, they could not turn a blind eye to the Israelite "strangers" who were steadily filtering into Ntabelanga. When Nightingale visited the location in early September, he noted the scores of new dwellings and estimated that of twelve hundred to thirteen hundred Israelite "settlers," one thousand were there illegally. How to deal with them was another question, and Queenstown officials tried various legal maneuvers to expel them. After a late July visit, Nightingale issued summonses to bring some twenty-one Israelites to trial for squatting. When only three appeared in court, Mgijima explained that it was impossible for his followers to show up on short notice because they were scattered about the region.[15] In October, after Nightingale confirmed more Israelites were moving in, the Queenstown magistrate, E. C. Welsh, instructed him to compile a register of Ntabelanga inhabitants. However, the Israelites were uncooperative because, as Enoch's older brother, Charles, put it, "Our names are written in God's book, and as God was greater than man, we would not be justified in allowing this."[16]

At this stage, the Israelites were dealing with low-level officials of the Native Affairs Department. Poorly funded and understaffed, the department had acquired a reputation in official circles for being the "Cinderella of the ministerial family."[17] In most Ciskei districts, the government administered "native" affairs through location superintendents (many of them sons of missionaries). They were under Native Affairs but reported directly to magistrates of the Justice Department. For decades local officials had practiced a benevolent paternalism that entailed gradually uplifting Africans to "civilization" in exchange for their deference to white authority and not challenging the established order. Typifying this view were the remarks at Kamastone in 1910 by the secretary for Native Affairs, Henry Burton, who said he was in "charge of several millions of human beings, just waking up from the sleep of ages, and needing fair, just and sympathetic treatment at the hands of the Government."[18] Thus the Israelites stood out because they were violating this understanding. By openly questioning the legitimacy of the state's authority and recognizing only God's dominion over human affairs, they were subverting the etiquette of what most whites believed constituted proper black-white relations.

For example, on 6 September, Charles Mgijima and Adonijah Ntloko took the Israelite case directly to Welsh to complain about Nightingale's summonses and to ask the government to leave the Israelites alone. God had directed them to settle at Ntabelanga to wait for the millennium, and all they were asking for was the opportunity to live in peace and pray without interference. Why, they asked, was the government acting as if they were at war? They also questioned why Nightingale was denying that he had permitted them to build houses.[19]

The Israelite intransigence can be attributed not only to their belief in the righteousness of their cause but also to their awareness that Nightingale and Welsh, without substantial backing from higher authorities, were incapable of moving forcefully against them. Matshoba confidently boasted to Enoch that white officials, despite their bluster, could not rely on black police if they confronted the Israelites.

> O! Father, O! Son of Jonas O! Lad of Makesa, do assist us with Faith, Father. The lads of Gogi [the British] are terror-stricken. . . . Oh these heathens, we have already overpowered them. They are extremely afraid of us. This is unique. . . . The wiseacres here say the Magistrate, Mr. Welsh, as also that of Kamastone say: Oh, these people should be left alone when they do not molest any person, and the sergeant says: No they cannot be give up allow me to personally have an attempt, I will come in with that nigger. The Magistrate then said: All right, then proceed. After saying that he then issued summonses. This sergeant instructed the police to go and serve them. They promptly refused, saying that the Mountain of the Sun (Ntabalanga) and its people is extraordinarily dangerous, we have never seen the one who is their chief, therefore we will not go; get other persons. He compelled them so much that the native constables nearly lost their senses as they (natives were unexpectedly and without having been told anything before hand called up), when they returned, so we are informed, they said if we are compelled to go and fight with Mgijima, we will go, but immediately on our arrival we will be on Mgijima's side.[20]

A controversial letter Enoch sent Ebenezer Mhlambiso, a Hlubi headman in the Amatole basin, revealed another element of Israelite thinking. Although the two had never met, Mgijima called for Mhlambiso's assistance because the government was persecuting him and plotting to drive his followers out of Ntabelanga. "The Day of the Lord has come," he pronounced. "We aborigines are that Stone which was visioned by Daniel, Chapter 2, verses 34 and 35. This determined and obstinate British race, with other European powers, is like the iron. We are living on their territory. We will be as is stated in Daniel, Chapter 2, verse 44."[21] Mgijima's reference to Daniel is telling because it is another biblical narrative set during the Babylonian captivity. Daniel, who had been captured in Judah and brought to serve in Nebuchadnezzar's court, had saved his own life by interpreting one of the king's complex dreams in which a great stone was supernaturally carved from a mountainside and crashed into the feet of a statue made of iron and clay.

Testifying at the Israelite trial in late 1921, Charles Mgijima clarified the metaphor in the letter to Mhlambiso that the Israelites represented a stone and the British the iron that it destroyed. The "monsters," he explained, referred to "our masters, the white people." And Enoch inserted the passage "Ho! Ho! Ho! I wish to sound the alarm" to dramatize the Israelites' growing distrust of government intentions.[22]

Charles's testimony affirmed that the Israelites had no intention of asking Mhlambiso or other chiefs to join in a seditious plot. However, their appeals for help and the references to a bloody war of retribution, to the government as a "monster," and to the Lord crushing Israelite foes disturbed officials in Pretoria, who pondered the possibility that Israelite resistance could very well take a violent course.[23]

At that stage, the Israelite presence did not unduly alarm Nightingale, who counseled against any precipitate action. "These people," he wrote, "are not . . . out for bloodshed or loot, it is purely a religious movement with them." But he added the caution, ominous in retrospect, "If there is to be any disturbance it will be at Ntabalanga [sic] where they are massed and when the law is enforced."[24]

With local officials unable to root out the Israelites on their own, communications began flowing back and forth between them and officials of various departments in Pretoria—Native Affairs, Justice, and the South African Police. In theory Native Affairs had jurisdiction over the problem, but in the Ciskei, it was complicated by the fact that the chain of command for "native affairs" flowed from the location superintendent, Nightingale, to the Queenstown magistrate, Welsh, representing the Justice Department, and finally to the Justice Department in Pretoria. Officials in these departments in Pretoria often held considerably different perspectives on how to handle "natives," but on this issue, they were in accord. Even though they anticipated having to bring force to bear at some point to uphold the law, tact and discretion were still the appropriate response, and they directed local officials to renew their efforts to persuade the

Israelites to disperse. On 13 September, Nightingale, Welsh, and the district police commandant, Philip Whitaker, went out to Ntabelanga to prevail upon the Israelites to end their squatting. The Israelites repeated their assurances that they would be gone by month's end. Welsh found the Israelites "very docile and humble and quite ready to do anything the magistrate wished them to do," and he and the other officials granted the Israelites additional time to complete their Passover ceremony.[25]

A Sanctuary for Lawless Desperadoes

In the meantime, local officials were coping with a chorus of complaints from the area's white farmers, who were distressed by the Israelites' "menacing" attitude. They characterized the Ntabelanga community as "a sanctuary for lawless desperadoes" and pinned the blame on landless paupers for a wave of stock thefts in the region.[26] The farmers were convinced that the Israelites were the culprits since they had no visible means of support. One longtime Kamastone area resident, Dixon Barnes, warned whites that the Israelites should be taken seriously and that if the stealing did not stop, "it is not to be wondered at if these families become desperate and take the law into their own hands."[27] However, Whitaker, after visiting Ntabelanga and the surrounding areas in September, came to a very different conclusion: "I do not anticipate any danger to farmers or other residents in the vicinity, from molestation from the natives in question. The alleged losses of stock is news to me, as no reports have been received by the police re such losses, this in my opinion, is mentioned in the petition with a view to its carrying more weight."[28]

While officials thought the grievances of white farmers had little basis in fact, they gave more credence to those of Kamastone Africans. Because the land was not well watered and was overstocked, many Kamastone residents were very concerned about rights to commonage and naturally resented the intrusion of strangers. They accused the Israelites of a host of transgressions. Not only were they encroaching on the location's commonage, their stock was eating residents' pasturage, foraging in their gardens, and damaging the maize crop. They also charged Israelites with pilfering other foodstuffs and threatening some residents to such a degree that several had left the area. In June, the local headman, Alfred Dondolo, called a meeting to warn the Israelites not to build any new huts on the commonage.[29] On 4 September, eight Kamastone headmen went a step further, blaming the Israelites for creating health problems and disrupting the stability of the area, and petitioned Nightingale to deal with the Israelites without further delay.[30]

The complaints of their white and African neighbors made no dent in the Israelite posture. They were creating a theocratic community. Therefore, the land they settled on was "holy ground" and not subject to European law. Since their sole purpose for gathering was observing their annual religious festival, they could not be accused of menacing white farmers in the area.

Despite Israelite assurances that their stay was temporary, Ntabelanga began to take on a permanent appearance with brick houses laid out along well-demarcated streets. At the center of Ntabelanga life was the Tent of the Congregation (*iTente yentlangano*), a structure patched together from tents. Church services were held four times a day—early morning, midday, sunset, and evening—in the tabernacle. The centerpiece of worship was the Israelite Ark of the Covenant, a large scroll with the Ten Commandments ornately inscribed on it in isiXhosa, which Adonijah Ntloko had recently brought from the Orange Free State. Next to the Black Kei (which the Israelites called the River Jordan) was a retreat, Gethsemane, reserved exclusively for the prophet.

By offering a sanctuary to the dispossessed and oppressed, Ntabelanga was fulfilling a similar function as European mission stations had for African converts in the nineteenth century.[31] The village was self-contained and self-sufficient, much like the Moravian settlement at Shiloh that Mgijima knew well. It was not true as some whites claimed that all the Israelites had impoverished themselves by selling off all their worldly goods. Many Israelites lived off the proceeds from selling their possessions, and their poor could draw on a communal fund. Some earned extra money selling firewood in Queenstown, while others moved in and out of Ntabelanga, returning to their homes to harvest crops and tend to their herds and flocks or even seeking jobs in the mines. A *Daily Representative* reporter posing as a labor recruiter asked a group of Israelites if they were worried about a famine, since they did not appear to have their own sources of food. "We have brought lots of grain; have you not seen it come by wagons?" they confidently responded. "When we want 'manna' will be sent from heaven—we are believers." Their autonomy was a source of pride to one Israelite who boasted that "they had always earned all they had from the Government, and owed it nothing. They had received nothing from the white man without earning it, and were independent of him."[32]

The Israelites were self-sufficient in many respects. They had their own surveyor, saddlemaker, cobbler, butcher, blacksmiths, builders, and police force. They set up a school for biblical instruction in English and isiXhosa. The women formed a nursing brigade.[33] New arrivals were taught that in order to achieve salvation, they had to undergo a personal transformation.

A court of elders regulated village life by trying those who transgressed the moral injunctions of the Ten Commandments and the Seven Keys.[34] Israelites had to give up fornication and adultery, forgo raucous living, and stop smoking and drinking.

Enoch and his brother, Charles Mcolela Mgijima, made the key decisions affecting the Israelites' relationship with the authorities. A member of his brother's movement since 1915, Charles had arrived in late June from Beaufort West, where he had been a schoolteacher for many years.[35] Although familial loyalty may have drawn Charles to Ntabelanga, there is no doubt that he was an ardent believer in his brother's message. He assumed the position of commander in chief, or *mpath'o mkhulu,* in charge of the Israelites' administration.

Charles was Enoch's Aaron. Enoch devoted himself to the role of visionary, while Charles handled the negotiations with the government. That Charles came to Ntabelanga when tensions escalated between the Israelites and the authorities was proof to officials that he was the real power behind the throne and that he, rather than Enoch, was responsible for Israelite intransigence. However, Israelite testimony as well as other evidence supports the view that Charles followed Enoch's directives. Charles remained in the forefront of negotiations because the Israelites feared the authorities would try to harm or kidnap the prophet. Israelites explained that his absence at critical stages of the negotiations was due to illness or to his retreats to the mountains for prayer and spiritual renewal.

The image of Ntabelanga as a peaceful, well-run village was not reflected in the reports of some white observers who thought the village was an armed camp. Reports circulated that the shaven-headed Israelite men were drilling daily with knobkerries and swords in hand. What most outsiders did not understand was that marching was an integral part of the Israelite service and the swords, although recently adopted, were ceremonial and never used as weapons, not even on the day of the massacre.[36] But if the reports of whites were often contradictory or fabricated, when pieced together, they conveyed the impression that the Israelites were not passively awaiting the coming of the Lord but actively plotting sedition.

They Must Remember They Are Fighting God

The patience of local officials had worn thin when Nightingale visited Ntabelanga on 3 October 1920 and discovered that thirty to forty new buildings had been built since early September. "I actually saw new buildings being erected, men working on them, women and girls carrying bricks on their heads to the building sites and also noticed large quantities of green brick made and ready for use." He discounted an Israelite claim that fifty of their number had gone away, and he suspected that even if they had left, it was only temporary. Indeed, when the Israelites asked for another extension of time, it confirmed his contention "that there is no intention on their part to disperse and return to their homes." He insisted that it was "imperative in the interests of both European residents and neighbouring farmers and the other native residents, that immediate action be taken to put an end to this most unsatisfactory state of affairs."[37] On 20 October, after Nightingale approached the Israelites about conducting a census, Edward Mpateni told him that since the Israelite names were written in God's book, they were powerless to provide him with their names because God was greater than man. Nightingale advised Pretoria that if the government decided on a show of force, the Israelites would likely adopt "passive resistance" tactics and "will seat themselves down and say to the Police, here we are, do with us as you like, we will not move from this place."[38]

As the Israelite stalling tactics became clear to officials in Pretoria, they began to debate possible courses of action. All were in agreement with Nightingale that since the Israelites were "under the impression that the government is weak and powerless to act and either cannot or will not interfere with them," the government could no longer defer decisive action.[39] They differed, however, on what option to follow. Some wanted to arrest Enoch, thinking his absence would quickly defuse the movement. Others argued that his jailing would provoke a counterproductive violent reaction; they expected the Israelites would leave if they guaranteed the prophet's safety. The government ruled out another idea, starving the Israelites into submission, as impractical. Finally, some thought a show of armed force would be enough to impress on the Israelites the gravity of the situation.[40]

Although the government ultimately adopted the last option, it was not an easy one to implement since mobilizing enough police on short notice was a major logistical problem. In the Queenstown region, there were only 119 white and 61 African police, and they could not be committed to Bulhoek without leaving the rest of the area unprotected. Police in the Transkei were already patrolling to allay feelings of insecurity among white settlers, and many Cape police were committed to Port Elizabeth to deal with a volatile strike by African workers. Thus it was not until early December that the police could muster a force of nearly one hundred to go out to Ntabelanga ostensibly to compile a register of Israelites. In this instance, Israelite intransigence and militancy in the face of government inertia and indecisiveness stripped bare the facade of white administrative control over Africans. The tenuous hold they maintained over rural Africans was often dependent on a mixture of intimidation and bluff and African acquiescence.[41]

By the time the police put together a mounted force of ninety-three men to go out to the Israelite village, the shootings of African strikers at Port Elizabeth on 23 October had complicated their mission. A massive crowd of demonstrators had gathered outside the Baakens Street Police Station calling for the release of trade union leader Samuel Masabalala. More than thirty white vigilantes had volunteered their services to the police, and after being issued guns and ammunition, they "took up positions on the balcony overlooking the crowd." [42] Around 5:30 p.m. the vigilantes and police without warning began firing indiscriminately on the crowd. In just a few minutes, at least several dozen protesters lay dead, and scores were wounded. Word of what African Political Organisation leader Dr. Abdullah Abdurahman labeled "South Africa's Amritsar" quickly spread throughout the region. A meeting addressed by SANNC president Z. R. Mahabane at the Cape Town location of Ndabeni passed a resolution condemning the "relentless and merciless shootings of an absolutely defenceless people" that was a prelude to a concerted policy of whites exterminating blacks to bring about a "white man's country." The resolution expressed the view that Africans might have to rethink their "allegiance and loyalty to the white peoples" and consider supporting a segregation of the land into equal shares of black and white land.[43]

Fearing that a confrontation with the Israelites so soon after the Port Elizabeth shootings would spark African rioting and disturbances elsewhere, the government authorized Maj. Edward Hutchons, Whitaker, and

Welsh to offer the Israelites rations and free railway passage home to in-
duce them to leave and instructed them to avoid a clash if at all possible.[44]
When the police force reached Bulhoek on 7 December, it judiciously
pitched camp about five hundred yards from the Israelite village.[45]

The following day's deliberations stretched from early morning to midafternoon and accomplished little more than to accentuate the vast gulf
between their positions. The Israelites were in an uncompromising mood
not only because of their religious zeal but also because Queenstown sympathizers had informed them that the police had instructions to act with
restraint.[46] They were also outraged by the shootings at Port Elizabeth
and feared that the police "wished to treat them in a similar manner and
pump bullets into them."[47]

The Israelite spokesmen, Edward Mpateni and Charlton Mzimkulu,
reiterated the sect's peaceful intent and its unwillingness to leave but
warned that if the government wanted to provoke a fight, "they must remember they were fighting God. . . . We are the children of God and under
Him. We only do that for fear of God and not against the Government."[48]
Hutchons assured the Israelites that although the government did not
want to interfere in their religion, they should refrain from any resistance
when he set up a day for registering Israelite "strangers."

The discussion broke off abruptly when the sight of a thousand Israelites drilling in the distance unsettled Hutchons. Realizing his unit was
too small to stand up to such a large force, he ordered Whitaker to refrain
from a confrontation and left for Queenstown to wire for further instructions. Although Hutchons did not expect trouble so long as the police
did not proceed with registering the Israelites, he still asked Pretoria for
airplanes and five hundred more men with machine guns.[49]

Whitaker had his men reposition their tents about seven hundred
yards from the Israelite village. In the late afternoon, two Israelites came
forward asking him to withdraw his force. He did not become alarmed,
though, until a short time later when about fifty Israelites wearing swords
and carrying knobkerries marched toward the police camp and proceeded
to put up their own tents next to and between the police camp and
Ntabelanga. Whitaker argued heatedly with the Israelites for a few minutes before matters took a turn for the worse when an Israelite, Philip
Mhlabane, reproached a black constable, Stanford Kati: "Have you heard
of the strikes at Johannesburg and Port Elizabeth where our brothers were
killed by the Europeans because they asked for money when starving? You

seem to be glad about our people being killed by Europeans. This is the third time you have been here with the white people. You will be glad to see Israel's blood spilt."[50] According to Whitaker, with this angry denunciation of Kati, the Israelites grew more agitated and threatening. When he saw about six hundred more Israelites approaching his camp, he called on them to turn back. But as soon as he realized that the situation was out of hand and a confrontation imminent, he ordered his men to abandon camp and withdraw to Stephen McComb's Welcome farm.

That evening, after Pretoria refused to send reinforcements, about 115 white volunteers (drawn from the Defense Association, the Comrades of the Great War, and the Automobile Club in Queenstown) responded to an appeal from McComb's wife and drove out to Whitaker's new camp. There they spent an uneasy night watching Israelites lining the ridges overlooking them and signaling to each other with lamps. At one point, Whitaker ventured out with twenty men to speak with the Israelites, who taunted him and defiantly challenged the police to cross the river bed and "come over to God's ground."[51]

The next day, the police returned to their camp to recover their equipment and found everything as they had left it because Enoch had ordered his followers not to disturb anything. The police stayed another eight to ten days at Welcome farm.[52]

The incident was significant in several respects. Stories that spread about the police retreat lay the basis for a myth that the Israelites believed they were impervious to bullets. One version related that before Whitaker and his men fled, they turned their guns to shoot at the Israelites but misfired. Another claimed that when some policemen returned the next day, the Israelites asked them, "Why didn't you shoot at us yesterday?" The police explained, "When we were running away, we wanted to shoot. But when we pulled the triggers we found the bullets had turned to water."[53]

Even if the stories were apocryphal, several points should be made about them. First, some Israelites believed them and a few of their evangelists as well as local Africans spread them throughout the area as added proof of their invincibility. Second, government officials, catching wind of the stories, became even more convinced that Mgijima and his followers were fanatics. There is no hard and fast evidence that Mgijima ever stated that bullets would turn to water, and only whites and Africans who indirectly heard the rumor attributed the story to him.[54]

The encounter was a turning point in the confrontation between the Israelites and the government. The Israelites had been reassured that the Lord was steadfastly watching over their resistance to the "heathens," while white authority suffered a devastating setback. White officials had to grapple with the sobering implication of a largely white force retreating without a fight from the lightly armed Israelites. Most white comment centered on the impact the incident would have on "native policy" and African perceptions. The Queenstown newspaper called it "the finest bungle in native policy that has occurred in these parts for many years."[55] Frank Brownlee, a longtime Transkeian administrator, warned of the contagion of resistance:

> I have always said that the Frontier districts must be watched. If things get out of hand there the people in these parts, law abiding as they generally are, will become contaminated and then God help us. It is by efficient administration that things are kept normal in the Territories but in this age of unrest and upheaval it will take a very small spark to kindle the fire. . . . One of the worst features of the whole business is the fact that the police had to withdraw. This will encourage the high priest and the people in their belief in Divine intervention and they will adopt further measures of defiance with the hope of being further protected. Natives are highly excitable and impressionable and I very greatly fear that this spirit will spread.[56]

What kind of image would this fiasco project to other Africans? If the control whites held over Africans was still open to question, then this unceremonious retreat was in some ways worse than if the Israelites had actually fought and defeated the police.

The December debacle forced officials in Pretoria to reappraise the situation thoroughly. The police tried to explain away the embarrassment of their retreat by arguing that if they had fired upon the Israelites, the whole countryside might have exploded in rebellion. Officials in the districts of Peddie, Alice, Cradock, and King William's Town had been submitting reports that Africans were holding secret meetings with the intention of organizing a general uprising.[57] The deputy commissioner for police in Grahamstown, A. T. Davies, cabled an explanation to his superiors in Pretoria: "That there is great discontentment amongst the Natives as a whole, in this Division, is very evident, the main causes for which are low wages, high prices and the drought."[58] Other reports speculated that an incident could have provoked Queenstown Africans to demonstrate since they believed the Israelites to have many sympathizers in the location. Indeed, police informers warned that if the Israelites were interfered with, African workers were prepared to lay down their tools and strike.[59]

Hutchons's hasty retreat came in for sharp criticism. His own assessment was that he erred in allowing the government to send out a large force rather than just him alone. Officials in Pretoria, after first thinking Hutchons probably "had lost his head," eventually agreed with him. They concluded that since he had been dealing with "fanatics," his strategy of showing moderate force without provoking a clash had been sound. Nevertheless, they still found it difficult to rationalize the retreat.[60]

Prime Minister Jan Smuts (who held the portfolio for Native Affairs) also took the position that brute force was not warranted. He recommended the government adopt a low-key attitude since he thought the Israelites had limited resources and could not sustain their defiance much longer. Writing to A. H. Frost, his party's candidate for the Queenstown district, he expressed his desire to refrain from taking extreme measures and avoiding bloodshed. "Bloodshed on a large scale at the present juncture would have the most lamentable political effects in many parts of South Africa. I am therefore for proceeding cautiously and giving time for the present effervescence among the Natives to calm down."[61]

The government followed Smuts's line of thinking and concluded the wisest course was to calm tensions by sending out a delegation of high-level officials to negotiate directly with the Israelites. Before this meeting took place, the police and the Israelites concluded a truce and agreed to keep at a distance from each other. The Israelites were to stay in their village and allow the police to patrol through African locations and neighboring white farms. Both the police and the Israelites were to withdraw all their pickets from Bulhoek.

If the government was still casting about for a formula to deal with the Israelites, its deliberations were measured and unhurried in the face of alarmist outcries of panic-stricken white farmers who were convinced that the Israelite rout of the police was the prelude to a larger rising. The stampede of white farmers seeking protection prompted a Queenstown African, B. S. Mazwi, to draw sarcastically on Aesop's fable of the fox and an ass in a lion's skin where the ass's identity was exposed once he brayed. In like manner, "The Government and the natives of this country have now learned the 'bray' of a certain class of farmers and traders in the country who have always been the cause of misunderstanding, conflicts and complications which had resulted in all the Kafir wars of the past and the forfeiture of lands by the Natives."[62]

The rumors of rebellion escalated in proportion to how far away white farmers lived from Ntabelanga. Those who lived farther away went into laager or sent their families into nearby towns such as Queenstown demanding protection. Those closest to the Israelite village were less apprehensive. Some had known the Mgijimas and other Israelites all their lives. They adopted a wait-and-see attitude because they did not believe the Israelites were plotting revolution. One exception was Archibald William, who claimed to be in close contact with Israelites. He warned that church members "seem to stir up the Kaffirs up to demand better food. Mealies are not good enough for them—they want wheaten meal, bread and butter, and plenty of meat. They say they are white people like us; as a matter of fact, they reckon themselves miles ahead of any European."[63]

One interpretation of white farmer hysteria was that the Israelites were attracting farm workers into their fold. Indeed, with some prescience, the International Socialist League predicted in December 1920 that "capitalism was planning a wholesale bloody slaughter of the Israelites probably because of the scarcity of farm workers."[64] Although the white farmers were acting more out of a fear of Africans rebelling than a simple desire to hold on to farm labor, one cannot discount this theory. Although accurate statistics on the supply of farm laborers after World War I do not exist, the Israelites probably did pose a nettlesome problem to white farmers. However, it was not so much because they were attracting farm workers into their fold—they were, but only to a limited degree—but because they threatened white control over African workers. The image of Ntabelanga as a self-governed, self-sustaining alternative for Africans was not a comforting thought to many white farmers.

The farmers' frenzies did not unduly concern government officials. The police in particular were skeptical since they believed some farmers were capitalizing on the Israelite affair as a ploy to get more firearms or as a convenient scapegoat for stock theft. A Grahamstown police officer thought it was "a revival of the agitation on the part of farmers—particularly the poorer class of Dutch farmers—to obtain a free issue of arms and ammunition, it being their inherent belief that they should be so armed."[65] When W. H. Quirk compiled a report on stock theft in the area in January 1921, he found that most farmers believed stock theft was actually decreasing. Moreover, his investigations convinced him the Israelites were not culpable. After checking out the complaints of Stephen McComb of Welcome farm adjoining Ntabelanga that Israelites were stealing his sheep, the police found that the actual number of sheep on his property, when properly counted, exceeded what McComb claimed he owned. Indeed, the police had previously tracked down several small flocks of stolen sheep to McComb's farm, but the owners had decided not to prosecute.[66]

Despite their reservations, the police moved to assuage the farmers' fears by stepping up patrols, calling on farmers not to take any precipitous actions on their own, and asking newspaper editors to refrain from running inflammatory stories about the Israelite menace. However, the situation had no time to calm down when, on 14 December, John Mattushek shot two Israelites.

Mattushek, whose Thornhill farm abutted Bulhoek, had waged a running feud with the Israelites for some months. Several times Israelites had prevented him from entering Ntabelanga, and local farmers remembered his repeated quarrels with Israelites. He accused them of breaking into his store and stealing his livestock. Footprints of the culprits, he claimed, invariably led to the Israelite village. He began to impound any of their cattle found grazing on his farm. In early December, he reportedly shot at several Israelites trespassing on his land. After the 8 December debacle he was warned that his life was in danger. He began carrying a revolver and sent his wife into Queenstown for her safety.[67]

Then, on 14 December, Mattushek and his Coloured laborers, Rudolphe and Christoffel Klopper, fired on three Israelites, Phillip Mhlabane, John Nkelenjane, and Charles Dondolo, who showed up at his farm.[68] According to the Israelite version of what happened, Enoch Mgijima had instructed them to see if Mattushek had any forage for sale. When they neared Mattushek's home, he asked them where they were going. They replied, "We have been sent to see you." Mattushek repeated his question, but before they could respond, he drew a revolver and fired. They claimed they attacked him in self-defense.[69]

Mattushek's recollection of the fracas was very different. He claimed he shouted at the Israelites when they came on to his property. They took no notice even after he fired his revolver in the air. After asking them what they wanted, he claimed they said, "We have been sent to get you," and he had no choice but to defend himself. A melee broke out. The

Israelites chased him around the house and knocked him down and struck him on his head and leg. Only then did he fire his revolver at Nkelenjane. Then the Israelites ran into one of the Kloppers, who fired a shotgun, killing Dondolo and wounding Nkelenjane.[70] Contrary to the rumor that the Israelites believed themselves impervious to bullets, these Israelites had no illusions about their effect. Nevertheless, the incident created one more point of conflict with the authorities because the Israelites later refused to honor subpoenas to appear as material witnesses at the trial of Mattushek and the Kloppers, who were charged with culpable homicide.

FIGURE 1 Enoch Mgijima. ("The Bulhoek Tragedy," *East London Daily Dispatch*, 1922)

FIGURE 2 Enoch Mgijima in the crimson robe he wore at Israelite services. (Author's collection)

FIGURE 3 Wesleyan Methodist Mission, Kamastone. (Photo by author)

FIGURE 4 A wedding party of mission-educated Africans. (Author's collection)

FIGURE 5 William Saunders Crowdy (seated on left) at Passover festival in Plainfield, NJ, April 1906. (*New York Tribune*, April 22, 1906)

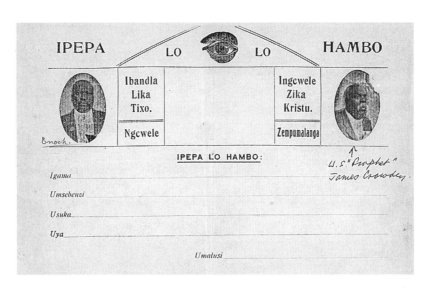

FIGURE 6 Handbill featuring photos of Crowdy and Enoch Mgijima. (Author's collection)

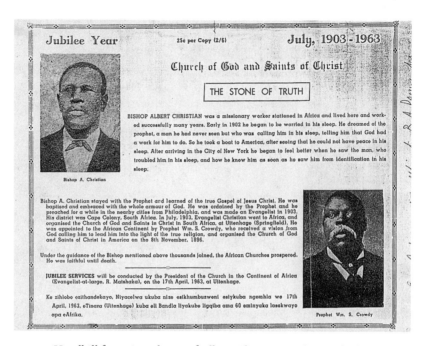

FIGURE 7 Handbill featuring photos of Albert Christian and Crowdy. (Author's collection)

FIGURE 8 The Israelite village at Ntabelanga. (Author's collection)

FIGURE 9 The Tent of the Congregation (*iTente yentlangano*), a meeting place for Israelites at Ntabelanga. (Author's collection)

FIGURE 10 An army unit displayed their machine guns before the battle. (Author's collection)

FIGURE 11 The commanding officer of the police, Colonel Truter, and army, General van Deventer. ("The Bulhoek Tragedy," *East London Daily Dispatch*, 1922)

FIGURE 12 An Israelite wearing a white tunic and carrying a ceremonial sword meets with the police after the battle. (Author's collection)

FIGURE 13 Charles Mgijima guarded by mounted police. He suffered a bullet wound during the battle. (Author's collection)

FIGURE 14 Israelite women gathered at Ntabelanga after the massacre. (Author's collection)

FIGURE 15 Israelite dead before their burial in one of three mass graves. This photo appeared on a picture postcard circulated after the massacre. (Author's collection)

FIGURE 16 A memorial erected at one of the three mass graves. (Author's collection)

MURDER! MURDER!! MURDER!!!

THE BULLHOEK MASSACRE

CHRISTIANS SLAUGHTER THEIR CHRISTIAN BRETHREN
GREAT EMPIRE DAY CELEBRATION.

How appropriate and how much in keeping with the Matabele Massacre, and other of their brutal Empire building tactics. And the Bullhoek tragedy was either by fate or circumstances enacted on their very Empire Day.

We accuse the responsible Government, whose forces are headed by a brutal assassin, of murdering unarmed strikers in Johannesburg 1913,— slaughtering unarmed natives in Port Elizabeth 1920,— and their latest debauch is the gruesome mutilation of hundreds of natives who were Christians and passive community.

Hence, this brutal invasion is truly symbolical of Governmental tyranny in their hysterical efforts to exploit the workers, irrespective of their particular colour or religous beleifs, and to maintain their position functioned by an idle and parasitic class; their armies are ever available to suppress any libertarian effort from the oppressing yoke of Capitalism.

A condemnation meeting will be held on the Parade at 11 a.m Sunday morning.

Sunday evening Adderley Street.

St. Marks Schoolroom, Tennant Street, Monday evening 30th at 7.30 p.m.

Published by The United Communist Party, 30 Plein Street, Cape Town, and printed by The Commercial Press, 64 Sir Lowry Road, Cape Town.

FIGURE 17 Handbill announcing a protest meeting in Cape Town in June 1921. (National Archives of South Africa)

FIGURE 18 The memorial to the Bulhoek massacre dedicated in May 2001. (Photo by author)

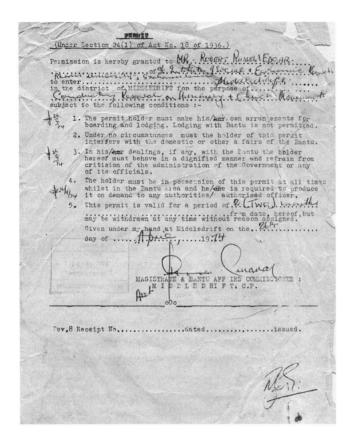

FIGURE 19 A government permit issued to Robert Edgar in 1974 to do research in a black area. (Author's collection)

FIGURE 20 Israelites celebrating the return of the Ark of the Covenant at the tabernacle in Queenstown, 1995. (Photo by Denver Webb)

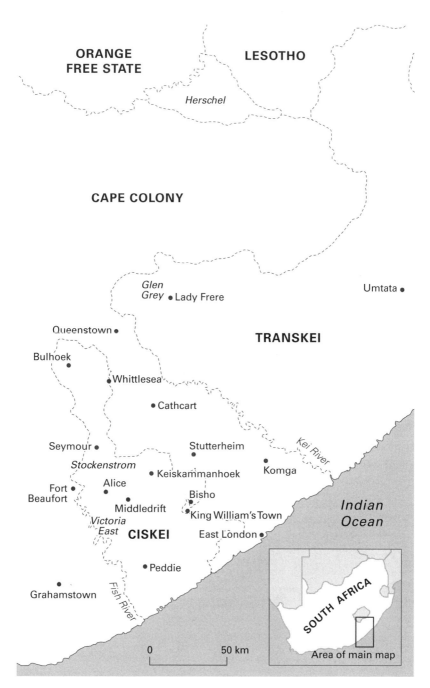

ORANGE
FREE STATE

LESOTHO

Herschel

CAPE COLONY

*Glen
Grey* ● Lady Frere

Umtata ●

Queenstown ●

TRANSKEI

Bulhoek
●

●Whittlesea

● Cathcart

Seymour ●

Stutterheim ●

Kei River

Stockenstrom

● Keiskammanhoek

Komga
●

Fort ●
Beaufort

Alice
●

● Middledrift

Bisho
●

●King William's Town

*Indian
Ocean*

*Victoria
East*

CISKEI

East London ●

● Peddie

Fish River

Grahamstown ●
●

SOUTH AFRICA

0   50 km

Area of main map

MAP 1 Eastern Cape. (Map by Nat Case)

MAP 2 The Kamastone region. (Map by Nat Case)

4 When People Rally Round the Word of God

When the earth is full of turmoil
When the earth is full of restlessness
The skies rumbling
You alone are our anchor

When the earth is full of restlessness
When nations are in conflict
The earth trembling
It is you alone who is our refuge

Zion heard and brought its blessing
And the young women of Judah
They looked up to Jehovah
They were fully blessed by God.

—Hymn composed by Enoch Mgijima in
prison after the Bulhoek massacre

Convinced by the police fiasco of early December that they had no choice but to break the impasse between local officials and the Israelites, officials in Pretoria swiftly assembled a delegation headed by Edward Barrett, the secretary for Native Affairs since October 1919, to meet the Israelites.[1] Many Native Affairs officials were sons of missionaries, and Edward's father had been a longtime Wesleyan Methodist missionary at Kamastone.[2] Despite being born in Queenstown, the secretary had little personal knowledge of the Israelites. That did not prevent him from concluding that their takeover of Ntabelanga was more than just the action of religious fanatics. Believing that impressionable Africans were falling prey to socialist ideals, he worried that the example of the Israelites, who had sold their possessions and were creating a communal society, could become the seedbed for another Communist revolution. "Shorn of all absurdities it simply amounts to a Bolshevik seizure of land. . . . The Israelite cult has spread, and other natives from elsewhere, attracted by the charms of a workless life, have joined the insurgents."[3] But Barrett's fear of Bolshevism did not become part of his delegation's exchanges with the Israelites.

Half of the delegation was South African police and army officers, including their respective commanding officers, Col. Theo Truter and General van Deventer.[4] The latter two were included to impress the Israelites with the seriousness of the situation and presumably to reconnoiter the area in case their services were required at a later stage.

On 15 December the delegation first conferred with Kamastone residents, who charged that the Israelites were illegally occupying land, threatening other residents, and allowing their stock to damage the land. Unless the government took immediate action, they feared that a civil war between them and the Israelites was inevitable. If such a confrontation took place, law-abiding Africans might lose their lands as well. Alfred Mpateni, a headman whose son Edward had joined the Israelites, expressed the "loyalist" point of view: "The location natives had always obeyed the law and were well aware how their forefathers had acquired the land, namely, that it was for their loyalty and to remain theirs so long as they were loyal otherwise it would be taken away."[5]

The next day, Barrett sent out a stalking horse in the form of four prominent African moderates, Meshach Pelem, Patrick Xabanisa, Chief Veldtman, and John Tengo Jabavu.[6] With the exception of Jabavu, they were members of the Bantu Union, a moderate African political organization formed after World War I whose principal base was in the eastern Cape. Jabavu was the most eminent member of the delegation. During his career he had achieved prominence as a church layman, an educator, and editor of *Imvo Zabantsundu*. Through his newspaper he wielded much influence over the development of African electoral politics in the eastern Cape. But by 1921, his influence among Africans was waning because of his conservative politics. For instance, he had supported the Natives' Land Act of 1913, and he had caused the defeat of Walter Rubusana, the only African ever to be elected to the Cape Provincial Assembly, by running against him, thus splitting the African vote and allowing the sole white candidate to win.

Despite the government's hope that they might be more persuasive than white officials, their efforts were just as fruitless.[7] In retrospect, this is not surprising since these African moderates symbolized all that the Israelites emphatically rejected—accommodation and compromise with a white-dominated system. They had associated themselves with the "heathens," a group of people that the Israelites defined less by color than by how they related to their cause.

The three-hour meeting at Welcome farm the following day between the government delegation and Israelite leaders accomplished little more than the two sides restating their respective positions. The government position was straightforward. Because the Israelites were squatting illegally on the Bulhoek commonage and were treating summonses with contempt, the government had no choice but to intervene. The Israelite "religion could not be made a cloak for defying the law." Barrett justified the necessity for obedience to state authority by reading a passage from Romans 13:1–4.

> Let every soul be subject unto the higher powers. For there is no power but of God; that powers that be are ordained of God. Whosoever therefore resisteth the power, resisteth the ordinance of God; and they that resist shall receive to themselves damnation. For rulers are not a terror to good works, but to the evil. For he is the minister of God to thee for good. But if thou do that which is evil, be afraid; for he beareth not the sword in vain; for he is the minister of God, a revenger to execute wrath upon him that doeth evil.

If biblical injunctions fell on deaf ears, Theo Truter's blunt statement of the state's position left little room for misinterpretation: "You must obey the Regulations. Every community has its rulers, but they are themselves subject to the laws. I rule the police but I must obey the law. Its [sic] no use awaiting an answer to your prayers."[8]

The Israelites rejected the legitimacy of the government and its stance, however it was phrased. Fearing an attempt to kidnap their prophet, the Israelites kept him away from this and future discussions. Their spokesman was Enoch's brother, Charles, who asserted that the Israelites were well aware of the gravity of the situation, however ridiculous they appeared to those in power who had "no regard for native rights."[9] They were not violating any laws. Nightingale had granted them permission to erect dwellings, local residents had consented to Israelites coming in, and any new buildings had been placed on Mgijima family, not Crown, land.

The Israelites could not reconcile their mandate from God with the secular laws of the South African state. Since the government could not prove any charges against them, their resolve had not wavered. "God has sent us to this place," Charles declared. "We shall let you know when it is necessary that we go." His lieutenant, Edward Mpateni, echoed him: "We wanted to live peacefully with all. We only want to pray, but we cannot introduce you to the secrets of our prayers. You can try to interfere with God's work if you like, that is not our affair."[10]

The Israelite stance had hardened since the confrontation with the police several weeks earlier. Operating on the belief that the government had judged their case prematurely, they claimed Nightingale no longer came near them. They also pointed to alarmist reports in the European press and the flurry of wild rumors that had inflamed whites in the region and prejudiced them against the Israelites. As the Israelites perceived it the police unit dispatched to confront the Israelites demonstrated that "the Government have already sent people to kill us. After sending enemies to kill, they send others to speak to us. In our view, the question is prejudged. . . . This is a serious matter and it must not be forgotten that already blood had been spilt. We cannot talk when surrounded by guns, and all were in a state of war. We are peaceful; the Government had declared war." The Israelites were only prepared to present their case "to the final court of appeal, and that is, General Smuts!"[11]

As Barrett departed, he warned the Israelites, "The Prophet you bless to-day you will yet live to curse." Although the government delegation had few illusions that the Israelites would leave Ntabelanga on their own, they still held out the slender hope that the movement might lose steam if left alone.[12] They passed on the Israelite request for a meeting to Smuts, who promised to grant them an interview "as soon as his engagements permitted."[13] However, he never set aside a definite time for it because he, too, hoped the movement would lose momentum.[14]

At least one eastern Cape official did not believe that Barrett and the Native Affairs Department were up to the task of dealing with the Israelites. After bumping into Barrett in Queenstown shortly after his meeting with the Israelites, Lady Frere magistrate Apthorp complained that Native Affairs officials based in urban centers had no experience in dealing with rural Africans. "I am afraid," he informed John X. Merriman, that "our Head Office is quite out of touch with the conditions outside Pretoria and Johannesburg."[15]

The Election and the Elect

Between 17 December 1920 and 6 April 1921, no representatives from Pretoria attempted to meet the Israelites. Smuts was not anxious to vigorously pursue the Israelite negotiations because he was preoccupied with an arduous election campaign. In his first electoral test in March 1920 after succeeding Louis Botha as prime minister, his South African Party (SAP) had eked out a slender majority in Parliament—and that was only through an alliance with the Unionist Party. On 3 December Smuts, believing that another campaign might win his party additional seats, called for fresh elections.

He labored the next three months on the hustings, battling the combined threat of the Labour and National Parties.[16] At one point, his campaign swung through the eastern Cape to Dordrecht, Burghersdorp, and Tarkastad, a town less than twenty-five miles from Bulhoek.[17] However, he was not tempted to venture nearer because the police debacle in December had complicated all dealings with the Israelites. In light of the futility of the efforts of other negotiators, he understood that his presence at Bulhoek would not have enhanced his image with white voters and could very well have lost him votes in surrounding constituencies in what everyone anticipated was going to be a close election. Smuts's letter to A. H. Frost, his party's parliamentary candidate for the Queenstown district and a prominent Tarkastad sheep farmer, affirmed his thinking that applying force at this stage would be detrimental. "Bloodshed on a large scale at the present juncture would have the most lamentable political effects in many parts of South Africa. There is not a border constituency where its repercussions would not be very grave."[18]

Another reason militating against swift government action was the presence of the Israelites' lawyer, A. B. Halse. Because Enoch Mgijima had hired a white lawyer in a land case in 1917, he recognized the advantage that Halse's skin color presented in any dealings with the government. This was not lost on Smuts either. Writing to C. P. Crewe, an old political confidant and managing director of the *Daily Dispatch,* he admitted that the involvement of a white lawyer prevented him from implementing Crewe's advice to summarily expel the Israelites. If they were taken to court, they would surely lose.[19]

Unlike Smuts, other white politicians were not reticent in soliciting Israelite votes. African men in Cape Province who met specific education, income, or property standards continued to vote on a common roll with whites until 1936, and white politicians avidly courted their votes since they could sway the outcomes of elections in certain constituencies. In Queenstown district, where over 20 percent of the electorate was black

(Coloured and African), both the SAP and the National Party regularly sent their candidates and "native" agents out to African locations to vie for their votes.[20] Although Queenstown's white electorate was over 50 percent Afrikaner, the district had long been represented by the Unionist Party's William Bisset Berry, originally a Cape Progressive Party member and speaker of the Cape Assembly from 1892 to 1908 and a member of the delegation sent to London in 1909 to appeal to the British to protect African and Coloured political rights in the constitution. In the 1915 election one of Berry's opponents was Lamb Brinkman, another lawyer who represented the Mgijimas. After Berry stood down in 1920 the SAP/Unionists put up A. H. Frost, who easily won the election.

Standing for the National Party in the district in his first election campaign was Eric Louw, a young Beaufort West lawyer and businessman. That the Israelites had successfully defied the government mattered little to him. "After all," he quipped, "a vote is a vote," and he was not about to ignore an estimated thirty to forty-five votes.[21] In an article Louw penned for *Die Burger* after the massacre, he claimed that early in the campaign he decided to steer clear of the Israelites.[22] But he changed his mind after holding a meeting at Kamastone, where he met several Israelites, including Charles Mgijima, who impressed Louw with his dignified bearing and his command of political issues. Thus, when a rumor later circulated that the National Party favored killing the Israelites (a rumor, Louw added, that a black South African Party agent planted), he decided to speak directly to the Israelites at Ntabelanga on a Saturday Sabbath. He has provided the only first-person white account of an Israelite religious observance.[23]

At the front of the tabernacle was a raised platform on which the prophet Enoch sat on a wooden throne. Church benches were arranged in a semicircle around the platform. Israelite men, wearing frock coats with stiff white collars, trousers, and sandals, sat on the left side, while the women, decked out in white blouses and dark skirts, were seated on the right.[24] All had on white neckties and long white bibs with photographs of Crowdy and Mgijima fastened to their lapels.[25]

The service began with hymn singing, and then the women were sent away before Louw made a brief speech. Heeding an Israelite admonition not to raise politics, he skirted around the issue by talking about how love of country went hand in hand with love of church. Then Charles recited verses from the book of Revelation in Dutch, while church elders read the same passages from seSotho and isiXhosa Bibles. Following a prayer came Enoch's thundering sermon: "Close to the platform a straw mat was placed and on this the preacher walked back and forth during the sermon. He began in a calm and reasoned manner and then he became serious and agitated. The sermon had the same effect on the congregation and at times members shouted out, which presumably had the same meaning as our 'Amen.'"[26] Among other things, he predicted a great slaughter over all the earth. Although Enoch's oratory dazzled Louw, he considered Enoch to be dour and uninteresting compared to his brother. As did many other Europeans, he thought the real skill and intelligence lay behind the throne with Charles.

Louw left Ntabelanga with a sense of respect for the Israelites, going so far as to call Ntabelanga a "model village." After the massacre, he sharply criticized the government's handling of the affair, though it is difficult to gauge whether his censure of the Smuts administration was prompted more by his political partisanship than by any real sympathy for the Israelites.[27] After losing the election, he claimed Mgijima told him that not even the arms of the government would deter him and his followers from voting for Louw.[28] This may well have been true, though not for the reasons Louw may have expected. During the 1924 national election, Mgijima asked Israelite voters to cast their ballots for the National Party candidate because a Hertzog victory would lead to intensified government repression of Africans, thus confirming Mgijima's prophecy that a period of strife and turmoil would take place before the coming of the Lord.[29]

Do You People Still Pay Taxes?

The election campaign provided a respite for both the government and the Israelites. However, the government's wait-and-see attitude waned after disturbing reports surfaced that Israelite blacksmiths were forging swords out of cart springs and scabbards from paraffin tins and distributing them to new converts throughout the countryside. Although the swords had been part of the Israelite uniform since 1916 and were worn purely for ceremonial purposes (Luke 22:36), the government suspected the Israelites might be arming other Africans for a coordinated general uprising. Reports filtering in that the Israelites were also acquiring rifles and ammunition generated even more alarm.

The Israelites recognized that the election campaign had given them a momentary reprieve but that it was only a matter of time before the government moved to evict them. Retreating even further into their village, they grew increasingly hostile toward all whites, forcing white farmers who had visited Ntabelanga in previous months to skirt around the village. In early April, Nightingale visited and found a dam under construction in place of a public road.[30] On several occasions, the Israelites refused entry to the district surgeon, John Cranke. On 13 January, when Cranke went out with his son to investigate reports of a typhus outbreak, he reported some Israelites "advised me to send him [his son] to Europe at once as the day of the Lord was coming and when it came it would not be like Port Elizabeth."[31] The Israelites treated tax collectors with particular disdain. J. Greyling, the tax collector for Kamastone and Oxkraal, came upon six Israelites in early April who warned him "that if I advance towards their Location or destroyed any of their dogs I would be a dead man."[32]

Israelite evangelists capitalized on their defiant spirit to win more converts. Apthorp, the magistrate at Lady Frere, about forty-five miles from Kamastone, reported that Israelite influence was spreading in his district as "messengers from Kamastone [were] telling the people not to worry about taxes."[33] After the Bulhoek massacre, he expressed his concern that landless Africans had been talking about the "simple method" of obtaining land the Israelites had adopted.[34] In that vein, Israelite evangelist John Sihlahla asked a crowd in the neighboring Glen Grey district: "Do you people still pay taxes, because we no longer pay taxes where we are? We have a prophet there and it has been given out that the time of the native people has come when we should rule ourselves."[35]

The Israelites, especially after their December triumph over the police, had come to symbolize for many Africans a successful challenge to white rule: land for the landless, an escape from burdensome taxes, and an opportunity to govern autonomously without white interference. Some Africans who were not Israelites still sympathized with their cause and joined in refusing to pay taxes or repay debts to white traders.[36]

While the Israelites solidified their base at Ntabelanga, their evangelists were actively proselytizing throughout the Ciskei and western Transkei. With the Israelite cause gaining strength, hundreds of new converts flocked to Ntabelanga. A register of Israelites confiscated after the May massacre recorded that in April 1921 there were 1,653 adherents.[37] But in little over a month, another 1,532 joined. Most came from the Ciskei and Transkei, and more particularly, from Kamastone, Glen Grey, Nqamakwe, and Cala districts. A smaller number trickled in from the Orange Free

State, Basutoland, and Transvaal and as far away as Rhodesia and Nyasaland. Those who arrived from farthest away were most likely labor migrants or farm labor tenants. Later in the year a government record of those put on trial classified almost two-thirds as "farmers" and almost one-third as "laborers." A small number were teachers, masons, saddlers, shoemakers, and clerks. There are no clues as to where the "laborers" worked—whether on white farms or the mines or for other Africans or whether they had been forced off the land. Similarly, the record did not define the term "farmers," so there is no indication of the extent of their land and stock holdings or their economic status.

Certainly Mgijima's image of a fiery and bloody war of retribution was a compelling factor behind many of the new conversions. There was a growing sense of urgency in having God's children gather at Ntabelanga since the conflict with the government was reaching a critical stage. Those who did not join were told they would soon die a fiery death. One Israelite bringing converts to Ntabelanga greeted Mgijima, "*Bota* [hail] Israel," to which he responded, "Are you returned?" "Yes." "Are these the men you have brought with you?" "Yes." "Tell these children that they have come to face death."[38]

Mgijima vividly impressed the image of a fiery end on all of his followers. Describing the expected millennium, Lunqwana Mtsha, a Glen Grey peasant, testified at the Israelite trial that the prophet had confirmed all his predictions and "further told me that I would be immune from the bullets of the white man."[39] Echoing his remarks was Tasman Jaxa, another Glen Grey resident. The Israelites, he said, "read of wars, fires, and destruction from this Book. They spoke of the Day of Judgment. . . . They said that if a man did not join them his own child would burn and stab him."[40] However, as persuasive as the Israelite millennium was, some converts like Jaxa could not accept the Israelite prediction of a war between black and white.[41]

Israelite evangelists finding fertile recruiting grounds in neighboring African reserves and new converts streaming into Ntabelanga every week reinforced the Israelite resolve to resist government interference. While this was going on, the Smuts government, having won modest gains in the election, prepared to renew its negotiations. However, Smuts reneged on his promise to meet face to face with the Israelites and instead delegated the recently established Native Affairs Commission (NAC) to go out to Ntabelanga in early April.

The NAC was set up in 1920 as a liaison between the state and Africans on a wide range of issues: education, pass laws, squatting, poll taxes, wages, housing, working conditions for laborers and labor recruitment, and African local and general councils. Some Africans, believing the NAC would be a constructive channel for airing grievances, welcomed its creation. In actual fact, it was an advisory body with no independent powers.

The Bulhoek negotiation was the NAC's first major opportunity to test its mettle.[42] Its members were Gen. L. A. S. Lemmer, Dr. C. T. Loram, and Sen. A. Roberts. The chief inspector of African schools in Natal and a member of Lovedale's governing council, Loram was well known in Cape educational circles, while Roberts had taught for many years at Lovedale, the school that had educated several Israelites, including Charles Mgijima.[43] Hence, some of those in government circles believed that Loram and especially Roberts might have personal influence and insight into African thinking that Native Affairs Department officials did not have. From its creation, the NAC had been at odds with the Native Affairs Department, and the commissioners certainly felt that Barrett and his officials had botched their negotiations with the Israelites. Roberts dismissed Barrett as the most ineffectual person he had ever met and derided the Native Affairs Department as the "cold storage vault of all living warm blooded servants."[44] However, Roberts, who had recently pronounced on the lack of unrest among Africans, and his fellow commissioners clearly had no idea of what lay in store for them.[45]

Meeting with the Israelites on 6 and 8 April, the commissioners explained that Smuts specifically appointed them to look after "native" interests and that since "they had come as the true friends of the Natives . . . they hoped that before leaving they could come to some friendly agreement which would be pleasing to the Prime Minister and to all parties."[46] To a large degree, their proposals were a rehash of earlier government offers. They promised to furnish free rail passage and rations for all Israelites who were not from Bulhoek and to settle those who were destitute or had sold their possessions in Crown locations. They went a step further by offering to consider an Israelite application for a permanent site at Ntabelanga so long as the church used it exclusively for religious purposes.[47]

If the commissioners showed some flexibility in the government's line, the Israelites did not budge from theirs. They questioned how the NAC could even presume to negotiate with them since they were there by the authority of a higher power, Jehovah. Scoffing at Roberts's contention that Jehovah also worked through him, they asserted that the Lord spoke through only one prophet and that was Enoch. As for the commissioners' offers, the Israelites contemptuously dismissed them. They were answerable only to the Lord, who determined how much land they needed and how long they were going to stay. "We cannot discuss these things because God does not deal with numbers. It is wrong to try to limit Him. If we limited Him that would make Him angry. We were called to this place, and until He said that we should leave, we will not."[48]

Despite the Israelites' unyielding stance, the meeting allowed an airing of viewpoints. Although the commissioners had concluded that the Israelites were fundamentally nonpolitical religious fanatics who would violently resist any attempt to root them out forcibly, they still asked Smuts and Parliament for another chance to mediate. That opportunity would not come for another month.

Meanwhile, relations between the Israelites and neighboring Africans were reaching a breaking point. The Israelites were competing for Kamastone's scarce resources with other residents who feared that if the Israelites laid claim to their land, the government would use the crisis as a pretext for confiscating all the land, Israelite and non-Israelite alike. In April, Alfred Dondolo lodged complaints with the Israelites about their hoarding of scarce firewood and their cattle destroying crops. But the Israelite spokesman, Edmund Magadla, took an aggressive line toward Dondolo. They had nothing more to say to him because they held him responsible for giving the land that the Israelites had taken from the police back to the whites. If the whites were defeated in the future, Magadla vowed that all non-Israelite Africans would be forced to leave as well.[49]

Other Kamastone residents also took the Israelites to task for their uncompromising stand. Edward Sokabo, a relative of the Mgijimas and Gilbert Matshoba, was skeptical that the whites would be driven into the sea and warned the Israelites about the implications of what they were doing. He did not buy their view that there was going to be bloodshed between the white and black races. "This can't be. These white people have their God also. How do you know God is going to be on your side? But the Israelites claimed that it was the time of Jehovah."[50]

A Kamastone headman, John Alfred Sishuba, aggressively attacked the Israelites. Speaking to a group of white farmers, he boasted that if the government supplied him with fifty sjamboks, he would soon drive the Israelites out.[51]

Relations between the Israelites and white farmers also further deteriorated. On 28 April, a white farmer caught an Israelite picking maize and pumpkins on T. Goosen's Tiger Klip farm adjoining Ntabelanga. In the ensuing fracas, the Israelite threw his sword at his pursuer, who shot at him before he escaped. Although the complaints of white farmers about a wave of thefts escalated, they never advanced any hard evidence to substantiate their allegations.[52] However, the Goosen incident reinforced their belief that the Israelites were running out of food and would start stealing more.

In the absence of government action, there was no lack of blustering settlers prepared to go on the warpath. Despite being advanced in years Gordon Turner of Lady Frere announced his readiness to join a commando against the "mob of black rebels" and protect the country from the "horrors of Black Bolshevism": "We must never forget that while we Europeans number a beggarly million and a half, the black races number some seven millions, and if once this damnable doctrine of the Israelites gets a firm grip of the native mind there will be horrors and misery throughout the land even worse than has been in Russia since the advent to power of Lenin and Trotsky."[53]

On 28 April, Mattushek's murder trial opened in East London, but the magistrate wasted no time in dropping the charges after the key Israelite witnesses, Charles Mgijima, Meshach Dondolo, Ebenezer Hjegesi, and Solomon Magadla, failed to appear. Based on his experience as a court interpreter Charles surely knew he would be called on to testify, but he saw no reason to obey the subpoena since he believed his testimony was hearsay and he had already given enough evidence to the police and the local magistrate to convict Mattushek and Klopper. To Enoch, the issue of testifying was less critical than bringing the wrongdoers to trial. Writing to Welsh in late March, he demanded "to know, what do you say about the murdered man Charles Dondolo and the murderers. This is the topmost matter which boils our blood and which I think should work in your minds more than the evidence of the previous firing [shooting]."[54]

Charles had more on his mind than testifying. He feared that if he moved out of the sanctuary of Ntabelanga, the authorities would arrest him immediately. He was also guarding against reprisals by local white farmers who he claimed had posted notices declaring they would summarily shoot any Israelite trespassing on their property.

However, the court was not sympathetic to his concerns.[55] Because the four Israelites refused to honor the subpoenas, the Native Affairs Department issued a notice stating that the government had bent over backward to indulge the "childish claims" of the Israelites, but it could not tolerate their defiance of a court of law. The judge of the East London Circuit Court issued a warrant to arrest the Israelite witnesses.[56]

A Sufficiently Strong Force

To officials in Pretoria, April's developments were clear proof that the Israelites were, if anything, digging in, and they finally gave the go-ahead to the police to assemble a sizable contingent to move on Ntabelanga. Because mobilizing one hundred police the previous November had demonstrated the difficulty of raising a force on short notice, Pretoria bought some time by giving the NAC one last chance to broker an agreement.

On the commissioners' return to Queenstown in early May, several Africans warned them that they had reliable information that the Israelites were planning to kill them when they approached the Holy City. That did not deter the commissioners. Roberts reportedly joked before they traveled to Bulhoek, "Well, anyway, let's have a good breakfast."[57]

Nothing constructive came from the 11 May meeting. The commissioners reiterated their proposals for repatriating Israelites to their homes, looking into individual grievances, and considering an application for a religious site at Ntabelanga.[58] This offer did not move the Israelites, and the meeting degenerated into heated arguments. Although the Israelites did not assault the trio physically, they sensed a distinct "spirit of defiance" on the part of younger Israelites. As the commissioners prepared to leave, one Israelite remembered Roberts warning Charles Mgijima, "I am leaving. We shall see what will happen. We part being very clear that things are not in order."[59] But Charles had the last word. "Very well, we thank you for your patience. And now it will be a matter between the Lord and the Government."[60]

Charles's parting comment was surely a disappointment to the commissioners. Perhaps because Loram and Roberts had known Charles as a student at Lovedale, they had tried to wean him away from Israelite militants, hoping he would serve as a counterweight to his brother and moderate the Israelite stance. At the commissioners' first meeting with the Israelites, Lemmer claimed that Charles had agreed to meet the commission on his own in Queenstown but had not shown up.[61] In late April, officials invited Charles to conduct a census of Bulhoek, for which they were going to pay him. He accepted, but never completed his task.[62] At the last visit of the commissioners, a headman, James Mtombeni, reported that Roberts appealed to Charles to get in his car and see if they could work out a solution with the magistrate. According to Mtombeni, Charles appeared willing, but an Israelite intervened, admonishing him, "You shall not go, you belong to us, and you will stay here."[63] And, in mid-May, Kamastone Africans informed officials that Charles was willing to compromise if there were a strong enough force to protect him.[64]

Once it became obvious that Charles would not soften his line, the frustrated NAC representatives finally resorted to coercion, threatening to withhold his teacher's pension and confiscate his private landholdings if he did not accommodate them.[65]

None of their tactics bore any fruit, and all the evidence suggests that Charles did not seriously consider working with the government at any point. Certainly his testimony at the Israelite trial in late November supports this. Charles and other Israelite leaders would have found it difficult to temper the Israelite position since their rank and file's uncompromising stance ensured that their leaders would not waver. Indeed, rank-and-file members were a crucial determinant in forging Israelite cohesiveness.

Their militancy was not because of a slavish obedience to their prophet. Rather, their common experience at Ntabelanga created another dynamic to Israelite resistance, which operated independently, not merely as an adjunct, of the leadership. Their months of communal existence, the material and physical sacrifices they endured, their successful defiance of white authority, and the infusions of zealous converts strengthened their discipline and bolstered their single-minded devotion to their cause.

The commissioners regarded the negotiations as hopelessly deadlocked. Lemmer candidly expressed their sense of frustration by relating that "even if we had sent an angel we could not have made these people listen to reason."[66] Believing the Israelites would capitulate before a show of force, they wired Pretoria, recommending "a sufficiently strong force to overcome natives if possible."[67]

Colonel Truter was already assembling such a force at the Queenstown Show Ground next to the African location. Eventually made up of around six hundred police drawn from all corners of the country (so that police work in other districts was not disrupted) and augmented by Maxim gun and artillery detachments from the army, the force was the largest unit of police put together up to that time for any action. Truter made a point of drilling his units in the open so that reports of what lay in store for them would reach the Israelites.

Government officials weighed several options about the kind and level of force they would marshal against the Israelites. One was to send airplanes overhead in a strategic display of power to gauge its impact on the Israelites (an airplane had first landed in the area in June 1920). If feasible, they would drop a series of bombs around the outskirts of the Israelite village. But the government decided against this tactic on the grounds that if the bombs missed their mark, it would greatly undermine the aircraft's "overawing influence" and "moral value" on Africans and stiffen the Israelite resolve to resist. Officials also feared the possibility that if the airplanes dropped bombs, they might hit Ntabelanga accidentally and wound and kill men, women, and children indiscriminately.[68] Another suggestion to dispatch a large force of soldiers to "surround and starve the Israelites into submission" was rejected because it would have adversely affected non-Israelites and required almost four thousand men to stay for a lengthy period. Even then they still may not have effectively sealed off Ntabelanga.[69] Although an artillery battery was added to the police force, it was to be kept out of any military action "unless and until an extreme situation arises which justifies drastic action and controlled rifle fire has been found powerless to effect object."[70]

Some observers believed that airplanes could have been used advantageously at Bulhoek. After the massacre, the *Johannesburg Star* editorialized: "The Israelite trouble might have been settled at very little cost and probably with far less loss of life, by using a few bombing aeroplanes."[71] A week before the massacre, a letter writer styling himself "Night Bomber" weighed in with his opinion: "When dealing with natives, and especially with the religious fanatics like the 'Israelites,' enough stress cannot be laid upon the value of moral effect. These natives are looking for martyrdom. Why not save white men's lives and natives as well by the 'martyrdom' really terrifying with as little bloodshed as possible! Half a dozen low-flying aeroplanes, using a few bombs or machine-guns, would clear up the trouble quickly, safely, and cheaply—besides creating a lasting impression on the rebel mind."[72]

With a final confrontation imminent, another African delegation made a last-ditch effort to mediate with the Israelites. On 14 May, the SANNC's James Ngojo, a relative of the Mgijima's and a boyhood friend of Enoch's, had approached NAC members at the Hexagon Hotel for permission for a delegation of local African and Coloured leaders to meet with the Israelites. At first they were reluctant to let the delegation go, but they finally relented and loaned a car to Ngojo's party to drive to Bulhoek.

Ngojo, C. M. Dantu, Reverend Solilo, and Matshikiza conducted an amiable meeting with Matshoba and the Mgijimas in Dutch. Ngojo's delegation warned the Prophet of the dangerous consequences of his stand and maintained that, despite the presence of the police force at Queenstown, Roberts was still willing to open a fresh round of talks. Enoch thanked them for their interest, but in a subsequent letter, he rejected their counsel and castigated them for offering their help at the last moment.[73] The Cape Native National Congress meeting in Aliwal North also voted on 19 May to send a deputation to the Israelites, but they were not able to do so before the massacre.[74]

Wild rumors circulating throughout the country heightened the tensions between the opposing sides. Newspapers published fabricated accounts of Israelite origins and history based on incorrect information and misinterpretations of their aims or reasons for gathering at Ntabelanga. An account in *Imvo Zabantsundu* (whose editor, Jabavu, had met the Israelites the previous December) is typical: "The Israelites . . . are a tough lot. . . . That the Israelites take themselves seriously is clear from the fact that they have sent . . . emissaries to native chiefs to urge them to adopt the damnable doctrine to rise up against the Government and every white man. One, we understand, came down to this neighborhood and another visited Khama's country. . . . The story of Garvey's Americans coming to assist them, and American aeroplanes have come as far as Queenstown from the territories. All this drivel is being circulated among the crowd."[75]

In light of African unrest in Port Elizabeth and other urban centers, the government decision to finally remove the Israelites pleased most whites as well as those Africans who had lobbied the government to take a firm stand. The Tarkastad newspaper advised that "serious illnesses demand severe remedies whether in the body physical or the body politic."[76] To most whites, the police presence was an "oracular demonstration of the fact the government has a power behind it, and that it would be folly to attempt to resist. . . . The demonstration is bound to do an immense lot of good."[77] The police force would impress and awe non-Israelites as well as Israelites.

Most white commentators concurred that the Israelites would put up no resistance to the formidable police contingent. One reporter thought: "Local natives say that the 'prophet' and his leaders will surrender readily and will not put to the test their own boast that a white man's bullet would be ineffective on an Israelite."[78] The *Queenstown Daily Representative* editorialized that just as Germany accepted the ultimatum to surrender during World War I, "so also will the Israelites accept the position and bow to superior force."[79] A day later, after the Native Affairs Commissioners returned empty-handed from their negotiations, the same paper confidently boasted: "Before many days are over they [the Israelites] will have a rude awakening, and they will be given occular demonstration that the power of their wonderful Prophet is as nothing compared to the mighty arm of the law, which, though, it may move very slowly, moves and strikes, when it does move, with deadly certainty."[80]

However, on the eve of the police moving to Bulhoek, some newspapers retreated from their confident pronouncements. The *Cape Argus* reported that "the police officers who were firmly convinced that the Israelites would tamely surrender, have changed their view, and now believe that resistance will almost certainly be offered."[81]

In the Queenstown African location, some of its six thousand residents were convinced the Israelites were preparing to fight the police.[82] A rumor circulated that a fire lit on the top of Ntabelanga would signal the beginning of a wider conflagration between blacks and whites. Location Africans had heard Israelite evangelists preaching many times about the war that was to start in the west at Ntabelanga. On 20 May, Banana Martins wrote a foreboding letter to the prophet, warning that he saw no good coming from the unarmed sect fighting the well-armed police.[83] He tried to frighten the Israelites off by dramatizing the heavy police armaments and a rumor of soldiers raping three African girls. Incongruously he still held out hope that the Israelites would triumph. At the Israelite trial, Judge Graham questioned him:

> *Graham:* What were you going to fight for? What have you got to complain about?
> *Martins:* We were told this was a war for freedom.
> *Graham:* Freedom from what?
> *Martins:* For the black people of this country.
> *Graham:* Aren't they free now?
> *Martins:* No.[84]

In the face of cautions from Africans and whites alike, the Israelites did not back down, and they and the government steeled themselves for a showdown. On 20 May, Wicks appealed to Charles and Enoch to hand over their witnesses for the Mattushek case.[85] Finally, on 21 May, Truter delivered a stern ultimatum to the Israelites, declaring that his police force had been empowered to arrest the Israelites who had not honored subpoenas, to send unauthorized residents back where they came from, and to demolish illegal houses.[86]

The following day Enoch sent two emissaries, Silwana Nkopo and Samuel Matshoba, with a letter to Truter at the Hexagon Hotel in Queenstown. In it Enoch recounted his prophetic career and reiterated his position that he had not invited any Israelites to settle in Ntabelanga, that they had not constructed houses without official permission, and that the police could freely take the men they wished. And he addressed the issue of the military and police force coming out to Ntabelanga.

> May it therefore be known by one and all that the arms and forces shall be ruled by God. As for myself, I am the messenger before the blood. I am not the causer of it, but God is going to cause it. I am a man of blood, said my God, the Lord of Hosts is His name. The time of Jehovah has now arrived. All nations are invited to the marriage of the Lord God of Heaven and earth, and also to the occupier of the God of heaven and earth (Rev. xix., 7–18; Ezek. xxxix., 17–20). God has now taken kindness away from the human being.[87]

Enoch had resigned himself to the probability that the government had set out not just to expel the Israelites but to eradicate them. The night the police moved out to Bulhoek, he called Israelite men together to inform them that even though the police were planning to evict them, he could not let them proceed without God's permission. He revealed a vision of the police arriving and entering Ntabelanga from many directions. His response was to send a party of men to confront them, but he saw the government forces firing on them and all the men falling down shot.[88] The Israelites understood that this confrontation was not going to be like the one with the police on 8 December. Bloodshed was inevitable. "When people rally round the word of God," John Tamana solemnly declared, "some must die."[89] If any thought their beliefs protected them from police bullets, it could not be attributed to their prophet's preaching. As one Israelite recalled, "No one would have had any such illusions on the 24th because the Prophet had said that on this day the brother will trod on the intestines of his brother."[90]

When some Israelites asked Mgijima if this prophecy came from him or from God, he simply responded, "God has sent me to prophecy." But his foreboding prediction did not diminish the Israelites' commitment. His followers reaffirmed that "whether you have seen death or bloodshed, we are not leaving. If there is death, let us die through our belief."[91] His nephew, Barrington Mgijima, added: "If you see death here, let the death begin with us Mgijimas."[92] Israelites were given the option of leaving or remaining at Ntabelanga, but none left during the night. In fact, a few more showed up during the evening.

As the police and Israelites braced for a showdown, the noted Gold Coast educator Dr. James Aggrey stopped over in Queenstown. Arriving in Cape Town several months before, he had been lecturing all over the country. Roberts hosted him at Lovedale, while Loram squired him around Natal. His lectures to black and white audiences invariably touched on the same themes—interracial bridge building by whites and blacks of good will reaching out to each other and Africans devoting themselves to their advancement rather than attacking whites for holding them down. In that vein his speech in Queenstown the evening of 22 May was titled "Co-operation." The local newspaper optimistically ventured that Aggrey was "out to make the black man understand the white better, and the black man to understand the white man better, and there is no reason why he should not be able to succeed in his aim."[93] But a few days later came the tragic massacre at Bulhoek.

Because They Chose the Plan of God

> *Because they chosed [sic] the plan of God the world did not have a place for them.*
>
> **—Inscription on tombstone of one of the**
> **mass graves of Israelites at Bulhoek**

> *Do not forget, Lord, to remember the plight of your people on the 24th of May, 1921. It is a very long time that we have been the butt end and sworn at by the foreigners.*
>
> **—From the Last Prayer of Enoch Mgijima**

Tuesday, 24 May, was the birthday of Queen Victoria (commemorated as Empire Day) and Jan Smuts, an auspicious sign for the looming showdown between the Israelites and the government forces. The previous day the

combined police and army units with 22 officers and 590 men had en-
camped several miles away at Potgieters Kraal, where Truter split his men
into two regiments. At dawn on 24 May the temperature was hovering at
the freezing point as one regiment and a signaler with a heliograph were
deployed on a northeastern ridge overlooking the Israelite village and
on the road to Bulhoek. At 9:00 a.m., the main force was deliberately
ordered to march slowly through the port leading to Bulhoek so that the
Israelites could understand the gravity of what they faced and reconsider
their position.[94] Truter deployed five detachments to positions south of
the Black Kei on the sloping hills overlooking the Israelite village and
placed the Maxim guns on a large kopje with artillery pieces behind them.
Truter, Van Deventer, and civilian officials set up a command center about
two miles away on a rise with a commanding view of the valley. All units
were in place by 10:00 a.m. Police heliographs busily flashed intelligence
on where Israelite columns were being positioned.

The Israelites followed their daily rituals, congregating before dawn
in the tabernacle for their morning service. By 8:40 a.m., the service
was over. Peering through binoculars, police scouts observed Israelites
milling outside the tabernacle. Several days earlier Sergeant Wicks had
reported the Israelite ritual dancing from a distance: "They were brandishing their weapons and thrusting at each other like lunatics."[95] Like
him the scouts mistook the Israelite ceremonial procession for a war
dance.

After sizing up the police forces, the Israelite men, numbering about
five hundred, split up into five regiments led by Samuel Mgijima, Silwana
Nkopo, Mafuya, and Barrington and Innes Mgijima. The regiments were
divided roughly by age—the elderly and lame (*amadoda amakulu*) in one
and younger men (*amadoda amancani*) in the others—and assembled.
Some were positioned in front of Ntabelanga, others next to the Black
Kei, and still others to the east. Israelite women and children remained
in the tabernacle praying and singing, while their men, chanting anthems
such as "Rejoice, Rejoice for Our King" and "Great and Marvelous Are Thy
Works, O Lord of Israel," awaited the police's next move.[96]

About 11:15 a.m., the police asked the Israelites if they were receptive
to another exchange of views. Two Israelites, Charlton Mzimkulu and
Edward Mpateni, lay down their assegais and stepped forward to meet
Wicks and Constable Boucher, who were fluent in isiXhosa.

"What are you here for?" the Israelites demanded.

Wicks firmly instructed them, "Go back to your people and tell them to lay down their arms and come out and surrender and if they fail to do so and oppose my advance, force will be used."

Was this a final ultimatum, Mpateni queried?

Wicks responded, "Yes, you must lay down your arms and surrender."

But Mpateni was undeterred. "If it is to be a fight, I warn you that Jehovah will fight with us and for us."

He and Mzimkulu then broke off the discussion with the words: "There is nothing more to say, it is finished."[97]

The police were positioned about six hundred yards from the Israelites. As soon as Wicks and Boucher passed on the Israelite reply, the police formed into three squadrons and were ordered to advance with fixed bayonets to within about four hundred yards of the main body of Israelites. Truter, thinking that the Israelites still might be induced to lay down their weapons, instructed Lieutenant Colonel Trew to have E. W. Woon meet with them one last time. Armed with assegais and swords, Edward Mpateni, Charlton Mzimkulu, and another Israelite came forward. Two gave their weapons to the third and approached Woon.

> *Israelite:* We have not received a reply from Queenstown to our message about a week ago.
> *Woon:* I know nothing about it.

When the Israelites asked why the police had come out to Ntabelanga, Woon stated that he was planning to occupy the Israelite village. "If that party in front there resists my advance I shall use force."

> *Israelite:* We will fight.
> *Woon:* You go back to that party and tell them to lay down their arms and surrender.
> *Israelite:* Is that your last word?
> *Woon:* Yes.
> *Israelite:* We will fight, and Jehovah will fight with us. Then that's all; it's finished; Jehovah will fight for us.[98]

Garbed in a red robe, Enoch stood on top of a hill behind the Israelite regiments. As the Israelite spokesmen left the meeting, one yelled to the ridge, "The Heathen want to enter the village," and Enoch shouted back, "Jehovah is not willing."[99]

What happened next is open to question since Israelite and government sources relate conflicting versions of how the battle was touched off. The official narrative conformed to its perception of the Israelites as a seditious sect. According to it, as soon as Mzimkulu and Mpateni reported back to Enoch, the prophet called out, "Jehovah says you must charge the Heathen," and the Israelites immediately surged forward into battle.[100] William Quirk reported that after Woon ended his exchange with the Israelites, he "had barely time to tell them the result of the interview, when the Natives advanced shouting, yelling, waving paper flags, and brandishing their weapons." Only then did the troops open fire.[101]

It is hard to believe, however, that anyone from the police ranks could have heard Enoch's commands distinctly from a distance of four hundred yards. Although some police were convinced the first shots came from the Israelites, this charge had little foundation since a Lee Medford carbine in serviceable condition and an old rifle in Enoch's home were the only firearms found among the Israelites after the battle.

Moreover, if the Israelites were indeed plotting to attack the police, why did they not draw nearer to the police ranks before charging? If they had attacked at a closer range, they might have inflicted casualties on the police. One explanation why the Israelites did not move closer is that some of them believed they were impervious to bullets. At the Israelite trial, several Israelites testified on this matter. Stephen Vanqa claimed: "I actually believed the bullets would not hurt us as we were told that this word had come from God. I did not fear the white man's bullets as I was told in public meeting by the Prophet that it was God's work that they would not injure me."[102] But other Israelites were just as adamant that Mgijima had not made such a prediction. John Sihlahla, an Israelite since 1912, contended: "I have never heard that bullets would turn to water. We had clear proof that bullets would not turn to water long before May 24. I knew water did not come out of fire-arms. Certain of our people were shot on December 14."[103]

Although Vanqa was a prosecution witness at the Israelite trial, this does not necessarily invalidate his testimony. Since the December rout of the police, some Israelites had accepted the story of bullets turning to water and no doubt passed on their belief to the new converts such as Vanqa. But this belief was not widely held and conflicted with Mgijima's own prophecies.

The Israelites laid the blame for the battle on the police and portrayed themselves as martyrs to God's plan. According to them, as soon as Mpateni and Mzimkulu reached the Israelite ranks, shots rang out. Charles Mgijima testified that the Israelite delegates ran toward him to report: "They say put down your weapons. If you don't put down your weapons we are going to shoot. As soon as they said that the firing started."[104] Even Israelite witnesses for the prosecution remembered clearly that they heard shots before Enoch directed them to engage the police line.

At that point the Israelites claimed they were left with no alternative but to charge. They had to protect their women and children. In his trial testimony Charles addressed the situation they were caught up in.

> *Charles:* We never expected the police to do us any harm, although we gave up hope when we saw that they had brought up cannon.
> *Question:* But why charge?
> *Charles:* What else could we do?
> *Question:* Put up your hands.
> *Charles:* If we had run away they would have shot us all the same.
> *Question:* Do you fell any remorse for all your comrades that are killed? Do you feel you are to blame for it in any way?
> *Charles:* No one can help but feel remorse.[105]

Many years later another Israelite survivor vividly remembered: "Have you ever been in war? When bullets are coming at you and people are in front of you, you can't turn back. No. You'll die going forwards. You face them rather than give your back."[106]

At least one alternative scenario to these accounts is feasible. Subinspector S. Chisholm reported that before the fighting erupted, he heard a single shot that he thought came from the Israelites.

> At 12:15 p.m., a shot was fired which I thought from the sound, was fired from the hill to west of village and commanding the road. A large number of natives lined the crest of this ridge.
>
> Almost immediately there followed a rattle of musketry and a general advance was made by the natives—those on my front and left crossed the river.[107]

The Chisholm account allows for the possibility that a single shot, perhaps fired accidentally, could have touched off the battle. Both sides were at an emotional peak. The police, believing the Israelites had firearms, expected fierce resistance from the aggressive Israelites, while the Israelites anticipated nothing but treachery from the heavily armed police. An unexpected movement from the Israelites or an errant shot by a jittery policeman could have ignited the battle instantly.

If the question of who initiated the battle is unresolved, the question of what happened next is not. The Israelites were at least several hundred yards from police lines when they charged. Dressed in white tunics and brown khaki shorts and armed with knobkerries and assegai (their ceremonial swords remained sheathed), they were conspicuous targets as they dashed toward the police. Mounted on a horse named Strike, Charles Mgijima's role was to relay messages and direct movements of Israelite regiments, but Woon had ordered his men to shoot the man on horseback. The machine gun unit wounded Charles in his left leg and he was quickly sidelined.[108]

In the event of an Israelite advance, Woon instructed a unit of twenty-five policemen to fire a volley at the Israelites to see how they would react. But because the bayonets attached to their rifles added some weight, the first shots fell in front of the Israelite line.[109] When one unwitting white farmer watching the battle unfold from a nearby hillside saw the Israelites advancing with bullets whizzing around them, he needed no further proof that they were invincible and he turned round and fled the scene.[110]

But after that initial volley as the rifles and machine guns sliced through the Israelite ranks, any illusions of divine protection evaporated. Moving against the main group of police, about fifty younger Israelites attacked the police flank to the right, where a squadron with machine guns mowed them down. Some charged head on, while others advanced steadily, clambering to whatever shelter—rocks, riverbed, dongas, kopjes—they could find. They were heard yelling "*Magwala* [cowards?] You will all die here." Their fanatical courage impressed the police, who were amazed at how wounded Israelites, after falling to the ground, kept pressing forward. All but one of the Israelites wounded or killed were shot in front.[111]

Despite their fearlessness, only a few Israelites made it to the police lines to engage in hand-to-hand fighting with the police, who relied on their bayonets and revolvers to defend themselves. The only injuries inflicted on the police were minor stab wounds. One constable was stabbed in the abdomen, a second suffered a superficial sword cut to his hand, and a third received a slight assegai wound to his upper arm. Woon himself had a close call as Israelite prisoners were being rounded up. An Israelite jumped out from behind some brush and grabbed him around the neck. Woon clubbed him in the face with his fist, and several troopers leaped forward to seize the assailant.[112]

As soon as the fighting broke out, two signal fires were lit on top of Ntabelanga. Some whites interpreted this as a signal to other Africans to commence fighting elsewhere, and indeed, one hundred police were held in reserve in Queenstown in case a simultaneous rising occurred there. But the Israelites claimed the fires were simply to "signal . . . our people outside not to approach the village" and to indicate to the Israelite regiments "who were not in sight of each other . . . that things were going wrong, and that we were being killed."[113]

While the shooting was still going on, Enoch proceeded to the tabernacle, where he interrupted the prayers of the women and children. "Look up to your God," he proclaimed, "the Israelites are finished." And then he prayed, "Is the blood required by you enough? Have enough Israelites been sacrificed?" As he implored the Lord to leave a remnant, the shooting ceased.[114]

In twenty minutes of fierce fighting over the two-and-a-half-mile front, several hundred Israelites were killed and nearly 130 wounded. The police arrested ninety-five Israelites. An accounting of those killed or arrested substantiates the broad appeal the Israelites had in the region. Of those killed, 66 were from the Queenstown area, 37 from the Transkei, and 66 from other areas. The rest were unidentified. Of the prisoners taken, 75 were Mfengu, 7 Basotho, 23 Thembu, 18 Ndebele, 2 Gcaleka Xhosa, 5 Ngqika Xhosa, 1 Khoikhoi, and 26 other Xhosa.[115]

When the shooting stopped, three Israelites bearing a white flag came forward to ask if the Israelites could tend to their wounded. Permission was granted so long as they carried white flags. The police regrouped, and at 1:30 p.m. they advanced on Ntabelanga. They forcibly disarmed about forty Israelite men who refused to lay down their knobkerries.[116] When Enoch was arrested, the police claimed they found him cowering in a house. But he retained his dignity and conviction to the end. Truter, when brought face to face with Enoch, told him: "Enoch, I hold you responsible for all this bloodshed." The prophet replied, "You take your orders from the Government. I take mine from Jehovah."[117] Despite all their derogatory remarks the white press had printed about Enoch, one reporter was moved by his bearing: "Standing there with his arms folded across his chest, his head up, and a defiant look in his eyes, the man seemed to radiate a strange sense of power, and it was easily understood in a measure, how he had persuaded his deluded followers to face certain death and die for his cause."[118]

The troops who remained at Ntabelanga guarded prisoners, while patrols fanned out searching for wounded Israelites. Israelite women joined in and continued the search throughout the night. They ministered to the wounded and took them water. Blankets served as stretchers for most of the wounded, but one woman went out with a wheelbarrow a dozen times. About 130 wounded Israelites were brought in, the last arriving around 4:00 a.m., and treated at a dressing station near the prophet's home that was manned by a police surgeon Major Welsh and Dr. Cranke. Some of the wounded who crawled away were hidden until their compatriots could determine what the police intended to do with them. The men who escaped injury worked through the night digging three mass graves for their dead, and a service was held to commemorate them at dusk.[119] The police escorted Enoch and the other prisoners to the Queenstown jail, while the wounded were conveyed to Queenstown's Frontier Hospital in ox carts and cars provided by the Automobile Club.[120] As they neared Queenstown, the Israelites suffered one last indignity: they had to pass through a gauntlet of angry whites waving Union Jacks who jeered, "Where is your God now?"[121]

The following morning the police registered Israelite women and children. Then Edward Barrett addressed the women. Although he expressed great sympathy for their plight, he felt compelled to speak candidly about several things—that they and their menfolk had broken the law, that their leaders had misled them into thinking that their cause was righteous, and that God was not the god of both blacks and whites but a god who would look after them only. The government had negotiated in good faith, but the Israelites had "turned a deaf ear to all the overtures." The government had no choice but to restore law and order after the negotiations proved fruitless. Barrett placed sole responsibility for the bloodshed on the shoulders of the Israelite leaders and chided the women: "The opposition was very foolish indeed, especially when they opposed rifles, guns, and, if necessary, artillery, with assegais, short swords and sticks. They might just as well have used toothpicks."[122] He did, however, promise the women that the government would assist them in returning to their original homes. Most, however, chose to stay in Queenstown to be near their menfolk. They remained there during their trial and imprisonment.

The authorities confiscated a variety of church possessions, including Mgijima's red robe; an exercise book listing Israelite regiments; a book, *The Chronicles of the Church of God and Saints of Christ*, containing Mgijima's prophecies; and the Israelites' most revered relic, the Ark of the Covenant, which disappeared from sight for seven decades. They ordered the demolition of Israelite dwellings after Israelite women and children salvaged doors and window frames from the homes. Later that day many white farmers and Queenstown residents as well as Africans from neighboring locations came out to view the battlefield.

Understanding the Massacre

At the heart of the showdown between the government and the Israelites was the clash between secular and sacred power. Like the nineteenth-century Xhosa prophets, Mgijima did not separate the two, while British colonial and South African government officials drew a clear line between them and saw the secular as the driving force. Hence, when the South African government and the Israelites had their showdown at Bulhoek, they had very different conceptions of what their states represented. The Union government, which had been in existence for a little more than a decade, was in fact a pigmentocracy representing the interests of its primary constituency, the white minority. It was a state without a nation, its claim to legitimacy tenuous at best. On the other hand, while Mgijima's message had universalist components, his dualistic view of the world strictly divided believers from unbelievers, the elect from the damned, and so limited the number of people who would join his community. He and his followers were creating an autonomous sacred space and were prepared to directly challenge the legitimacy as well as the authority of the state. To borrow the words of Saul Dubow, the goal of the Israelites was "deliverance of freedom from, rather than inclusion in a white-dominated state."[123] In this respect they had much in common with many other African social movements of the post–World War I era.

One of the most troubling questions the Bulhoek massacre poses is why the government ultimately resorted to lethal force against a religious group that was doing nothing more than illegally squatting on Crown land? In looking for an answer to this question, one can draw on the insights of James Scott, who created a framework for analyzing how power relations between dominant and dominated groups are expressed and negotiated.[124] He sets out two "transcripts" that govern relations between the dominant elites and their subordinates. One is the "public transcript," which includes "open interaction between subordinates and those who dominate."[125] Relations between the two groups follow a script in which the dominated wear a mask of deference that acknowledges and reinforces their subordinate status. The South African government's "public transcript" with black people was a paternalistic understanding of how "natives" should act in their dealings with white officials. Even when "natives" were critical of the government, they were expected to accept the prevailing order by showing deference to white authority and keeping their rhetoric within a prescribed boundary.

The other transcript Scott lays out is a "hidden transcript," in which the dominated express "a critique of power spoken behind the backs of the dominant."[126] This transcript is expressed in a subtle "discourse that takes place 'offstage,' beyond direct observation by power holders."[127] According to Scott, a crisis ensues when the hidden transcript intrudes on the public transcript. As he observes, "The first open statement of a hidden transcript, a declaration that breaches the etiquette of power relations . . . carries the force of a symbolic declaration of war."[128]

Although Scott's analysis provides important insights that can be applied generally to the power relations between whites and Mgijima and the Israelites, it does not capture the full range of relations between the two groups and the fact that Mgijima and the Israelites made a number of "declarations of war" expressed in many different ways over an extended period of time. They were transgressing the public transcript long before they confronted the government head on in 1920 and 1921.

We can examine the shifts in relations between Mgijima and his followers and white authority in two phases. The first encompassed the years after his call to prophecy in 1907 until his invitation to his followers to congregate at Ntabelanga in 1919. As an independent evangelist he initially worked cooperatively with Wesleyan and Moravian missionaries but eventually broke with them to establish his own group, the Israelites, which challenged the spiritual power and legitimacy of the missions. Drawing on the beliefs of William Crowdy and his African American Church of God and Saints of Christ, he created a liberatory theology centered on the book of Exodus that defined the Israelites as a chosen people destined for salvation. As with other independent churches, Mgijima was openly transgressing the public transcript. White officials were uncomfortable with Mgijima and his disciples and harassed and arrested them in certain locales. But as long as Mgijima's transgressions were restricted to the spiritual realm, he was allowed to proselytize and bring his followers together for their annual Passovers.

The dramatic change in power relations between Mgijima and the state began when he issued his call to his followers to congregate at Ntabelanga in 1919 to await the end of the world. That is when the "hidden transcript" began aggressively challenging the state's "public transcript." When Israelite "strangers" stayed on after the Passover, the prophet began negotiating with the lowest rung of officialdom, Kamastone's superintendent of natives, Geoffrey Nightingale. Although he assured Nightingale that he had no intention of allowing the "strangers" to stay on indefinitely because his own landholdings were not large enough to accommodate all of them for an extended period, he still asked the superintendent for permission for his followers to stay longer.

Nightingale was initially accommodating, but by September 1920, he could no longer ignore the fact that the Israelite "strangers" were not leaving Ntabelanga. Although he believed that the Israelites were primarily motivated by their religious beliefs, he still issued summonses to twenty-one of them for illegal squatting. When his followers did not honor them, Mgijima explained that many of them were unable to make their way to Queenstown because they had gone back to their homes and were too far away to make an appearance in court.[129]

By October Nightingale tried to break the stalemate by kicking it up to the next level of officialdom, the Queenstown magistrate Welsh, who attempted to bureaucratize the issue by ordering the Israelites to compile a register of their community at Ntabelanga. The Israelites turned him down, stressing that their fundamental disagreement with the government was over their devotion to the laws of God and not the laws of secular authority. Charles Mgijima explained that they could not countenance counting members of their community because they were already enumerated in "God's book." Moreover, they were praying in accordance with God's wishes and were no longer operating on European time "for it is God's time now." Despite ample evidence that the Israelites did not intend to budge, Welsh still found them "very docile and humble" to deal with and granted them more time to finish their Passover.[130]

By creating their own autonomous theocratic community, one that was self-governing and self-sustaining, the Israelites were upsetting proper relations with the government as well as challenging what the South African state represented to them—intrusive and oppressive control over their lives and arbitrary laws legislated by and for the white minority.

Government officials in Pretoria monitoring the situation found Mgijima's references to war and retribution disturbing and were concerned about the alarmist cries of white farmers who regarded Ntabelanga as a threat to their livelihoods because of the presence of so many "strangers" who, they claimed, were stealing their crops and cattle. They also heard the concerns of black farmers living around Ntabelanga who expressed their fears that the government might associate them with the Israelites' defiance and punish them as well.

The confrontation was taken to a higher level when the central government finally decided to send out police to intimidate the Israelites with a show of force. However, it took several months for Pretoria to muster a hundred white police from around the region. When they finally pitched camp near the Israelite holy village on 7 December, the confrontation was an absolute disaster for white authority. The police retreated the moment the Israelites stood up to them. After that the Israelites gained confidence in defying the government and the tone of their rhetoric dramatically shifted—from warning that the government was in a fight with God to contending that Jehovah would actively intervene on their side against secular authority. And the government began interpreting Israelite resistance in political terms by concluding that they were plotting a rebellion.

Jayne Docherty, a professor of public policy at Eastern Mennonite University, captures how confrontations between governments and end-of time movements can end disastrously. "Acting out of their own fear or suspicion, public officials may approach a millennial group in ways that feed further the suspicion and distrust of the group. The result can be an escalatory cycle of encounters that end in violence"[131] This describes what happened at Bulhoek.

The gulf between the two sides was accentuated a week later when a government delegation met with the Israelites. The police commander,

Theo Truter, stressed the primacy of secular over spiritual law, while the Israelite spokesmen reiterated their belief that God had sent them to Ntabelanga to pray. They were not the aggressors; the government had "declared war" on them. It was noteworthy that the Israelites also refused to compromise with a delegation of black moderates the government sent out to negotiate with them.

Since it was concentrating on a closely contested election campaign, Smuts's government refrained from any direct contact with the Israelites for several months. During that time the Israelites grew even more defiant. They prevented whites from entering their holy village and refused to pay taxes. They prohibited those who had been subpoenaed from appearing at the Mattushek murder trial in East London and rejected the offers of the recently established Native Affairs Commission, which had been delegated to hold discussions with them in early April. In addition the Israelites' use of swords and drilling in their daily religious observances led the government to conclude that they were actively preparing for an armed uprising.

The South African government found itself in a classic dilemma. Any strategy to cope with the Israelite stance, described as "armed passive resistance" by police Lt. Col. H. F. Trew, was fraught with difficulty.[132] If the Israelites were allowed to remain at Ntabelanga in the hope that the movement would lose steam and the faithful disperse, it would be seen as a sign of weakness and other Africans might be encouraged to flaunt the law. On the other hand, relentless government pressure likely would have strengthened Israelite resolve and unity and validated their self-image as martyrs persecuted for adhering to God's word.

After considering their options, government officials decided that the "public transcript" had to be restored and ordered police and army commanders to mobilize a squadron in May to forcibly expel the Israelites. Once that decision was made, it was almost inevitable that a massacre would ensue. While the Israelites clung to their conviction that God would protect them, their spiritual arsenal was no match for the state's vast array of modern weapons—rifles, machine guns, and cannon. On 24 May several hundred Israelites were mowed down at Bulhoek.

After the massacre, the state quickly moved to restore its authority. It arrested Israelite leaders and members, demolished their houses, and lectured their womenfolk on the error of their ways. Officials took a census and seized spiritual plunder, including the most important symbol of

Israelite identity and legitimacy, the Ark of the Covenant. At the end of the year they staged a show trial to convict the top three leaders and over a hundred rank-and-file members and drove home a clear message that the state had reinstated the public transcript of proper relations between blacks and whites—or so it thought.

5 The Bulhoek Aftermath

Since 24 May 1921 South Africans have been debating and pondering the Bulhoek massacre's meaning and significance, deciding on and administering its implications for policy and determining how it should be publicly represented, memorialized, and remembered. In the months after the massacre, whites and blacks carried on spirited exchanges between and among themselves in newspapers, in Parliament and in trials about how the government dealt with the Israelites and whether it was justified to use force to uproot them. Over the next decade the government, based on its experience with the Israelites, addressed the issue of how to respond to other prophetic and millennial movements, which continued to appear in the eastern Cape and Transkei, and the larger issue of how to regulate African independent churches nationally. From 1921 to the late twentieth century whites and blacks also contested the representations of Mgijima, the Israelites, and Bulhoek, with whites generally justifying how the government dealt with the Israelites and presenting their version of the story in museum displays and supporters of the freedom struggle citing the massacre as a chapter in their heroic struggle to win freedom. Since 1994, the current government's representation of the massacre has dramatically changed by consciously promoting its memory and erecting a memorial at the massacre's site as part of its emphasis on creating heritage sites. In recent years the prophet Mgijima's image has become a unifying force in communities in the Queenstown area suffering from internal splits, while interpretations of the massacre are being injected into contemporary party rivalries.

"Dead Shocked": Reactions to the Bulhoek Massacre

Even though there were some biting criticisms of the government's handling of the confrontation with the Israelites in the months after the massacre, very few commentators, European or African, believed the government could have avoided bloodshed in the face of Israelite intransigence.[1] Although African opinion was heavily opposed to the government, a handful of African journalists commended the government for its patience throughout the negotiations and uncritically accepted the charge that the Israelite movement was a cover for revolutionary political action. *Imvo*'s editor John Tengo Jabavu contemptuously dismissed the Israelites, arguing that the government would be wise to monitor similar movements with care.

> That the people were demented there remains no room to doubt; and no inquiry, however searching can reveal anything. The whole history of the matter has been enacted by an open diplomacy on both sides and cannot be glossed over. . . . Some with wisdom after the event, say that the Government should have dealt drastically with the movement at the start. We believe that they mean when Msikinya brought the sect from America. At the bottom it is a political movement identified with worship. The main object being to drive the white man from the country. The "prevailing unrest" comes from the same cause. Where an "Israelite" is or any semi-religious movement exists we have sermons from the same text and if Government were wise they would closely watch movements with this root of bitterness before it becomes prosperous as Mgijima's at Ntabelanga.[2]

Jabavu's stance was not surprising. A staunch Methodist, he was generally hostile to any religious group tainted by Ethiopianism, and he was especially contemptuous of the Israelites, who had rejected his mediation in December 1920.

The editors of *Umteteli wa Bantu*, financed by the Chamber of Mines, had originally intended to print a hard-hitting editorial fixing blame on the government, but after government officials supplied them with new information about the Israelites' sinister message, the editors dramatically changed their line. Their revised judgment was that Mgijima's emissaries had been actively expanding the movement around southern Africa "and that if allowed to continue the movement would have spread more and more rapidly, with consequence to white and to black which we do not care to contemplate." They found the carnage at Bulhoek was not "so merciless" as it seemed at first glance because it spared "the country from the rapine and violence which would follow its extension." *Umteteli* parroted the unfounded charge that Ntabelanga was a sanctuary for criminals by revealing that the Criminal Investigation Department had made a "rich haul" of well-known criminals from among the Israelite prisoners. Thus, while *Umteteli* regretted the deaths of so many Israelites, it concluded that "we might hold the resulting good as justification in some measure for the evil done."[3]

Oxkraal and Kamastone residents, while passing a resolution lamenting the loss of life at Bulhoek, nevertheless believed the government had tried every option possible but had no recourse but to use force. They called for freeing the Israelite rank and file but vigorously prosecuting their leaders.[4] The headman of Hukuwa sublocation, Kamastone, John Alf Sishuba, pinned the blame on the Israelites for the "blood that flowed at Bulhoek." Because he had followed the situation closely, he thought the government had shown extreme patience, though he was uncomfortable with the police action.[5]

However, these unsympathetic views did not generally reflect African opinion. *Abantu Batho*, the SANNC mouthpiece, warned the government not to delude itself into believing that the views of the editors of *Imvo* and *Umteteli* and progovernment loyalists were accurate gauges of African thinking. "We take not the slightest notice of the betrayal of Israelites by their countrymen in the Cape who have passed nauseating resolutions supporting the principle of blood spilling with all the recklessness that the Government could command; and it would be childish on our part to take any notice of the half hearted attitude taken by our two native contemporaries in King Williamstown and Johannesburg in supporting the Government in its callous action." *Abantu Batho* thought the massacre could have been averted if the government had explored other options in dealing with the Israelites. Could it have called on chiefs or relatives of people residing at Ntabelanga or the SANNC to mediate or convened a conference provided for in the recently passed Native Affairs Act?[6]

The SANNC also took a sympathetic interest in the plight of the Israelites before and after the massacre. Opening its annual congress in Bloemfontein on the morning before the massacre, the SANNC passed a resolution appealing to the government to exhaust every possible alternative and to refrain from using brute force to uproot the Israelites. It called on the government to convene a conference to explore alternatives ways to resolve the dispute. President S. M. Makgatho admitted that the SANNC had no direct connections to the Israelites, but claimed that if his organization had taken charge of negotiations with the Israelites, a showdown would have been avoided. [7]

After learning of the massacre, the SANNC decried the "pogrom" against the Israelites and passed a resolution calling for repeal of the 1913 Natives' Land Act, which had caused the evictions of many African farm workers and may therefore have contributed to Mgijima's appeal to the landless. SANNC officials believed the incident would undermine African confidence in the government and questioned whether the government would have acted in the same way against a European church and why force was levied on a group charged only with misdemeanors. After adopting the resolution the conference adjourned and staged a procession through the Bloemfontein location. A band played the "Dead March" and Congress delegates held a brief memorial service.[8]

Others questioned whether the Israelites' relatively minor transgressions warranted their brutal suppression and whether a white religious sect would have been treated in the same way. *Ilanga lase Natal* wondered: "When we consider that Enoch and his followers were not breaking any law of the land, but only a Location bye-law regulating the number of huts which may be built on an allotment the tragedy suggests a sad mishandling of a serious situation."[9] *Abantu Batho,* citing the killings of Africans during the Bambatha Rebellion and the Port Elizabeth strikes, remarked "that it is now the custom of the whiteman to kill us, the natives."[10] In similar vein, Moses Mphahlele judged Bulhoek a showdown between religious and political fanatics on both sides and thought that the government's real motive was to intimidate Africans.[11]

The Industrial and Commercial Workers' Union (ICU) passed a resolution establishing 24 May as a national holiday for black workers and "condemning the Bulhoek happenings which were symbolic of the capitalistic determination to drive the natives off their land, to force them out to work in industries, and to cheapen their labour."[12] The government was compelled to crush the Israelites to prevent future movements of the landless. A delegate at a meeting at Ndabeni, Cape Town, of the Non-European National Industrial Union, affiliated with the ICU commented: "If Mgijima had perpetrated a murder he could not have been treated worse. The whole thing was to compel me to go and work on the mines in Johannesburg to suit the ends of the capitalists. The people at Bullhoek had been shot down just because they had had the courage to say that Christ was their Lord and that the place they dwelled in was the Lord's ground. For that the Government had declared war on them without permission." At the same meeting another leading ICU official, Selby Msimang, blamed the massacre on the land laws and asserted that "if Enoch Mgijima had ordered his proselytes to indenture their labour to the surrounding farmers of Kamastone or to give it gratis in the name of his Church, the killing and wounding of 400 natives would not have taken place."[13]

Queenstown Africans expressed deep regret for the tragedy and sympathy for the families who lost husbands and sons and strongly urged that the Israelite rank and file be released from jail. Suggesting that violence might have been avoided if Smuts had personally intervened, they called for the inclusion of two local Africans and two Israelites on a commission to investigate the incident.[14]

News of the massacre reached as far away as the United States, where a few African American newspapers commented on what had happened. The *Chicago Defender* noted that "tribes" settling in the Queenstown area had "seized large estates which belong to the Europeans" and prompted the South African government to send troops to quell the disturbance. Its editors sympathized with the Israelite plight.

> Call these natives religious fanatics if you will, they are at least honest in their convictions. Their leaders do not preach one thing and practice another. And who has a better right to African land than they? Why should they be driven from pillar to post, robbed of everything they hold dear at the point of a civilized man's guns?
>
> IN THE SO-CALLED CHRISTIAN WORLD we find bands of men and women with their own little particular kind of a god to worship, and their rites are quite as outlandish in the eyes of others as are the rites of these uncivilized Africans. But do the other ninety and nine attempt to check them? Not so, they are busy with their own feticisms.[15]

A month after the massacre Marcus Garvey's *Negro World* republished an account, "A Queer Story by General Smuts," that had first appeared in London's *Daily News* on 27 May 1921.[16] Six months later (25 June 1921), it ran an editorial, "Negro Martyrs," on Bulhoek. Blaming the massacre on the machinations of British prime minister Lloyd George, the newspaper compared Mgijima to Irish patriots and Mahatma Gandhi. They claimed Mgijima at some point had visited America and "caught the vision of an Africa Redeemed.—Boiling with race pride, he went back to Africa, determined to organize the natives into strong, self-governing units. From coast to coast the doctrine of this violent lover of freedom created a furore, a realization of the slavery and thralldom in which the natives have been for centuries held. At once the blacks, in fearless parades, told the white overlords of their determination to throw off the yoke of imperial domination."[17]

Writers of the mainstream white press generally spoke with one voice about many aspects of the massacre. They consistently lauded the government's performance at Bulhoek as valiant and unavoidable and characterized the Israelite "enemy" as deluded fanatics. They dissected how the confrontation between the Israelites and the government had unfolded and how the latter had bungled it.[18] They were virtually unanimous in attributing Israelite defiance to government vacillation. Some newspapers editorialized that because the Israelites probably had more insight into how the government might act than vice versa, they took advantage of the government's pusillanimity.

Inevitably the massacre was another opportunity for the white press to rehash the government's handling of "native" affairs. One letter writer accused the Native Affairs Department of being "hopelessly inefficient and incompetent" and "reared on a diet of sentimental pap. . . . It [the Israelite challenge] was not nipped in the bud with the result that it grew and grew."[19] Paternalistic "native" policy was the target of the Afrikaans newspaper *Het Westen*, which counseled that Bulhoek would never have happened if the government had adopted the firm Voortrekker approach to Africans rather than the sickly "*Engelse*" (English) one or if it had shown it was more interested in retaining the support of Africans as a trump card against Afrikaners who wanted to sever relations with the British Empire.[20]

The white left launched the most caustic attacks on the government. A Communist Party flyer distributed in Cape Town blared the headline "MURDER! MURDER! MURDER! Christians Slaughter Their Christian Brethren, Great Empire Day Celebration" and contended that the slaughter taking place on Empire Day represented the sheer brutality of British imperialism. Communist Party speakers branded Truter a government assassin. The South African Peace and Arbitration Society held a protest meeting on Bulhoek at the Cape Town city hall. H. M. Fridjohn wondered what the government meant when it stated the Israelites had broken the law. If the city council had violated sanitary regulations, would that have prompted the government to mount a police force against it? Even though Fridjohn acknowledged that the Israelites were guilty of trespass and taking over land that was not theirs, he asked whether the "punishment should fit the crime": "He asked whether what the 'Israelites' had done was of such a nature that they should be mown down by machine guns? A Government which did not fear ignorance because it knew that, when that ignorance became dangerous, it could exterminate it, was never likely to take an interest in uplifting and enlightening the people."[21] Another society member, S. C. Cronwright-Schreiner, added that a massacre such as Bulhoek would have been widely condemned before World War I, but the large-scale loss of life in the war had inured people to this kind of brutal behavior.[22]

The independent weekly the *Cape* sarcastically commented that there were two hundred fewer Africans for whites to govern now that the Israelites had been mowed down with "a hose-pipe of bullets." The *Cape* asked: "Are there to be no medals struck to commemorate the 'famous victory' of Bulhoek? Think how the South African Policemen will hand down such a proud token to their children and their children's children in memory of that historic morning when our spurred and gauntletted constabulary rode into the midst of these religious maniacs."[23] A week later, the *Cape* added, "Why the boasted charge of the Light Brigade was nothing to it."[24] When the Israelites refused to move off Crown land, the police gave "him a taste of that wonderful invention of our civilization, the machine gun."[25]

One of the few other publications that questioned the outcome of the massacre was the Catholic *Southern Cross*, which questioned why, given the large loss of Israelite lives and the few wounded among the police, it was necessary to use so much force against the Israelites, who, it was clear, were not heavily armed. It asked why the government did not call on Catholic spiritual leaders to help mediate (as had been done in America and India). Because the government treated the issue as a civil matter—trespassing on land, defiance of civil authorities—it did not take into account its religious significance. If it had, the Catholic journal was convinced, the blood of martyrs would not have been spilled. The *Southern Cross*, however, took a paternalistic line when it came to African

Christians. Arguing that the government had to take cognizance of African religious beliefs, it maintained: "The natives are but the children of our civilisation, and you can no more bring up a native without some sence [sic] of religion than you can train an unreasoning little child to be good without telling it that there is a God above."[26]

Government departments, especially the South African Police, closely monitored the reactions to the massacre. Sensitive to criticism, the police responded quickly to a story that their force had trapped unarmed Israelites in a hollow and mowed them down in cold blood. They were worried about the inevitable comparisons to the massacre at Amritsar, India, in April 1919, where British Indian army troops commanded by Gen. Reginald Dyer slaughtered nearly four hundred protesters in ten minutes.[27] To dramatize that the Israelites were not unarmed innocents, they placed five Israelite swords in the lobby of the House of Assembly. When the deputy commissioner of police caught wind of the fact that Merriman was preparing to deliver a speech in Parliament criticizing the police, he took preemptive action by meeting Merriman at a club and setting him straight.

Merriman's subsequent speech backed the government's stance, arguing that if the film circulated overseas it would be harmful to South Africa's image. For example, the League of Nations was then monitoring South Africa's mandate in South West Africa, and a film of the Bulhoek massacre could have been taken as an example of how the government administered its African subjects. Merriman also warned that Americans "would be interested . . . at seeing how South Africa treated a religious sect."[28]

The police, trying to bolster their case, lobbied for a public showing of a newsreel that documented the confrontation from beginning to end. *Defiant Native Israelites at Bulhoek,* produced by the Gaudium company (Africa Film Productions), opened with the police assembling at the Agricultural Show Grounds in Queenstown and followed their march to Bulhoek, the final attempt at negotiations, the battle itself, Mgijima's capture, shots of Ntabelanga and the tabernacle, and ended with the Israelite village's demolition.[29] The police thought the film portrayed them in a positive or at least a credible light, but after Native Affairs officials and some members of the cabinet and Parliament viewed it, on 4 June the government suppressed its showing to the general public on the grounds that it might provoke an outcry and generate unnecessary political damage.[30]

The Board of Film Censors, which had the responsibility for reviewing films, cited the precedent of the suppression of the fight showing the black boxer Jack Johnson defeating his white opponent, James Jeffries, on 4 July 1910. The board reasoned: "Apart from the possibility of hurting the religious susceptibilities of a section of the community, it may be held that as films showing pugilistic encounters between natives and Europeans should be barred, a fortiori should one depicting an armed encounter such as that at Bullhoek be prevented from public exhibition."[31]

But the decision also prompted B. G. Phooko to write in *Abantu Batho* that many Africans would interpret the suppression of the film as a sign that what happened at Bulhoek was far worse than what had been reported. The government "was desirous of covering itself with fig leaves in order to conceal its nakedness. . . . Natives have seen atrocious pictures, such as from the German territories, the Belgian Congo, etc. perpetrated to their next of kin; and if the Bulhoek pictures are forbidden, one may conscientiously imagine that they present brutality in its worst form not such as was indulged in even by Tshaka or Kaiser. . . . It stands to reason therefore that the films—which have for some 'solid' reason been buried in a Golden coffin—are doubtlessly indescribable."[32]

The parliamentary debate over the government's handling of the confrontation with the Israelites took place while the prime minister was out of the country. Smuts had left the day after the massacre to attend an Empire Conference in London, but before he departed, he had commented that the government had gone to great lengths to avoid bloodshed. However, it had been left with no choice but to uphold the law. In the final confrontation, "it was a case of so many hundreds of police well-armed, and so many thousands of poor deluded natives, armed with such weapons as they had, but they came out and seemed determined to swamp the police and there was no alternative."[33]

If Smuts exhibited restraint in not expelling the Israelites during the initial stages of the confrontation, it is also true that he might have sent in a massive force early on if he had the means to do so and, perhaps more important, had he not been in the throes of a closely contested election campaign. When it might have changed the course of the negotiations, Smuts did not get personally involved; instead, as his emissaries he sent two delegations with little power. In either case the dreadful result was a senseless massacre. The Israelites were not the victims of a bloodthirsty tyrant. Nevertheless, Smuts invariably resorted to the force of arms to quell dissenting voices—witness similar responses to the Bondelswarts revolt and the Rand Rebellion in 1922. Roy Campbell's stinging characterization of Smuts as "the Saint who . . . fattened up the vultures at Bulhoek"[34] may be unjustly overdrawn, but another of his barbs is nearer the mark: "Statesmen-philosophers with earnest souls whose lofty theories embrace the Poles. / Yet only prove their minds are full of holes."[35]

With the prime minister out of the country, the primary official response to the massacre took place in the House of Assembly, but the partisan warfare characteristic of debates was restrained. General Lemmer, a member of both the Native Affairs Commission and Parliament, laid out the laborious efforts of both the government and the commission to negotiate with the Israelites. In the end, he argued, "Even if we had sent an angel, we would not have made these people listen to reason."[36] Opposition spokesmen were less concerned with rebuking the government and the police than they were with insuring that Africans did not believe the Israelites had been callously slaughtered and that the government would use excessive force to quell other African movements.[37]

The National Party leader, J. B. M. Hertzog, argued that African political and labor unrest after the First World War should have impressed on everyone that unless the rising consciousness of blacks was positively addressed, then the confrontations at Port Elizabeth and Bulhoek would be mild compared to future conflicts. Whites could not ignore or subdue the spirit of black resistance. "The native had come to a consciousness of independence—of native independence—to a consciousness of himself and that no authority would ever be able to suppress. That spirit, that consciousness, was not necessarily an evil, it was a spirit which in the white population also asserted itself." In fact some Africans had already conveyed their belief to Hertzog that Bulhoek "was a slaughtering,"[38] Hertzog stressed that an official commission of inquiry was necessary not because of what happened or because it was unjust but because it was critical for Africans to believe that the government had exhausted all alternatives before using force against the Israelites. They would want to know why it had been necessary to kill nearly two hundred in order to arrest four hundred and to wonder if the government would have acted the same against a European church. He even recommended appointing Africans to a commission investigating the affair. [39]

Smuts's deputy, F. S. Malan, was not receptive to Hertzog's recommendation. The government, he felt, had already placed the facts on the table in its report to Parliament. But Malan's dogged refusal to appoint a commission of inquiry stirred up more controversy than the massacre itself. After a sharp debate, Malan backed down and agreed to establish a Native Churches Commission but refused to appoint an African to it.[40] When an African challenged him on this at an election meeting, Malan responded that since he could not think of any one African who represented all Africans, he would not appoint any.[41]

The Israelite Trials

Before the trial of the Israelites began in late November 1921, two legal proceedings relating to the massacre took place in October. The state treated the first one as a warm-up for the main event. It accused Cape Town socialists Wilfrid Harrison, William Dryburgh and his son, David, and W. Green of libeling Truter because they had called him a "brutal assassin" in the flyer "Murder! Murder! Murder!" issued after the massacre. Its star witness was Truter, who used the opportunity to put on display an array of Israelite spears, swords, and assegais that the police had confiscated after the massacre. According to his testimony, the police had no choice but to fire on the Israelites or they themselves would have suffered many casualties. Harrison, in a fiery defense, stated that Truter was merely doing the state's bidding. The real indictment, he charged, should have been leveled against Parliament. David Dryburgh and Green were found guilty of criminal slander for "calumniating and traducing the Prime Minister of South Africa" and fined forty pounds or three months in jail, while Harrison was fined seventy-five pounds or six months in jail. He and William Dryburgh were also fined ten pounds or fourteen days for violating a Dutch *placaat* of 1759 that prohibited "offensive, rebellious and libelous lampoons and prints." However, their lawyer, Morris Alexander, pointed out that the *placaat* had only been used over the previous century—and during the Anglo-Boer War. An appeals court agreed with Alexander and overturned their convictions on the grounds that the archaic Dutch law was no longer in effect.[42]

The second trial, which took place in East London, was that of John Mattushek, the farmer charged with culpable homicide and assault with intent to kill in the shooting of the Israelite Charles Dondolo in December 1920. Because Phillip Mhlabane, another Israelite Mattushek attacked, had died in the massacre, John Nkelenjane was the principal witness for the Israelite side. He testified that he went with Dondolo and Mhlabane to Mattushek's farm to buy forage, but as they neared the main house, Mattushek confronted them and asked where they were going. When they answered that the Israelites had sent them, Mattushek repeated his question and then pulled out a revolver, fired, and wounded one Israelite. The others then attacked Mattushek and chased him around the house until they ran into Klopper, who fired his shotgun and killed Dondolo.

In his defense, Mattushek spoke of the spate of stock thefts on white farms since the Israelites began settling at Ntabelanga, so when he saw the three on his property, he began to shout at them. Since they did not pay him any notice, he fired his revolver in the air and again asked them what they wanted. But they rushed at him without provocation, giving him no choice but to fire in self-defense. Once his testimony concluded, the all-white jury wasted no time in returning a verdict of not guilty.[43]

Meanwhile over one hundred Israelites remained in jail awaiting trial. Queenstown Africans took up several collections—"The Israelite Defence Fund" and "The Israelite Destitute Women and Child Fund"—to pay for defense lawyers and to support penniless Israelite women and children.[44] The ICU, the African Political Organisation, and the SANNC contributed donations, and the ICU held a benefit concert in Cape Town for the families of those killed at Bulhoek.[45] However, the fund-raising netted only twenty pounds for the Israelite defense.

When the case finally got to court, the Israelites were tried collectively. Probably mindful of the verdict in the Mattushek case, they asked for a trial by judge rather than jury. Since the Israelites had scant resources to hire lawyers, the court appointed A. B. Halse and S. M. Mallett to defend them.[46] This was an unusual step since an attorney had not served as a barrister for a half century, but an exception was made in this case because Queenstown had fewer than three advocates. Bisset Berry, a prominent Queenstown politician, wondered why Halse, a young attorney "fresh from his indentures" rather than an experienced lawyer was allowed to represent the Israelites before the formidable presiding judge, Thomas Graham, who "frightens every man who comes before him."[47] However, Halse's main qualification was that he had already represented Mgijima in an earlier proceeding.

Graham assembled a seasoned team of assessors to handle the case. Broers was a magistrate from Grahamstown and Norton was an assistant chief magistrate from the Transkei. The lead prosecutor was W. S.

Bigby, the solicitor general of the Eastern Cape, who had made a name for himself in show trials of dissidents—Zulu rebels during the Bambatha Rebellion, the Zulu king Dinuzulu after the rebellion, and Indian rioters in strikes in Natal in 1913. An interpreter translated the English testimony into isiXhosa for the accused.[48]

The government chose Queenstown as the site for the trial because it was near Bulhoek and was an important African center. Officials were worried about how Africans would perceive their handling of the case, and they hoped that many would observe the proceedings firsthand and see that the Israelites were receiving a "fair and impartial trial." The sensational trial also riveted the attention of the region's whites, who packed Queenstown hotels and even rented cottages from homeowners. The white enthusiasm irked a black letter writer, "Amicus Africae," who argued that since Queenstown whites had prejudged the Israelites, the trial should be moved to Grahamstown. He also called on the government to put Africans' taxes to more constructive uses since they had "received nothing in return except the bullets and maxims of last May"[49]

The two-week trial commenced on 21 November. Thirty of the 141 defendants had not been granted bail, so armed police escorted them, with numbered cardboard tickets hanging from their necks, from jail to the court. Enoch and Charles Mgijima and Gilbert Matshoba, dubbed by Graham as the "ringleaders," bore the numbers 1, 2, and 3. As the defendants arrived, there were no demonstrations; onlookers were silent as testimony to the carnage at Bulhoek—defendants missing limbs or hobbling on crutches—passed before them. Before the trial Mgijima had reportedly instructed his fellow defendants to sit in a disciplined manner, to refrain from smoking or spitting, and to plead not guilty. Their witnesses were told not to swear an oath but to respond truthfully to any questions the assessors posed.[50]

State prosecutors dramatically groomed the courtroom with grim reminders of the massacre—an assortment of confiscated Israelite swords, scabbards fashioned from paraffin tins, assegais, knobkerries, "an ancient looking rifle," and an Enfield carbine. They hung the prophet's crimson robe and several caps on a wall. They even reserved space for six prominent African "loyalists" in seats normally occupied by the jury.[51]

The state charged the Israelite defendants with "wrongfully, unlawfully, willfully and seditiously taking up swords, assegais and other weapons" and asserted that they "did establish and maintain themselves in an armed camp or settlement and did defy, resist and obstruct the lawful authority of His Majesty his Government and officers aforesaid." To win a conviction, the prosecution had to prove that the Israelites had intentionally used violence and force against the state. To that end, it called forty witnesses to support its case.[52]

The outcome of the ten-day trial was never seriously in doubt. The trial was just as much a pulpit for restoring state legitimacy as it was a way for determining the guilt or innocence of the Israelites. Hence, Graham drove home the message that since the government had tried every peaceful avenue to convince the Israelites to leave Ntabelanga, the police/army force was justified in firing on the Israelites on 24 May.

At the same time as he condoned state violence, Graham also skewered Native Affairs officials, both at the local and national level. In his eyes, their misjudgments in dealing with the Israelites contributed to the disaster and were ample evidence of the department's inability to rein in Africans. To him, the first mistake of Geoffrey Nightingale, Kamastone's superintendent, and E. C. Welsh, the Queenstown magistrate, was to grant recognition in administrative matters to Mgijima instead of to Kamastone headmen. When he questioned Welsh, the state's first witness, Graham asked if he and other officials had considered telling the Israelites that they could not meet Prime Minister Smuts until they obeyed the law. Then he aggressively took on Edward Barrett, the secretary for Native Affairs, asking: "Was not there something wrong with the administration of this location that hundreds of unlawful squatters were allowed to be there?" and "Would it not have been better if you had taken a firmer attitude, and instead of preaching to these people told them they were committing breaches of the law in drilling and arming, and it must be stopped?"[53]

Graham grilled Hutchons and Whitaker on how the police dealt with the Israelites at the 8 December fiasco and why they retreated from the Israelites. Hutchons justified the police withdrawal, arguing that if they had fired on the Israelites then, the "whole country would have been alight, and this place would have been burnt down." But Graham challenged his line of reasoning. "Why did you take all these men out fully armed and camp within 500 yards of the village unless you intended to do something?" Whitaker responded that it "was done to overawe the native," but Graham countered that it achieved the opposite, and he worried about the implications of their behavior for maintaining white control.[54]

"I am not aware of any other instance in the long history of native disturbance in South Africa, where a body of nearly a hundred armed and disciplined men were compelled to retreat before a body of natives armed with swords, assegais and [knob]kerries, and abandoned their camp without firing a shot."[55]

Only a few Israelites took the stand. Because Enoch refrained from testifying, their most prominent witness was his brother Charles, who eloquently narrated his church's version of the events that led to the massacre.[56] He reiterated the Israelites' contention that they had congregated peacefully at Ntabelanga to await the end of the world before the government unjustly disrupted their prayers. They were innocent of any wrongdoing, and they never sought temporal power. They had built houses on the commonage with Nightingale's permission; they had cooperated with summonses until they were overcome with fears of what white farmers would do to them if they appeared for trials; they had been receptive to the idea of meeting Smuts; and they had understood that bullets would not turn into water. The government had not understood that Israelite drills and their wielding of swords and knobkerries were only for ceremonial purposes and had mistaken them as signs of preparation for an uprising. Charles was delegated commander in chief because he was leading the religious community, and they adopted military titles for their leaders in much the same way as the Salvation Army. He adamantly stated that the regiments of the army of Israel listed in an exercise book confiscated from Enoch's home after the massacre contained the names of members and office bearers. On 24 May he instructed the Israelite regiments to refrain from confronting the government force, but as soon as the Israelites who met with the police returned to their lines, the police commenced shooting. The Israelites charged only after they saw their brethren fired upon. "If we ran away," Charles maintained, "they would have shot us the same."[57]

Charles Mgijima also testified that there was a bitter feeling between the Israelites and the government after they pressed to see Smuts at the 17 December 1920 meeting and they heard that he was willing to receive an Israelite deputation in Pretoria. He also maintained that they learned from the location superintendent that Smuts was willing to come to Queenstown.

Did Smuts actually promise to meet the Israelites? After the massacre, Barrett thought the government case against the Israelites at their trial would be strengthened if they made it clear that at no point were the Is-raelites told that Smuts would receive a delegation. At the 17 December meeting Barrett promised to relay the Israelite request for a meeting to the prime minister. Smuts's office sent a telegram to the Queenstown magistrate on 30 December that the "[Prime] Minister will be prepared to meet deputation in due course but owing to political engagement he has as yet been unable to fix a date." But Barrett maintained that Smuts's willingness to meet the Israelites was never passed on to them. "This no doubt accounts for the fact that the Israelites ignored any question of a meeting with the Prime Minister when negotiating with the Native Af-fairs Commission which the Government sent as its delegate to Bulhoek to deal with the matter in April and May."[58] However, Barrett overlooked the fact that on 8 January at a public meeting in Queenstown of about 130 whites a letter had been read in which Smuts stated that he would meet a deputation of Israelites when his schedule permitted.[59]

In his closing statement for the defense A. B. Halse struck the chord that white misunderstanding rather than Israelite aggression precipitated the final confrontation. He suggested that the outcome may well have been different had Smuts kept his promise to personally meet the Israel-ites. But Halse revealingly was not prepared to absolve the Israelites of all responsibility. According to him, they were misguided and were suscep-tible to extremist ideas because they had a "veneer of civilization." Indeed Africans generally had advanced very little since their initial contacts with Europeans. While he was convinced the Israelites were genuinely motivated by religious fervor and that they had gathered at Ntabelanga because of their passionate belief in Mgijima and his vision of a Day of Judgment, in the end, the prophet and his followers were all victims of a delusion.[60]

Judge Graham clearly had made up his mind long before the testimony ended. His verdict, rendered a half hour after Halse's statement, was a foregone conclusion. Mindful that whites and blacks all over the country were anxiously awaiting the trial's outcome, he took two hours to read his judgment, a judgment that emphasized the political implications of what had happened at Bulhoek. He took pains to recount all the devel-opments that led up to 24 May to show that the government had gone to great lengths to negotiate with the Israelites before resorting to force. He rejected the Israelite contention that they were solely motivated by their religious beliefs and expressed his conviction that they were prepared to resist and attack the police. Graham not only dismissed the charge that the government had interfered with the group's religious practices but charged that their beliefs were being used as a ruse for attracting dissidents from all over the country who were rallying around "the crazy notion that the day was coming when the black man was to have his freedom."[61]

Graham's verdict did not stop there, however. He also heaped scorn on the government. He faulted the government's vacillating approach to "native affairs" and the manner in which local and national officials did not take responsibility and shifted the blame for mistakes on others. From the outset he pointed out that Mgijima had taken advantage of the government's unwillingness to use force. Officials were chided for forgetting that "in dealing with natives a legacy of sorrow and blood invariably follows in the footsteps of misplaced clemency." In his estimation, the worst mistake occurred when the police retreated on 8 December, thus violating David Livingstone's dictum that "no [white] man should ever threaten a native with a firearm unless he intended to use it."[62]

In passing sentence Graham singled out the leaders, Enoch and Charles Mgijima and Gilbert Matshoba, for special opprobrium, blaming them for misleading their followers. They were sentenced to six-year terms with hard labor at DeBeers Convict Station in Kimberley. Twenty-seven Israelite office holders were given terms of three years with hard labor; most were sent to Pretoria to work on public buildings. Eighteen-month terms were handed down to seventy-four rank-and-file Israelites who were sent to the Cape peninsula to work on road crews. The rest—eighteen elderly men, seven boys, and three seriously wounded men—received twelve-month terms, but their sentences were suspended for two years.[63]

During the time that the convicted Israelites were serving their sentences, Queenstown Africans and the African Political Organisation petitioned the government to grant them an amnesty so that they might return home and provide for their families. In January 1923, over half the prisoners were released and by September all but the leaders were freed. Charles Mgijima died of chronic Bright's disease and apoplexy at De Beers Prison Hospital on 12 March 1924, while Matshoba and Enoch were released in May 1924 and arrived in Queenstown on the third anniversary of the massacre.[64]

During his time in prison Enoch had tried to keep his church alive. The massacre had created many widows among the Israelites, and Mgijima sanctioned a special polygyny, permitting Israelite men to marry the widows and allowing their children to bear the name of the deceased husband. Before he died, however, Mgijima reversed this decree and forbade Israelites from having more than one wife.[65]

Passovers went unobserved during the leaders' imprisonment, but many Israelites settled in Queenstown after the massacre. On Enoch's release he moved there also, and the town council gave the group a site on which to build a tabernacle. The building began in 1925. Israelite women and girls collected sand and sifted the ash, while the men prepared the bricks and baked them in the ovens. The temple was completed in 1927.

Throughout his life Mgijima's focus had been on spiritual deliverance, but after his release from prison, he began to address political liberation as well. He urged his followers to pray for freedom and said that they should cooperate with iKongolesi (African National Congress, ANC) in its efforts. He stated, "We are pushing the same mountain. We are pushing it spiritually, and they the fleshy way." The "fleshy way" referred to the secular struggle. And he allowed the ANC in Queenstown to hold meetings in his home before the new tabernacle was built. At the new tabernacle he organized a meeting with ANC officials Theo Mvalo and Mandaba at which an ox was slaughtered. Later Bishop Gwazela allowed the ANC anthem to be sung during church services.

Mgijima had a premonition that his life was coming to an end. He visited the branches of his church, telling them, "I have pointed the way of life, [and] the time has come that I will sit down and fold my hands."[66] Shortly before he died on 5 March 1929, he anointed Silwana Nkopo as his successor, telling him that he "wished the Israelites to live in peace, that they would hear rumours of big wars and fighting, that they were to take no notice of them. But to go their ways in peace."[67] He was buried in the evening near the Black Kei River at Ntabelanga. His last prayer was

Here, Lord, Jehovah I stand before you together with your servants and the congregations of Israel, before you who remembered our fathers through the spilling of blood. And here oh Lord they are kneeling, with tears falling in your face Jehovah. I with your servants and all the congregation of Israel, you who remembered our fathers with the spilling of blood. And here oh Lord when your people kneel, their tears falling on the ground may their prayers ascend and reach you Lord, through the spilling of blood do not forget oh Jehovah the 24th Zive [May] 1921.

We have endured being the laughing stock. Arise! Arise! Ye Jehovah in your omnipotence.[68]

The South African Government and Millennial Movements

The final trial and the verdict to imprison the Israelites prompted the government to review its "native" policy and how it dealt with the Israelites and independent churches in general. Although the Smuts government did not hesitate to use force the following year to quell a mine workers strike on the Witwatersrand and the Bondelswarts rebellion in South West Africa, it sought to gain leverage over but not engage in the kind of direct confrontation with independent religious groups that led to the tragedy at Bulhoek. The government tasked the NAC to set up a Native Churches Commission—made up of Roberts, Loram, and Lemmer as well as P. van der Merwe—to examine "the origin and nature" of the Israelites and to assess whether the hundreds of independent churches that had blossomed in the black community were actually forces for conservatism or seedbeds of sedition in the black community. Their investigation of the Israelites was perfunctory and the commission's report quoted verbatim Judge Graham's judgment at the main Israelite trial. On independent churches the commission recommended that the government should tolerate these religious groups because they were sincere expressions of black religious beliefs. One lesson the commissioners drew from their examination of what happened at Bulhoek was that individuals could take over a group and use it for subversive ends. Hence the government had to maintain oversight over these churches and advised officials to control their activities by setting strict requirements for gaining official recognition from the state. An unrecognized church could not obtain sites for building churches and schools. Its ministers could not act as marriage officers, buy wine for sacramental offerings, or qualify for cheaper railway tickets. Because the government set high qualifications and required churches to submit considerable data, only a handful were granted recognition—and they were churches with close ties to white missionary groups.[69]

At the policy level the South African government assumed a stance of moderation and accommodation regarding independent African churches, but that did not prevent officials or the press from casting suspicion on their motivations and the potential for public disturbances that prophetic movements could cause during and after World War I. Such movements flourished in both the white and black communities, but they were especially plentiful in the eastern Cape. Typical was a report in 1922 in the *Daily Dispatch:*

> A correspondent from Molteno writes to say an African "prophet" has been active there and this message is similar to Garvey's. He says . . . a change of government would come soon with new leadership being black. He also predicted the coming of a great plague which would wipe out the whole universe, and said he was the first man to receive such a message from the Lord. The prophecy greatly alarmed his hearers, who had vivid recollections of the heavy mortality caused by the influenza epidemic of 1918. Among the signs which heralded the coming of the plague, said the prophet, is the fact that native ministers are becoming the "detectives" of the Europeans, and that the moneys which they collect for Church funds are really for the private use of the white man. Another sign is that "unusual blessing from God is falling upon those native churches which have no European ministers," the moral to be drawn being obviously that the natives, if they desire this blessing should cut themselves adrift from the white man. It seems to us that the authorities would do well to keep a watchful eye upon this so-called prophet. From such teachings as his mischief may easily arise.[70]

In 1925 the *Blythswood Review,* a mission journal, reported the appearance of a "witchdoctor" who preached that "the days of all men are over and that the days of women have at last dawned. It is not to the prophet but to the prophetess that people have to look for instruction and guidance."[71]

These examples indicate that despite the hands-off policy, a strong strand of official thinking continued to regard prophets and independent churches as potentially subversive. Although it never again used brute force against them, the South African government worried about a repeat of the Israelite disaster and kept a watchful eye on these movements. On some occasions the authorities intervened before a movement could reach a stage where it could no longer be controlled. The 1922 *Annual Police Report* noted that a mobile squadron had been dispatched to patrol districts in the Transkei where a prophet was stirring up unrest. Although the prophet was arrested on a charge of vagrancy, they could not muster the evidence to convict him.[72]

Another example of this kind of surveillance comes from Natal, where the police monitored Isaiah Shembe's movement near Durban. While Maj. W. E. Earle investigated reports of immoral behavior, he did not recommend a government clampdown on Shembe and his faithful women followers: "At present their does not appear to be anything seditious in the teachings and there is no danger to be feared as far as Europeans are concerned for the reason that there are a few males in the congregation the chief evil being the attraction of so many females from their kraal allegiance and the immoral conduct that is alleged that goes on at the prayer meetings. This is much resented by kraal heads but they appear to be powerless to prevent their women going."[73] Apparently a perception of licentious behavior was not sufficient grounds for state intervention.

Shembe's movement differed from Mgijima's Israelites on several other scores. First, the twenty or so parcels of privately owned land Shembe bought with church offerings between 1913 and 1927 were from white farmers or were allocated by local chiefs. Some were within the historic Zulu kingdom, while others were black spots in predominantly white farming areas. Although he rented some of the land holdings to individuals, several became sacred sites of pilgrimage and ritual, such as his principal sanctuary, Ekuphakameni, the thirty-eight-acre center of his healing ministry and site of an annual three-week assembly in July. To his amaNazaretha faithful, Ekuphakameni was both an earthly Zion and a court of heavenly worship.[74]

Furthermore, Shembe enjoined his followers to pay their taxes and respect the law. Although he did not regard the South African state as all-powerful, he did recognize its legitimacy. He stressed the injunction of Romans 13:7 on how religious bodies should deal with the state: "Render therefore to all their due; tribute to whom tribute is due."[75]

Like Mgijima and Shembe, some black religious leaders creatively articulated a theology of the land and adopted a strategy of defensive segregation by establishing "holy villages" or "New Jerusalems" in which their communities of the faithful could create sacred landscapes, safe havens where, even if for a brief time, they would be protected from European oppression. To these prophets their Zion cities were natural extensions of Zionist and Pentecostal religious teachings—gathering places for their followers devastated by land shortages.

A prominent example was Ignatius Lekganyane, the prophet-leader who founded the Zion Christian Church in 1925, bought land from a white farmer, and established Moriah (near Polokwane in Limpopo Province), which became the site of an annual Passover festival that now attracts millions of the church's faithful. Moriah became the church's central sacred space free from white domination and interference; Zion Christian congregations in other localities developed their own sacred spaces.[76]

Before its confrontation with Mgijima and the Israelites, the government relied on the legal system to deal with prophetic movements. But in Bulhoek's immediate aftermath officials worried that if they did not deal with a millennial group right away, it might lead to a tragic confrontation. A notable case of state intervention was that of Nontetha Nkwenkwe who, like Mgijima, was called to prophesy in the Ciskei. The influenza pandemic of 1918 killed hundreds of thousands of people in southern Africa. And as the influenza raged, Nontetha fell into a deep coma and had a vision in which God informed her that he had sent this cataclysm (called by Xhosa *umbathalala*, or "disaster") as punishment (*isibeto*) for people's sinful behavior.[77] Moreover, the *umbathalala* was a prelude to a doomsday that was coming soon. Therefore, he gave her a special mission and directed her to preach his message to the *amaqaba* (the "red" or illiterate people). The message was that the present and future generations had to acquire a formal education.

Nontetha began her preaching in the area between King William's Town and Middledrift, but after the Bulhoek massacre, government officials, suspicious of prophets and wanting to head off a confrontation before it escalated into another Bulhoek-like standoff, debated about how best to deal with her. The whole question of how to appropriately deal with religious dissidents—to give them space or wield the law to silence them—had still not been resolved. The superintendent of "natives" at Middledrift, Clement Gladwin, had held the same position at Kamastone during World War I and had dealt with Mgijima. Gladwin counseled against any precipitous action against Nontetha because he had concluded that she was a positive force in her community and that her preaching might well have a moderating influence on Africans.[78]

But Gladwin was in the minority. Most state officials were alarmed by the reports that Nontetha was making antiwhite statements, and they saw her preaching as a cloak to cover more sinister designs. So remembering their inability to contain Mgijima, they backed moves to silence her before her movement spiraled out of control and posed a threat to the status quo. A King William's Town official asserted: "In view of the Bullhoek developments the subsequent steps of the movement here can be readily visualized." A report from Pretoria took a similar tone: "The religious aspects of Nonteta's activities are regarded as cloaking a more serious objective, for information has been received that her followers discuss the overthrowing of the Europeans by a combination of the black races and the coming of the American Negroes."[79] Some officials also thought Nontetha had the potential to become another Nongqawuse because goats were slaughtered at her meetings.

The officials who were convinced that Nontetha was a threat to peace and order eventually won out, but they had to find a pretext to arrest her. She was not encouraging her followers to resist the government, so they had no legal grounds for an arrest. Instead their solution was to direct a King William's Town magistrate to diagnose her as "manic depressive," and in December 1922, she was committed to a mental hospital at Fort Beaufort some fifty miles away.

A month later she was released on the understanding that she would not resume her preaching. When she violated the order, the authorities moved her six hundred miles away to Weskoppies Mental Hospital in Pretoria in 1924 in an attempt to isolate her and discourage the regular visits her followers made to Fort Beaufort. The move did not stop almost a hundred followers from starting a "Pilgrimage of Grace" in 1927. They walked all the way to Weskoppies to visit her. The hospital psychiatrists who evaluated her did not think she would be a threat if released, but they deferred to state authorities who wanted to keep her institutionalized. So she remained at Weskoppies until her death from cancer in 1935. She was buried in a pauper's grave without a marker and officials resolutely refused to hand over her remains to her family and followers until 1998.[80]

Another millennial movement that challenged the government was the American movement led by a disciple of Marcus Garvey, Wellington Butelezi, who burst onto the Transkeian scene in the mid-1920s predicting that salvation was not to be brought about by a vengeful Jehovah but by African Americans who were soon arriving in airplanes to expel whites and liberate Africans. These African Americans were modernizers who wielded twentieth-century weapons of war and who aimed not only to end white domination but also to transfer their material wealth to the people.[81]

Born about 1895 at Emtonjaneni in the Melmoth district of KwaZulu Natal, Elias Wellington Butelezi was educated at Mapumulo Training

College, a Lutheran school, and Lovedale. He held positions as a clerk at a labor-recruiting firm in Ekuluteni and at the African Life Assurance Society, but around August 1923, he was practicing medicine under various guises. Although he had been legitimately granted a license to practice as an herbalist in Natal, he was now touting himself as a medical doctor and his stationery stated that he was a "homeopathic medical practitioner."[82] A few years later Butelezi embellished his credentials by claiming that he had trained at Oxford as well as Cambridge and that he had earned a bachelor of medicine degree at Rush Medical College in Chicago through a correspondence course at Swits College in Delagoa Bay, Mozambique.[83]

Undeterred by his lack of formal medical training, he moved his base of operations in February 1925 to Qachas Nek on the southern border of Basutoland, where he began peddling his medicines on a circuit throughout the northeastern Transkei and Griqualand East. Armed with a stethoscope and a dry cell battery (which he used to administer mild shocks to some patients), he claimed to be a specialist in diseases of women and children and treated everything from tuberculosis to water on the womb.

Butelezi's conversion to the Garvey movement probably came in the early 1920s through Garveyites such as James Thaele, head of the Western Cape African National Congress who had recently returned from a fifteen-year stay in the United States,[84] and a West Indian, Ernest Wallace, who arrived in Qachas Nek about the same time as Butelezi. Wallace had joined the Universal Negro Improvement Association after World War I and, with several African Americans, had moved to Basutoland to organize chapters. Black unity, freedom, and salvation were at the core of Wallace's message. But it was the redemptive element that Butelezi seized on in crafting his message that African American liberators were dispatching a fleet of airplanes to free Africans from their European oppressors.

Butelezi's message tapped into a popular image of African American modernizers that had appealed to many black South Africans since their initial contacts with African Americans in the late nineteenth century.[85] A widely circulated belief was that African Americans had overcome the bonds of slavery and succeeded in America, and, untarnished by any association with European rule, they would now bring back their educational accomplishments, technical skills, and Christian beliefs to benefit Africans. After World War I the role of liberator was added to the imagery of the African American and projected the idea that blacks in America were not an oppressed and downtrodden people but a dynamic and creative race who ruled America and was now playing a pivotal role in global politics.

Many blacks welcomed the message of Garvey because it offered hope that the yoke of European domination could be thrown off. Indeed, the imagery was so strong that even those who were inimical to the ideas of Garvey found themselves transformed into liberators. The Ghanaian educator James Aggrey, who toured South Africa in 1921 with the Phelps-Stokes Commission on education and who spoke in Queenstown on the eve of the Bulhoek massacre, had spoken publicly against Garvey's idea of an African republic and dismissed the belief that a black fleet was coming from America. However much he contended that Garvey's promises were a "Midsummer Night's Dream," many in his audiences still looked to him as a savior.[86]

Butelezi rode this wave of popular enthusiasm for African Americans and channeled it to his advantage. He reinvented himself, changing his name to Butler Hansford Wellington and began claiming that he was in fact an African American whose mission was to prepare people for the imminent appearance of the African American liberators.[87] "Dr. Wellington," as he was popularly known, concocted his version of contemporary history to bolster his view that African Americans were bringing a new day for black South Africans. He claimed that although African Americans had long been planning to return to Africa, the American government had blocked their efforts. However, during World War I, America and her allies, needing additional troops, called on African Americans for assistance. In exchange for their help, black leaders had extracted the promise that after the war, they would be allowed to return to Africa to take over administration from European colonizers.

"Dr. Wellington" cut a distinctive figure. He consciously cultivated symbols of modernity. He wore glasses and was nattily attired, possessing a half dozen suits that he would regularly change throughout the day. For public meetings he donned an academic gown and mortar board and boasted of his educational accomplishments. Since he claimed to be an American, he kept up the ruse by addressing crowds in English with interpreters translating his speeches into isiXhosa.

The American movement's strongest concentrations of followers were initially in the districts of Griqualand East, Mount Fletcher, Mount Ayliff, Qumbu, and Tsolo, but disciples spread the movement to other districts in the Transkei. Those who joined wore red, green, and black buttons and bought membership cards for 2s. 6d. Once people joined, they swore secrecy and expressed their solidarity with one another by joining Wellington's organization, *Amafela Ndawonye* (those who die together). Tremendous pressure was exerted on nonmembers to join. Those who sat on the fence or who opposed Wellington were branded as *witwoete* (white feet)—or collaborators with whites.

In 1927 Butelezi set specific dates on several occasions for the arrival of African American liberators who would fly over in airplanes casting down balls of charcoal on all those, black and white, who had not joined the UNIA.[88] Members were enjoined to paint their homes black, to discard needles and cups and saucers, and to kill pigs and destroy any items derived from them such as candles. If the planes happened to bombard any live pigs, their fat would turn into paraffin and burn their owners and their homes.

Even when they did not appear, his followers remained steadfast because Butelezi told them his prediction could only be fulfilled if they practiced unswerving obedience. Thus he could rationalize why the airplanes had not come, because some doubters had not slaughtered all their pigs.

One government response to Butelezi's prediction of an American fleet was to send its own airplanes to awe Africans and to reassure whites, but it did not achieve its intended effect. An Anglican missionary commented on how his black congregation responded: "Have we not seen aeroplanes flying over us each of the last two Sundays? And who can prove that they are not the ones predicted by Dr. Wellington?"[89]

While Butelezi's effervescent personality and his message of the African American liberator are the most dramatic and conspicuous elements of the American movement, they should not overshadow the movement's attacks on white-dominated institutions of control such as churches and schools. Butelezi argued that the mission schools were imposing Western cultural values on African children, alienating them from traditional values and beliefs, and conditioning them to accept subservient positions in a white-controlled system. He proposed that that to break this monopoly, Africans should establish their own schools and churches so that their children would be raised in institutions that enshrined African values. Despite a lack of money, buildings, and trained teachers, Butelezi achieved a measure of success. In the late 1920s, thousands of students deserted the mission schools for the American schools. In 1930 Butelezi boasted that he had established 181 schools and 200 churches.[90]

Butelezi's movement took off because he tapped into grievances that many Africans, especially those living in the rural reserves, held against the government. In 1926, the Hertzog government had proposed several "native" bills that would have demarcated the "native" reserves and abolished the qualified vote in the Cape Province. Although these laws were not passed for another decade, they aroused African opposition. In 1925 the Hertzog government also levied new taxes, imposing duties on imported cotton blankets and secondhand clothing that raised prices 300 percent, and implementing the Native Taxation and Development Act, which was aimed at creating taxes for Africans throughout the union but which raised taxes in the Cape Province.[91] One of the act's provisions stipulated that unmarried adult men had to pay a poll tax of one pound annually.[92] The American movement also spoke to the resentment of dipping regulations, which many Africans hated not only because the fees were burdensome but because they believed that dipping was a white ploy to decimate their cattle herds.

Government officials closely monitored Butelezi's activities. Policemen attended his meetings and arrested him dozens of times on an array of charges. But after paying fines he immediately resumed his crusade. That he never served a day in jail only enhanced his reputation that the government could not confine him because truth was on his side. The government was also aware that if he had been sentenced to jail, it might have provoked an aggressive response from his followers.

The government concluded the American movement had gotten out of hand when rumors spread that Qumbu and Tsolo were going to be attacked. It dispatched a mobile police squadron and a fleet of airplanes to the districts of Tsolo, Qumbu, and Mount Fletcher. The government turned to the newly enacted Native Administration Act, which allowed officials to expel individuals summarily from reserve areas without bringing charges against them. Hence, on 1 March 1927, they officially banished Butelezi from the Transkei, and although he made several attempts to reenter the territory, he was either turned away or arrested.[93]

Butelezi carried on his mission outside the Transkei, although he never again roused the same enthusiasm he had previously generated. He suffered a severe blow in mid-1927 when the UNIA denounced his Transkei odyssey: "You are warned against an individual who calls himself Dr. Wellington and claims to represent us. This man is an impostor."[94] Undaunted, he carried his movement elsewhere. He moved to Edendale near Pietermaritzburg, where he called together his assistants and instructed them to continue organizing in the Transkei, and he established another American school, the St. Booker Washington Memorial Industrial College.

Butelezi also made excursions to Johannesburg and Bloemfontein but eventually concentrated his activities in the Ciskei, where he founded American schools and Garvey chapters in Aliwal North, Queenstown, and King William's Town. In the Herschel district he connected with *Amafela* groups who were attracted by his antitax and anticouncil positions.[95] He occasionally appeared in places such as Tylden on the Transkei border, where he held rallies with Transkeian followers.

In the Ciskei Butelezi came full circle with other millennial movements when he made contact with Enoch Mgijima and Nontetha Nkwenkwe. In Queenstown, where he had started an American school, he held some activities in the Israelite tabernacle. He placed a small plaque on one of the mass graves of Israelites at Bulhoek. Before Mgijima died, however, he denounced Wellington for subverting his authority and trying to poach followers from the Israelite fold and forbade him from having any further contact with them.[96]

Nontetha's followers were among those who heard the stories of American liberators. When Jongile Peter was jailed in King William's Town for refusing to kill locusts, he fully expected African Americans to unlock their cells and free them. He recollected: "We used to dream in the hope that the Americans were coming to release us. . . . There was always hope throughout that the Americans would free us. As oppressed people we always had heard that we would be released."[97] Wellington even journeyed to Pretoria to visit Nontetha at the Weskoppies Mental Hospital in which she was institutionalized. Although she was favorably inclined toward him because of his message of unity, her followers ultimately decided not to join forces with him and established the Church of the Prophetess Nontetha.

Remembering Bulhoek

Memories of Bulhoek have reverberated in South Africa over the decades. To borrow James Scott's terminology, while whites controlled the government, they continued to put out a "public transcript" that justified their version of the massacre and portrayed Enoch Mgilima in a derisory way.

Whether their rendition was aimed at winning over a significant segment of the dominated is debatable because the latter created a "hidden transcript" that characterized Bulhoek as a chapter in their freedom struggle.

In the decades after the massacre, there was a gulf between white and black commentators and the lessons they drew from the confrontation at Bulhoek. On the whole whites sympathized with the government's resort to force to deal with the Israelites and pinned the blame for the massacre on a combination of African inability to evolve beyond what whites thought was a primitive state and the Israelites' heretical religious beliefs. The British publication *Round Table* referred to the Israelites' subversive reading of the sacred text of the Old Testament as a cause for the confrontation with the government. "Indeed, the Old Testament record at its more primitive levels understood as only a primitive people could understand it, seems to afford the real key to a mysterious episode."[98] An underlying message was that because Africans were inherently backward, only a handful could ever achieve a thin veneer of Western civilization and a sophisticated understanding of Christianity. Hence the eminent jurist Manfred Nathan could assert "that some of the more absurd ebullitions of feeling on the part of natives were attributable not so much to lawlessness or hostility to white rule as their want of discipline, their recent emergence from savagery, and the megalomania of some of their leaders."[99] James Rose Innes, South Africa's chief justice from 1914 to 1927, thought the historical roots of Israelite fanaticism could be traced back to the Xhosa cattle killing of the 1850s, which led to disaster for its adherents. "In the one case [the cattle killing] the motive force was superstition, in the other religious mysticism. But both were cases of the impressionability of the Bantu race, and of its recklessness when roused, which lawgivers and administrators would do well to bear in mind."[100]

Before and even after 1994 the "public transcript" infused several museum exhibits on Bulhoek. Depending on the curator, a museum display can reflect an official perspective on an event or be used to critically examine traditional interpretations. Two museums—at Queenstown until the last years of the twentieth century and the South African Police Museum at Muizenberg near Cape Town—featured displays on the Bulhoek massacre. Both exhibits featured Israelite swords and spears that the government confiscated after the battle. Their narratives stressed that the clash between the Israelites and the state was primarily over maintaining law and order and drove home the lesson that because the Israelites were not only deliberately violating the law but actively plotting a rebellion, officials were justified in using force to deal with them. They depicted Enoch Mgijima as cowardly and the purveyor of "hare-brained" beliefs that drove his deluded, fanatical followers to a disastrous end.

In contrast, those who fought to overthrow white rule saw Bulhoek as one in a long litany of injustices that they cited to mobilize their followers to action. This would not have surprised the editor of the Afrikaans newspaper *Die Burger,* who worried shortly after the massacre that its memory might be taken up as a rallying cry by politically minded Africans in the same manner that Afrikaner nationalists exploited the memory of Slagter's Nek, an eastern Cape rebellion of Afrikaners against British rule in the early nineteenth century.[101] African politicians in later decades wove the memory of Bulhoek into their speeches. At the Treason Trial (1956–61), in which the South African state prosecuted 156 leading anti-apartheid campaigners, Prof. Z. K. Matthews recounted how the massacre "is talked about to children and so on, as an incident that has passed into what we might call the political history of the people."[102] In 1962, Nelson Mandela educated delegates at the Pan-African Freedom Movement of East and Central Africa in Addis Ababa, Ethiopia, about the meaning of Bulhoek. "Almost every African household in South Africa knows about the massacre of our people at Bulhoek in the Queenstown district where detachments of the army and police, armed with artillery, machine-guns, and riles, opened fire on unarmed Africans."[103]

A handful of left-of-center whites also wrote sympathetic portraits of the Israelites. One was Edward Roux, a former communist whose *Time Longer Than Rope* was for many years the standard work on resistance to white domination in South Africa. His discussion of the massacre noted that "the struggle for racial freedom . . . has often taken a religious form."[104] In the year after the Sharpeville massacre of 23 March 1960, a communist activist, Lionel Forman, who wrote numerous newspaper pieces on South Africa's past, contributed a column on Bulhoek in 1961 and called it the "Sharpeville" of 1921.[105]

As resistance to the government intensified during the 1970s and 1980s, the Israelite community was divided over the freedom struggle and how to relate to it. One faction argued that the Israelites had suffered enough because of the massacre and should maintain a low profile. Others believed that their mission was to sustain the resistance. Some Israelites joined political organizations and served prison terms for their activities. When

Mandela was released from prison in 1990 and resumed leadership of the African National Congress, there were members of the church who interpreted his actions as fulfillment of what Mgijima had prophesied in the 1920s—that he was the Joshua who led black people to their freedom.

Bulhoek and Public History since 1994

Since Mandela became president of South Africa in 1994 following the first democratic elections in which all South Africans could vote for the first time, the government has been looking at the past in a different way.[106] The "hidden transcript" has now been elevated to a "public transcript" although it is no longer a communication between the dominant and the dominated. Now the government has been raising new questions about how history has been written in South Africa and how it was (and occasionally still is) presented around the country in memorials, monuments, and museums—sites that deliberately excluded black people. In many school textbooks used before 1994, the past focused on whites and ignored black actors and their contributions, and the apartheid government's version of events was presented as unquestionable truth.

In a post-apartheid South Africa the government has encouraged people to reconsider the past and to research the lives of forgotten people and overlooked events. This has largely not been done at the expense of monuments from the colonial and apartheid eras; few have been removed from their sites. Instead, at the national level, new memorials have been erected to remember significant people and groups: for instance, at the homes of Mandela at Qunu and Albert John Luthuli at Groutville; at Freedom Park at Tshwane; to Zulu warriors who fought at the battle of Ncome (Blood) River in 1838; at the site where the plane of Mozambican president Samora Machel crashed at Mbuzini in Mpumalanga; and at the Hector Pieterson Memorial to commemorate the June 1976 Soweto uprising.[107]

In 1999 Parliament passed the Heritage Resources Act, which created a Heritage Resources Agency, and the government encouraged "heritage studies" and the establishment of heritage offices in provincial governments. The Eastern Cape's Department of Sports, Recreation, Arts, and Culture, for example, has been active in identifying new sites at which to establish memorials that highlight the experiences of black people, particularly their struggles against white oppression. Hence, memorials have been built to remember the Cradock Four, the Bhisho and Port Elizabeth massacres, the Khoisan genocide, and the homes of D. D. T. Jabavu and James Calata, and statues were commissioned to honor Oliver Tambo, Steve Biko, King Sabata Dalindyebo, and Vususile Mini.

Special attention has been paid to the Bulhoek massacre. Not surprisingly, over the years the memory of the tragedy has been a central event in the lives of Israelite church members. In the early 1970s they started a ritual of remembrance, holding special services on 24 May to honor those who died on that day in 1921. In the late 1980s they approached the Ciskei homeland government several times about erecting a Bulhoek memorial at the site of one of the mass graves, but their request attracted little interest until after the democratic elections of 1994. After the Eastern Cape's Heritage Office held discussions with Israelite church leaders, a decision was made to build a Bulhoek memorial, which officially opened on the eightieth anniversary of the massacre on 24 May 2001.[108]

The ceremony was a solemn but inspiring affair with several thousand people in attendance. The organizers had carefully thought about what happened on the day of the massacre, and they opened the proceedings by making a statement about how much things have changed since then. The honored guests included provincial government dignitaries and high-ranking officers of the South African police and army. An Israelite regiment dressed in tunics similar to the ones worn in 1921 marched to the gathering. The names of those known to have died in the massacre were inscribed on the memorial and were read out as part of the ceremony.

Israelite church members and eastern Cape political leaders delivered speeches reflecting on the meaning of the massacre. The minister of public enterprises, Jeff Radebe, observed:

> The irony of the Bulhoek massacre was that a government that professed to be Christians mercilessly killed people because "they chose the plan of God." Their only crime was perhaps that they chose to respond to the call of God in their own way, in a manner that arguably suited their cultural and traditional value system.[109]

Rev. M. A. Stofile, who was then premier of the Eastern Cape, offered these remarks:

> South Africa is notorious for the lopsided way in which her history is recorded. Many villains are commemorated as heroes and many heroes are not ever mentioned. As in the rest of life in our country, this

dichotomy tends to assume racial characteristics. The latter being the most accurate reflection of our history viz: a racially segregated past. In this situation "right" was always associated with the fairer colour.[110]

Referring to the Bulhoek massacre, he added:

This forced-removal-turned-into-a-massacre was acclaimed by the media and the apologists of the regime as a commendable step to "put the natives in their place." Smuts and his troops were condemned by the world and by patriotic South Africans. None could return the dead.[111]

Some speakers pointed out the lessons that could be learned from past injustices and how they might help heal the divisions of the past and build unity in the present. Nosimo Balindlela, then minister of Sports, Recreation, Arts and Culture in the Eastern Cape government, said:

The episode of 24 May 1921 must serve as a constant reminder of who we are and where we come from as a nation and our religious beliefs. It is a history that must be related to our children as one example of what must be avoided at all costs in this country if we are to take the development of our country to higher levels.[112]

Since the memorial's opening it has become a popular stop on heritage trails in the eastern Cape, and the Israelites and the eastern Cape government have maintained the annual commemoration at the memorial. As we near the massacre's centenary, Mgijima's public image has also undergone a dramatic change from how whites depicted him in a derisory manner to one in which he played a positive role. In 2016 the municipalities of Tsolwana, Nkwanca, and Lukhanji in Chris Hani district were combined into one municipality named after him. Local officials opined that these municipalities had been scarred by so much "instability and discord" in recent years that they believed the Mgijima name, which is not linked to any particular political faction, could potentially be a unifier. Speaking at the Enoch Mgijima memorial lecture in Queenstown, Vuyani Booi, a Fort Hare University historian and archivist, challenged his audience not to dishonor the prophet's name and he "warned that bringing the legacy of Mgijima into disrepute could unleash the wrath of the great prophet Mgijima."[113]

The meaning of Bulhoek has generally not been fodder for disputes between contemporary political parties, but an essay by Sam Matiase, commissar for land and agrarian reform for the Economic Freedom Front (EFF), may change that. Dissident ANC Youth Leaguers who established the EFF in 2013 charge that ANC leaders have compromised on their commitment to fundamental change and have avoided addressing the gross racial inequalities in land ownership. To Matiase, the heart of the massacre was a showdown between white settlers and blacks who had been dispossessed of their land.[114] He argues that although the land issue remains central to understanding the economic inequities of modern-day South Africa, the ANC "has never recognized the massacre for expedient reasons" and has tepidly supported land reform.[115] In contrast he lauds his own party for aggressively championing large-scale expropriation of white land without compensation. If his speech is a portent, then the rhetoric over the meaning of Bulhoek may well intensify in the years leading up to the massacre's centenary.

6 The Lost Ark

Conducting historical research in southern Africa in the 1970s and 1980s was challenging.[1] To cope with a tense political and racial environment, I developed instincts and skills—not learned in the classroom—for tracking down sources of documentation outside archives and libraries and coping sensitively and tactfully with racial and political barriers that governed all research undertakings. Through social networking (long before the advent of Facebook), I patiently established enduring relationships with people and groups that eventually paid dividends over the decades. However, what I did not anticipate was how I became part of the historical narratives of some of the religious groups I dealt with and how they interpreted my actions as a social scientist in spiritual terms.

On numerous occasions before 1994 I had to deal with the skepticism many black South Africans had of any researcher—especially a white researcher—who came into their lives. Based on long and painful experiences with political authority, their assumption was that anyone asking questions was not likely to be gathering evidence that would benefit them. There was not much I could do to overcome this stigma except to be honest and forthright and hope that with time people would begin to trust and open up to me. In some cases that took a long time. A schoolteacher who assisted me in the Ciskei and Transkei in 1974 told me several years later that he had kept a close eye on my behavior for several months before he began to trust me.

Recovering the Ark

Gathering material in South Africa in 1973 and 1974 for my Ph.D. dissertation on the Israelites and the Bulhoek massacre, I first started in the state archives and libraries in Pretoria, Cape Town, and Grahamstown, and then turned to making contacts with people in two eastern Cape Bantustans, the Ciskei and Transkei, who had firsthand knowledge of the movement. At a time when most historians of South Africa were basing their studies almost exclusively on written documentation, I was one of the few historians conducting interviews in these areas. But because apartheid was in high season, I had to conform to the rules of racial engagement that the government set for any white going into a black area, whether a township or a Bantustan. One had to have a permit. In my case the government issued me a permit that I had to submit to the white magistrate in each district that I visited. The permit stipulated that "lodging with Bantu is not permitted" and that "under no circumstances must the holder of this permit interfere with the domestic or other affairs of the Bantu." Moreover, I "had to behave in a dignified manner and refrain from any criticism of the administration of the Government or any of its officials."[2] Government officials and chiefs and headmen scrutinized me wherever I went; indeed, on several occasions, local people pulled me aside to inform me that security police were making inquiries about what I was up to.[3] Although the permit restricted me from staying with Africans (and South African whites often warned me that I would have my throat slit in my sleep if I did so), I was allowed to reside in African areas so long as I was housed in a "white spot," typically Moravian, Anglican, and Catholic mission stations and schools such as the Federal Theological Seminary at the eastern Cape town of Alice.[4]

The Israelites generally were welcoming and were prepared to talk with me but with some reservations. Although the Israelites had already had dealings with several anthropologists such as Katesa Schlosser and Vincent Masters in previous decades, some of them questioned my motivations for digging into what had happened at Bulhoek. Why was I resurrecting such a painful episode in their past that might reopen wounds and that might lead to more unwanted government attention? However, some Israelite elders were keen on relating the history of their church and took me under their wing. They introduced me to a dozen or so Israelites who had extensive knowledge of their church's history or who had been at Bulhoek the day of the massacre. I attended a number of services, including one of the first Israelite services of remembrance held at Bulhoek on 24 May 1974 for those who had died in 1921. Although I knew that most of the Israelites I spoke to were restrained in their recollections, I was confident that I had enough written and oral documentation for my study.

For several extended periods of time—from 1977 to 1980 and 1985 to 1990, for example—I was prohibited from entering South Africa because of my involvement in anti-apartheid activities in the United States, but I maintained contact with the church's historian, Gideon Ntloko, and shared with him my documentation on the Israelites. One of the times I was persona non grata in South Africa, I took advantage of the government's policy of granting a bogus independence to the Transkei in 1976. Even though I did not have a visa for entering South Africa, I could cross the Lesotho border at Telle bridge into Transkei's Herschel district, which was separate from the rest of the Transkei. I had no choice but to travel through South Africa before reentering Transkei. Since there were only a handful of border posts for entering Transkei, as long as the police did not stop me at a roadblock, I could make discreet detours to visit people in South Africa. One was with Gideon Ntloko in Queenstown, who informed me that the security police had recently warned him against speaking with some foreign researchers who were in Port Elizabeth intending to do research on the Israelites. I did not want to compromise the Israelites, so after that incident, I refrained from further visits with them until after I was allowed to reenter South Africa in 1990.

In retrospect these extended sabbaticals from entering South Africa were actually a blessing in disguise because I shifted my research focus to exciting projects in neighboring Lesotho. In January 1990 I was allowed to reenter South Africa at precisely the same time as President F. W. de Klerk was making his historic speech to Parliament lifting the government bans on organizations such as the African National Congress, the Pan Africanist Congress, and the South African Communist Party and preparing to release Nelson Mandela from prison. Because of the dramatically changed political environment and the willingness of black people to talk more openly about the past, opportunities opened up to probe issues that I had had to defer.

My ties to the Israelites were renewed in late 1994 when I was affiliated with the Institute for Social and Economic Research at Rhodes University in Grahamstown. My curiosity was piqued by an essay on historical resources by Denver Webb, a leading eastern Cape heritage specialist, who related that an Israelite artifact, a "wooden box containing a large parchment scroll with religious texts," was stored in the basement of the

Albany Museum. When museum officials allowed me to examine the box, I found it contained a six-foot-long parchment scroll on which the Ten Commandments were inscribed in ornate script in isiXhosa.

Although I was not sure of the box's provenance, I knew that after the massacre, the police had taken spiritual treasures from Mgijima's home and the tabernacle: the prophet's red gown, hats, and walking sticks; silver vessels and plates; brass bugles; lamps; and, most important, the Israelite Ark of the Covenant, which had originally been brought from the Orange Free State by Adonijah Ntloko and was a revered holy relic.

Following Mgijima's release from prison in May 1924, he wrote the Queenstown magistrate requesting the return of the confiscated items from the police, but they claimed that they did not have them in their possession.[5] We now know that they were lying when they made this statement. While we do not know how long the Ark remained in their hands, the staff at the Albany Museum documented that around World War II an anonymous person donated the Ark to the museum. Although the box containing the scroll had a tag stating that it was the property of Enoch and museum officials were vaguely aware that it had something to do with the Israelites, they had no idea of its significance and never displayed it in public. The Ark remained forgotten in the museum basement for more than a half century.

I was also unclear as to the scroll's importance, so I decided to consult Gideon Ntloko in Queenstown. As I was describing my find in detail, he grew visibly excited. As a young man he had heard his uncles describing the box and scroll, and he was sure that I had discovered the missing Ark of the Covenant. Because he was concerned that the Israelite faithful would be extremely excited about this find and might have unrealistic expectations about its immediate return, he appealed to me to keep the news to myself until he had a chance to look at the Ark in person. When we met some months later in mid-1995 at the Albany Museum and viewed the Ark, he nearly passed out on the spot. He knelt and went into an extended prayer. We agreed that he would convey the good news to the Israelite leadership at an appropriate moment and that I would talk to museum officials about the significance of the box and scroll in their basement.

Meeting with the museum's director, Wouter Holleman, I related the story of the Bulhoek massacre and how the Ark had eventually been deposited in his museum and what its importance was to the Israelites. Since I was leaving soon for the United States, I did not see myself as an intermediary between the museum and the Israelites. My hope was that he and other museum officials would not treat the Ark as the museum's private property even if they had had no hand in its seizure from the Israelites. I also suggested that it would be a major public relations coup for the museum, especially in the context of post-1994 South Africa, if they cooperated with the Israelites and facilitated a transfer of the Ark. Otherwise I envisioned a scenario in which the aggrieved Israelites would be staging protests at the museum. I was elated months later when I learned that with the assistance of the Eastern Cape provincial government's Department of Sports, Recreation, Arts and Culture (DESRAC), the Ark had been transferred to the Israelites in late 1995 in a moving ceremony at the Israelites' main tabernacle in Queenstown. The Israelites reconsecrated the Ark and placed it in a vault in the tabernacle to be displayed every three years.[6]

I did not pick up the whole story about the transfer until the following year, when I learned that museum officials initially had refused to surrender the Ark to the Israelites and instead offered to restore and display it at the museum and create a facsimile of the Ark for the Israelites. They believed that the Ark would be preserved better under their oversight. As might be expected, their stance threatened to inflame the situation, but eventually they backed down and arranged for the transfer.

After the transfer Israelite elders debated my role in discovering the Ark. When I stopped in Queenstown in mid-1996, several elders sat down with me and related their discussions about why I, an American, was the one who had solved the mystery of what had happened to the Ark and set in motion the process for its return. Their interpretation was that an angel had possessed me without my knowledge and guided me to the Ark's location. I may have thought that my search was guided by my instincts as a social scientist rather than providence, but they knew better.

A Grave Injustice

My interest in the eastern Cape prophetess Nontetha Nkwenkwe featured even more providential twists and turns. I had first learned of her through Native Affairs and police files that I located in my 1973 research in the state archives in Pretoria. Because of the fifty-year rule then in effect, researchers were prevented from looking at documents written after 1925. I could piece together the early stages of Nontetha's movement after she began preaching but not what happened to her after the state committed her to a series of mental hospitals. I decided that I would follow through on leads from the handful of documents I had located and then visit the African locations in the Ciskei mentioned in official dispatches. Since I was going to conduct research in the Ciskei, I arranged for accommodation at the Federal Theological Seminary in Alice. After securing permission from local chiefs in the Debe Nek area, I learned that two of Nontetha's children were still alive. They informed me of the existence of the Church of the Prophetess Nontetha headed by Bishop Reuben Tsoko, one of Nontetha's leading disciples since the 1920s. After I contacted him, he invited me to attend a church service, where I explained my research and arranged to interview him and church members both individually and collectively. By the time I left the area, I knew that I had gathered enough information to reconstruct the main outlines of the story but that there were still enormous gaps that were going to be difficult to fill until I had access to all the government files. Indeed, after returning to the United States to write up my dissertation, I found that I had enough source material to piece together a cursory essay on Nontetha and her movement but too little to write up a full study. I intended to return to the story in the future, but that would not take place for more than two decades, and I lost contact with Tsoko and his church.

In 1994 and 1995 I was on sabbatical leave in South Africa when another historian, Hilary Sapire, informed me that she had learned about a substantial file on Nontetha in the state archives that had become available in recent years. Because of her interest in African conceptions of mental illness, western psychiatry, and mental hospitals, Sapire was preparing to do a study on Nontetha's (and other Africans') experiences in the mental hospitals and the diagnoses of European psychiatrists and wanted to consult me about my previous research. After communicating with each other about what we had each discovered, we decided to pool our research findings and write an extended essay on Nontetha's story.

After consulting the new government documentation, I decided to return to the same rural locations I had visited in 1974 to see whether I could unearth any fresh sources of information. I had no idea whether the church was still in existence, but I thought it was worth a try since the climate for interviewing people had dramatically improved since the establishment of South Africa's democracy in 1994.

With a close friend, Luyanda ka Msumza, I set out on an overcast Sunday in mid-1997 to a village about ten miles from King William's Town where I had conducted interviews in 1974 and asked some men on the side of the road if they knew whether Nontetha's church was still in existence. After confirming that it was, they directed us to an elderly woman standing nearby. Although she acknowledged her membership in the church, she was reticent to speak with us. But she pointed to the home of another member, a middle-aged woman, and recommended that we talk to her.

When she appeared at the front door of her home, we did not have a chance to introduce ourselves before she began looking at me intently. She asked, "But aren't you Bob Edgar?" Her question took me by surprise. After acknowledging that I was indeed Bob Edgar, she chided me: "But what happened to you? You left many years ago and we did not hear any more from you." She had been a teenager when I attended church services in 1974 and had a clear memory of me. She said church members placed great stock in my visit and were very disappointed that I had disappeared and not remained in contact. She also queried me about my appearance. "Your beard is now getting gray and you're not as thin as you once were." I laughed and explained how the decades had altered my appearance. She recommended that we go next to the home of the church's leader, Bishop Mzwandile Mabhelu, Tsoko's successor, at nearby Thamarha.

I had not met Mabhelu on my initial visit in 1974, but when I reached his place and introduced myself, his eyes lit up as soon as I said my name. He was visibly excited that I had returned and warmly welcomed me. Word circulated quickly in the village that I was around and, within a short time, a stream of people flocked to Mabhelu's home. I was once again surprised to learn that I had become part of their community's oral history—"the American who had visited many years before"—and I was heartened by their gracious reception. We agreed that I would return in a week's time for a feast and a meeting with the congregation, where we both would have a chance to catch up on what had happened over the years. The following Sunday they shared a history of Nontetha's life that they had compiled, and they introduced me to two people in their nineties who had known Nontetha as young people and who had participated in the "Pilgrimage of Grace" in 1927. The congregation conveyed how anguished they remained over how government officials had mistreated and institutionalized Nontetha and refused to return her remains to her family after her death. I shared with them the documents that we had recently collected and an essay on Nontetha that Sapire and I had drafted.

After leaving them that day I reflected on the occasion and determined that at the very least I was going to look for Nontetha's burial place in Pretoria, regardless of how remote my chances were of finding it. Even if I could locate the cemetery where she was buried, I questioned whether I had any chance of finding her grave in a pauper's field with no gravestones. I had two bits of information to work with—the date of her death in May 1935 and the name of the cemetery, "New," where she was buried. However, once I arrived in Pretoria and called around to the main cemeteries, I learned that there was no cemetery still bearing that name. I then decided to visit each of the cemeteries in turn, beginning with Rebecca Street Cemetery, the one nearest Weskoppies Mental Hospital. When that cemetery's superintendent, Johan Green, volunteered that his cemetery's original name was Newclare, I knew I had probably found the right place. In line with segregationist rules prior to 1994, the cemetery had maintained separate burial areas for Europeans, Coloureds, Indians, and Africans, but its register listed all burials in chronological order regardless of racial classification. After Green brought out an oversized ledger for 1935, we soon found a listing for a "Nontetho" with a burial date of 22 May. The entry noted that she had died at age sixty-two of liver and stomach cancer. The entry mistakenly listed her as a male, but we speculated that since she was wrapped in a blanket when she was brought to the cemetery, officials probably did not bother to ascertain her sex. Three bodies were normally placed in a pauper's grave, but the ledger listed the name of one other man who had been buried below her a few days earlier and indicated that no one had been buried above her.

More important, the ledger identified Nontetha's burial plot. Although I assumed that would not be helpful in a pauper's field where graves had no markers, Green informed me not only that he had a detailed map of every plot in that area but also that, with the help of surveyor's pins, he could pinpoint the precise location of her grave. Driving to that area, he showed me roughly where he thought her grave should be. Since this remarkable discovery came as I was preparing to return to the United States, I called on Mzumza to report this exciting news directly to Bishop Mabhelu and to Nontetha's family. As I anticipated, they were ecstatic to hear about these developments.

The next year was spent preparing the groundwork for an exhumation of Nontetha's grave. DESRAC was exceptionally cooperative. Its staff had considerable experience in working with local communities to memorialize historical events and was sensitive to the cultural issues that we would have to contend with. They advised that we should put Nontetha's family foremost in our consultations before bringing the church or anyone else into the dialogue. In spring 1998 Hilary Sapire and I met Nontetha's descendants from several branches of her family at the East London home of Vuyani Bungu, a world champion boxer and Nontetha's great-grandson. We were fortunate that all the branches were in agreement about how to proceed.

I returned to South Africa in mid-1998 to prepare the way for the exhumation. Sapire had approached Coen Nienaber and his team of archaeologists attached to the University of Pretoria's Department of Anatomy about conducting the exhumation.[7] Although their specialty was Iron Age archaeology, they were receptive to performing an exhumation of a person from the recent past. They were also well versed in the complex bureaucratic process of securing the necessary permits from offices at four different levels of government in the Eastern Cape and Gauteng Provinces.

All the stakeholders in the process—family members, church leaders (including ninety-three-year-old Tobi Mokrawuzana, who had participated in the Pilgrimage of Grace in 1927), government officials, archaeologists, a journalist, and myself—finally converged on Pretoria at the Holiday Inn on the morning of 13 July. But since Gauteng Province had not issued the last permit for the exhumation, the archaeological team was not prepared to commence work until all the paperwork was in order, including having a policeman at the grave site. Since they had only a small window for conducting the exhumation, they would not be able to reschedule for the foreseeable future. I was a nervous wreck since I felt responsible for bringing all these people together. The church leaders, however, calmed me down by assuring me that their prayers and Nontetha's spirit would see to it that the last permit was issued. Indeed, within the hour, the permit arrived, and we drove immediately to the cemetery, where Green had marked off with twine a rectangular area that he was confident was Nontetha's grave.

After Nontetha's family and church leaders held a prayer service at the grave site, a worker cleared off a foot or so of topsoil, and Nienaber's team began their patient work. They dug six-inch trenches at the end of the grave, where they expected the femurs, the strongest bones, to be. When struck, those bones would not crumble as more fragile bones would. If they did not uncover any skeletal remains, they would then clear off the six-inch layer for the whole grave. As they methodically dug down, they turned up many bones. To my untrained eye, they had to be human remains, but the archaeologists quickly identified them as animal bones that were strewn throughout the landfill and had been spread throughout the pauper's field. By the end of the first day they had dug down three feet without any indication that there might be any bodies in the grave. I was getting very nervous about the whole undertaking.

The next day, as the archaeologists inched deeper, my sense of foreboding grew, since I anticipated that at least some evidence should have turned up by then. It was not until midafternoon that a team member unearthed evidence of the foot bones. With a whisk broom he meticulously exposed the imprints of foot bones that had decomposed in the acidic soil. At the same time, another team member began uncovering the skull at the grave's opposite end. Within an hour they uncovered what was left of the skeleton and made some preliminary observations of what those remains revealed. They determined the rough height (a little over five feet), the general age (at least over fifty), and the sex (female) of the person and noted that there were traces of cancer on her arm bones. They also found the remains of a second skeleton below the first. That confirmed what we knew about there being two bodies in this grave. They reasoned that since Nontetha was wrapped in a blanket when she was buried, she was likely placed on top of the wooden casket of the other person. Then, as the casket decomposed—and evidence was found of the casket—her body sank lower and lower.

The archaeologists carefully placed her remains in a storage box to be examined further by an anatomist at the University of Pretoria. Their reading of the physical evidence led them to conclude that the remains were indeed Nontetha's. Nontetha's family and church leaders followed their own cultural and spiritual truths, and they, too, accepted that the remains were those of their beloved prophet. In this case scientific and cultural logic came to the same conclusion.

We left that day with a great deal of satisfaction (and relief on my part). Plans were set in motion for Nontetha's remains to be returned to her home at Khulile a few months from then for a reburial service. The archaeological team had become personally invested in Nontetha's story and insisted that some of them accompany her remains on the long trek from Pretoria to the eastern Cape. In a moving ceremony in October 1998 attended by several thousand people, Nontetha was finally laid to rest.

Even though I was personally involved in the process, I was not fully aware of how the church interpreted my actions. In August 1999 I attended a service of the Church of the Prophetess Nontetha so that we could review all that had taken place. In a discussion after the service, a woman stood up and divulged something that they had not revealed to me before. In the 1920s Nontetha had prophesied that her followers should look to the Americans because one day "they would do something miraculous." Her prediction then was most likely influenced by the ideas of Marcus Garvey and a popular myth that was widely circulating in the Ciskei and Transkei that African Americans were arriving soon to liberate South Africa from white oppression. To her followers my appearance and disappearance in 1974 was a source of discussion and disappointment precisely because I was American. And when I reappeared almost a quarter century later and played a critical role in locating Nontetha's grave, they interpreted my actions as the fulfillment of her prophecy.

A Restless Spirit

The story of Nontetha's exhumation and reburial was featured on a news magazine on SABC TV's evening English and isiXhosa language services. Many viewers, especially in the eastern Cape, faithfully watch these programs. Among the viewers were Israelite elders who remembered my earlier intervention in the return of their Ark and decided to call on me again to solve the mystery of the location of the grave of Charles Mgijima, who had died in DuToitspan prison in Kimberley of Bright's disease on 12 March 1924 and been buried in a Kimberley cemetery. Although his widow and a few Israelite leaders knew where his grave was, they had not followed through with a request by the prophet Enoch to erect a gravestone with his name on it. Only an iron rod marked his grave site, and they carried the knowledge of the exact place with them when they died.

After several Israelite leaders requested my assistance in locating Charles's grave, I agreed to attend an Israelite religious ceremony and to hold a meeting with a group of elders to learn all I could before agreeing to take on this project. Because of my previous involvement in helping to return the Ark, I did not want their expectations to be unrealistic. Although I may have acquired a reputation for achieving miraculous feats, I never lost sight of the reality that I was relying on my investigative skills and that I was following whatever factual leads were at hand.

The twenty-five elders and I talked for three hours on a wintry Saturday evening in 2000 in the chilly Queenstown tabernacle. They offered compelling reasons for wanting to locate Charles's grave. One was his pivotal leadership in the early years of the Israelites, his central role in the negotiations with the government in 1920 and 1921, and his actions as the Israelites' commander during the Bulhoek massacre, where he had been prepared to sacrifice his life. When he fell gravely ill in prison, Enoch had prayed that the Lord should take him instead so that Charles could return and hold the church together. Another reason that they wanted his remains buried with other church leaders at Bulhoek was so that he could be reunited with his ancestors. Finally, they noted that since they were involved in a partnership with the Eastern Cape DESRAC to develop the site of the massacre (and a new memorial was dedicated to those slain at Bulhoek on the massacre's eightieth anniversary on 25 May 2001), it was crucial for his remains to be returned to complete the process.

As our deliberations wound down, one elder took me aside and explained an unstated but crucial reason—and one that would not be voiced publicly—why locating Charles's grave was so important to them. Before Enoch died, he enjoined his followers to bring Charles's remains to the family cemetery at Bulhoek. Since that had not happened, they interpreted it as a breach of Enoch's wish, which itself contributed to generations of turmoil in the church. Moreover, Charles's restless spirit would continue to disrupt church affairs until his remains were returned. The Israelites had indeed split into two factions in 1947 over the laying of a stone to commemorate the fortieth anniversary of Enoch's first prophecy, which represented their (and the biblical Israelites') years in the wilderness. One faction, led by S. P. Mgijima of Shiloh, favored laying the stone on Wednesday, 9 April, the actual date of Enoch's prophecy, while the Stephen Shweni faction in the Queenstown tabernacle pragmatically supported holding the ceremony on 13 April, a Sunday, when those who worked on weekdays could attend. The rift between the factions became bitter. The Shweni faction refused to give S. P. Mgijima access to the Queenstown tabernacle, and even though a court order of April 1948 directed them to keep the tabernacle open to all worshippers, services conducted by Mgijima were disrupted. In April 1949 Mgijima's opponents assaulted him and his followers at a service.

Over the decades the rivalries continued to simmer. By the 1990s the rivalries over leadership between and within Israelite branches had grown so destructive that fistfights were breaking out in tabernacles, and some members were even being killed. Israelite leaders attributed the troubles to Charles's restless spirit and believed that no healing could take place until his grave was located and his remains were brought home.

During our discussions I quizzed the elders about the availability of any documentation that might give me clues to work with. They had none, but they volunteered that a few years before, several Israelites had traveled to Kimberley to search for Charles's grave. Their inquiries had been fruitless. Armed with a few scraps of information, I set out for Kimberley, where I consulted with officials of the Northwest Province Heritage Office and librarians at the Africana Library. The latter held municipal records and death notices, but aside from a listing with the date and cause of Charles's death, there were no other leads about where his grave might be. Du-Toitspan prison, where the Israelite leaders served their jail terms, had subsequently been converted into a mining compound and its records destroyed.

My next stop was Green Point Cemetery, several miles from the city center. Unlike the segregated Rebecca Street Cemetery, which maintained detailed records of burials, the Green Point Cemetery was for blacks only, and most of its records had been destroyed in a fire at some point. A few surviving records that were deposited in a nearby school contained no leads. The cemetery itself had fallen into disrepair. Few gravestones were still erect, and only a handful had names on them. I walked around an older section hoping to stumble on some overlooked clue, but I gave up after several hours. My search this time had faltered, but as I reflected on my experiences with the searches for the Ark and Nontetha's grave, I understood clearly how extraordinary these undertakings had been.

During the apartheid era, whether I was interrogating official records or negotiating with people to talk about their recollections of the past, the "politics of inequality" set the ground rules and boundaries for my research undertakings. However, with South Africa's independence in May 1994, the research landscape underwent a seismic shift. "Freedom" unlocked the memories of many people who previously had been unwilling or reticent to speak with me openly. While collecting oral history is challenging even in the best of circumstances, at least the apartheid state's repressive machinery was no longer such an intimidating and intrusive factor.

Independence in May 1994 also created opportunities for rectifying some of the injustices of the past that were amply documented in my researches. Although historians are trained to maintain their objectivity by keeping a distance from their subjects, I believe that historians have to engage with and serve the wider community. So my personal relationships with individuals and church groups compelled me to take a different path. I applied my investigative skills to search for the Israelites' holy relic, the Ark of the Covenant, which the police confiscated after the Bulhoek massacre, and Nontetha Nkwenkwe's anonymous grave in a Pretoria cemetery. Those experiences exposed both the limits and possibilities of South Africa's changing landscape as South Africans grappled with the legacy of the old order and the possibilities of the new. Thus, Albany Museum officials were at first reluctant to concede ownership of the Israelite Ark, but eventually they made the right decision and facilitated handing it over. In the case of Nontetha's remains, government officials, archaeologists, and even a cemetery superintendent embraced the transformation and reconciliation process and fully cooperated in exhuming her remains and returning them to her home.

Notes

Introduction

1. This does not mean that there were no religious overtones in the other massacres. In the Duncan Village massacre, police fired on an African National Congress prayer meeting on 9 November 1952. See Leslie Bank and Benedict Carton, "Forgetting Apartheid: History, Culture and the Body of a Nun," *Africa* 86, no. 3 (2016): 472–503.

2. Solomon T. Plaatje, *Native Life in South Africa, before and since the European War and the Boer Rebellion*, 2nd ed. (London: P. S. King and Son, 1917), 255.

3. Studies on nineteenth-century Xhosa prophets include Julia Wells, *Rebellion and Uproar: Makhanda and the Great Escape from Robben Island* (Pretoria: University of South Africa Press, 2007); Janet Hodgson, *Ntsikana's Great Hymn: A Xhosa Expression of Christianity in the Early 19th Century Eastern Cape* (Cape Town: Centre for African Studies, University of Cape Town, 1980); J. B. Peires, *House of Phalo: A History of the Xhosa People in the Days of Their Independence* (Johannesburg: Ravan, 1981); and Peires, *The Dead Will Arise: Nongqawuse and the Great Xhosa Cattle-Killing Movement of 1856–1857* (Bloomington: Indiana University Press, 1989).

4. Edith Bruder, *The Black Jews of Africa: History, Religion, Identity* (Oxford: Oxford University Press, 2011); Merrill Singer, "Symbolic Identity Formation in African American Religious Sects: The Black Hebrew Israelites," in Yvonne Chireau and Nathaniel Deutsch, eds., *Black Zion: African American Religious Encounters with Judaism* (New York: Oxford University Press, 2000), 55–72.

5. Charles Freeman, *A New History of Early Christianity* (New Haven, CT: Yale University Press, 2011); Norman Cohn, *Cosmos, Chaos and the World to Come: The Ancient Roots of Apocalyptic Faith* (New Haven, CT: Yale University Press, 1993).

6. Some of the more important studies are Norman Cohn, *The Pursuit of the Millennium: Revolutionary Messianism in Medieval and Reformation Europe and Its Bearing on Modern Totalitarian Movements* (Fairlawn, NJ: Essential Books, 1957);

Peter Worsley, *The Trumpet Shall Sound: A Study of "Cargo Cults" in Melanesia* (London: MacGibbon and Kee, 1957); Vittorio Lanternari, *Religions of the Oppressed: A Study of Modern Messianic Cults* (London: MacGibbon and Kee, 1973); Jean Rosenfeld, *Island Broken in Two Halves: Land and Renewal Movements among the Maori of New Zealand* (University Park: Pennsylvania State University Press, 1999); Kenneth Newport and Crawford Gribben, *Expecting the End: Millennialism in Social and Historical Context* (Waco, TX: Baylor University Press, 2006); and Stephen O'Leary and Glen McGhee, eds., *War in Heaven / Heaven on Earth: Theories of the Apocalyptic* (Oakville, CT: Equinox, 2005). Studies on southern Africa include George Shepperson and Thomas Price, *Independent African John Chilembwe and the Origins, Setting and Significance of the Nyasaland Native Rising of 1915* (Edinburgh: Edinburgh University Press, 1958); Bengt Sundkler, *Bantu Prophets in South Africa*, 2nd ed. (London: Oxford University Press, 1961); Karen Fields, *Revival and Rebellion in Colonial Central Africa* (Princeton, NJ: Princeton University Press, 1986); and David M. Gordon, *Invisible Agents Spirits in a Central African History* (Athens: Ohio University Press, 2012).

7. Stuart Wright, ed., *Armageddon at Waco: Critical Perspectives on the Branch Davidians* (Chicago: University of Chicago Press, 1995); Kenneth Newport, *The Branch Davidians of Waco: The History and Beliefs of an Apocalyptic Sect* (Oxford: Oxford University Press, 2006); Jayne Docherty, *Learning Lessons from Waco: When the Parties Bring Their Gods to the Negotiation Table* (Syracuse, NY: Syracuse University Press, 2001); James Tabor and Eugene Gallagher, *Why Waco? Cults and the Battle for Religious Freedom in America* (Berkeley: University of California Press, 1995).

8. On Sharpeville see Ambrose Reeves, *Shooting at Sharpeville: The Agony of South Africa* (Boston: Houghton Mifflin, 1961); Philip Frankel, *An Ordinary Atrocity: Sharpeville and Its Massacre* (New Haven, CT: Yale University Press, 2001), and Tom Lodge, *Sharpeville: An Apartheid Massacre and Its Consequences* (Oxford: Oxford University Press, 2011).

9. *Abantu Batho,* 23 June 1921.

10. *Abantu Batho,* 9 June 1921; *Queenstown Daily Representative (QDR),* 27 May 1921.

11. Letter, Mr. Waterston to the Editor, *Cape Times,* 24 June 1921.

12. Sarah Gertrude Millin, *General Smuts* (Boston: Little, Brown, 1938), 328. A decade earlier Millin had published a novel, *The Coming of the Lord* (London: Constable, 1928), which featured a story line whose events and dialogue closely followed what had happened at Bulhoek. One of her lead characters was an Mfengu prophet, Lucas M'fula, who had broken from the Wesleyan Methodist Church and had gone to the United States, where he "found a religion which really suited him" (17). On his return to South Africa, he changed his name to Aaron, patterned his beliefs on the Old Testament Israelites, held Passovers, and attracted a following called the Levites. After the sixth Passover, he called

on his followers to stay on and establish a village in defiance of the local white authorities in the nearby town of Gibeon. Similar to what happened at Bulhoek, the Levites were finally routed in a massacre by police units, which utilized airplanes to attack the encampment. Their prophet Aaron was killed in the battle.

Enoch Mgijima and the Israelites inspired Mike Nicol's novel *This Day and Age* (New York: Knopf, 1992), in which his prophet, Enoch Mistas, challenged contemporary South Africa by appealing to the poor and disenfranchised. The massacre was also the centerpiece of the first African opera, *Enoch, Prophet of God*, composed by Michael Williams and Roelof Temmingh and performed in 1995.

13. Millin, *General Smuts*, 352.

14. Robert Edgar, "The Fifth Seal: Enoch Mgijima, the Israelites and the Bulhoek Massacre" (Ph.D. diss., University of California at Los Angeles, 1977).

15. Carolyn Hamilton et al., eds., *Refiguring the Archive* (Boston: Kluwer Academic, 2002), 9.

16. See D. H. Makobe, "The Price of Fanaticism: The Casualties of the Bulhoek Massacre," *Militaria* 26, no. 1 (1996): 38–41.

17. Clifton Crais, *The Politics of Evil: Magic, State Power and the Political Imagination in South Africa* (Cambridge: Cambridge University Press, 2002), 119–21. The bias toward the state version of the massacre is also reflected in Clifton Crais and Thomas McClendon's selection of a primary document on the massacre for *The South Africa Reader: History, Culture, Politics* (Durham, NC: Duke University Press, 2014), 211–18. The excerpt they selected is from *The Bullhoek Tragedy: The Full Story of the Israelite Settlement at Ntabelanga* published by the *East London Daily Dispatch* in late 1921, which favors the government's version of the massacre.

1. The Promised Land

1. On this period see Carolyn Hamilton, ed., *The Mfecane Aftermath: Reconstructive Debates in Southern African History* (Johannesburg: Witwatersrand University Press, 1995); and Norman Etherington, *The Great Treks: The Transformation of Southern Africa, 1815–1854* (London: Longman, 2001).

2. John Wright, "Turbulent Times: Political Transformations in the North and East," in Carolyn Hamilton, Bernard Mbenga, and Robert Ross, eds., *The Cambridge History of South Africa* (Cambridge: Cambridge University Press, 2010), 1:223.

3. The best accounts of these wars are Noel Mostert, *Frontiers: the Epic of South Africa's Creation and the Tragedy of the Xhosa* (New York: Knopf, 1992); Ben Maclennan, *Proper Degree of Terror: John Graham and the Cape's Eastern Frontier* (Johannesburg: Ravan, 1986); and Peires, *House of Phalo*.

4. Much of my summary of the Mgijima family history is based on *Umprofite Enoch Mgijima*, compiled by Silwana Nkopo (copy in possession of author).

On Hlubi history, see John Wright and Andrew Manson, *The Hlubi Chiefdom in Natal-Zululand: A History* (Ladysmith: Ladysmith Historical Society, 1982), 8–20.

5. The best academic treatments of Mfengu history are Richard Moyer, "A History of the Mfengu of the Eastern Cape, 1815–1865" (Ph.D. diss., University of London, 1976); and Poppy Fry, "Allies and Liabilities: Fingo Identity and British Imperialism in South Africa's Eastern Cape, 1800–1935" (Ph.D. diss., Harvard University, 2007). An attempt to list the mélange of groups that composed the Mfengu is Richard T. Kawa, *Ibali lamaMfengu* (Lovedale: Lovedale, 1929). See the 2011 facsimile reprint by the Cory Library with an introduction by Vathiswa Nhanha and Jeff Peires. See also W. T. Brownlee to W. G. Mears, 8 November 1927, Native Affairs (NTS) 9816 1/403, National Archives of South Africa (NASA), Pretoria.

6. W. T. Brownlee to W. G. Mears, 8 November 1927, NTS 9816 1/403.

7. Moyer, "A History of the Mfengu," 106–7. While I do not accept the myth of "Fingo" slavery that missionaries and British officials constructed, I also do not subscribe to Alan Webster's argument that the Mfengu who crossed the Kei were largely composed of "mission collaborators, mercenaries, refugees, and voluntary labourers." See his article, "Unmaking the Fingo: The War of 1835 Revisited," in Carolyn Hamilton, ed., *The Mfecane Aftermath: Reconstructive Debates in Southern African History* (Johannesburg: Witwatersrand University Press, 1995), 240–76. For a critique of Webster's interpretation, see Fry, "Allies and Liabilities," 63–65. Families that I interviewed in the Queenstown area who would have been called Mfengu historically often could trace their lineages back to their home areas in KwaZulu/Natal and still maintain relationships with them. Oral evidence does not figure in scholarship on the Mfengu.

8. For the Mfengu role in the Xhosa Wars of Resistance, see Richard Moyer, "The Mfengu, Self-Defence and the Cape Frontier Wars," in Christopher Saunders and Robin Derricourt, eds. *Beyond the Cape Frontier* (London: Longman, 1974), 101–26.

9. John Ayliff, *Memorials of the British Settlers of South Africa* (Grahamstown: R. Godlonton, 1845), 9.

10. Ibid., 10.

11. John Ayliff, "History of the Wars Producing the Dispersion of the Fingoes," MS 1110, Cory Library, Rhodes University, Grahamstown.

12. Ibid.

13. John Ayliff and Joseph Whiteside, *History of the Abambo: Generally Known as the Fingos* (Butterworth: Gazette, 1912), 20.

14. John Ayliff, *Notes on Various Matters, Including a Fairly Lengthy Discussion of Native Affairs*, John Ayliff Papers, A80(6), NASA, Cape Town.

15. Ibid.

16. Ibid.

17. Some Xhosa and Thembu groups also served as British allies in wars.

18. James Alexander, *Narrative of a Voyage of Observation among the Colonies of Western Africa in the Thalia, and of a Campaign in Kaffirland on the staff of the Commander-in-Chief* (London: Henry Colburn, 1837), 2:146.

19. J. Whiteside, *History of the Wesleyan Methodist Church of South Africa* (London: Elliot Stock, 1906), 203.

20. John Ayliff, Diary, July 1835, A 80 (2), NASA, Cape Town.

21. Ibid., 3 September 1834.

22. Ibid., 7 September 1834. Ayliff may be best remembered for his relations with the Mfengu, but in 1853, he was a founder of the Wesleyan school at Healdtown, which eventually rivaled Lovedale as the premier African school in the region. He died in 1860.

23. This did not mean that all Mfengu became Christians. Indeed, the 1904 Cape Colony census stated that of the 310,000 Mfengu in the Cape Colony, 50 percent were Christian and the rest were not. Ayliff and Whiteside, *History of the Abambo,* 76.

24. Janet Hodgson, "The Battle for Sacred Power: Christian Beginnings among the Xhosa," in Richard Elphick and Rodney Davenport, eds., *Christianity in South Africa: A Political, Social and Cultural History*(Berkeley: University of California Press, 1997), 68–88.

25. Quoted in Hildegarde Fast, "African Perceptions of the Missionaries and Their Message: Wesleyans at Mount Coke and Butterworth, 1825–1835," (master's thesis, University of Cape Town, 1991), 31.

26. William Moister, *A History of Wesleyan Missions in All Parts of the World from the Commencement to the Present Time* (London: Elliot Stock, 1871), 248.

27. Eugene Casalis, *The Basutos, or Twenty-Three Years in South Africa* (Morija: Morija Museum and Archives, 1992), 302–3.

28. Quoted in Fast, "African Perceptions of the Missionaries," 57.

29. Ibid., 58.

30. J. W. D. Moodie, *Ten Years in South Africa: Including a Particular Description of the Wild Sports of That Country* (London: Richard Bentley, 1835), 284–85.

31. Hildegarde Fast, "'In at One Ear and Out at the Other': African Response to the Wesleyan Message in Xhosaland 1825–1835," *Journal of Religion in Africa* 23, no. 2 (1993): 149. Young may have understood the hard questions being thrown at him, but he was not hesitant about claiming that Africans lived in "moral darkness" and that they were "without God and without hope in the world." He also argued that the ancestors of Xhosas he met were "more civilized and educated" than the ones he was meeting. See Samuel Young, *A Missionary Triumph of Grace; As Seen in the Conversions of Kafirs, Hottentots and Fingoes* (New York: Lane and Scott, 1849), 25.

32. On William Shepstone at Kamastone, see chapter 8 in Ruth E. Gordon, *Shepstone: The Role of the Family in the History of South Africa, 1820–1900* (Cape

Town: A. A. Balkema, 1968). Shepstone died in 1873 after spending a quarter century at Kamastone.

33. Kamastone was an amalgam of Kama and Shepstone.

34. This picture of African life in Kamastone location is largely pieced together from the annual reports of European administrators. For further details, see the *Cape Blue Books on Native Affairs*, 1870–1910.

35. *Queenstown Free Press* (*QFP*), 2 May 1865. See also *QFP*, 31 March 1866. The agricultural show lasted only a few years. For more details, see Megan Voss, "Urbanising the North-eastern Frontier: The Frontier Intelligentsia and the Making of Colonial Queenstown, c. 1859–1877" (master's thesis, University of Cape Town, 2012).

36. *QFP*, 8 November 1864.

37. *The Report of the Wesleyan Methodist Missionary Society for the Year ending April 1870* (London: Wesleyan Methodist Society, 1870), 53–54. In his book *The Reminiscences of an Albany Settler* (Grahamstown: Grocott and Sherry, 1958), Dugmore referred to the Mfengu exodus to the Cape. "The movement was compared by some to the exodus of the Children of Israel from the land of Egypt. They had suffered under cruel task masters in the house of bondage. Crossing the Kei was like the passage of the Red Sea and they had spoiled the Egyptians on setting out or the land of promise" (87–88). Dugmore translated the Bible as well as many Methodist hymns from English into isiXhosa.

38. On Pamla, see Daryl Balia, "Bridge over Troubled Waters: Charles Pamla and the Taylor Revival in South Africa," *Methodist History* 30, no. 2 (1992): 78–90; and Gordon Mears, "Charles Pamla," *Methodist Missionaries*, no. 2 (Rondebosch: Methodist Missionary Department, 1959). African evangelists were instrumental in translating the words of European missionaries. See Richard Elphick, *The Equality of Believers: Protestant Missionaries and the Racial Politics of South Africa* (Charlottesville: University of Virginia Press, 2012), 32–37; Tolly Bradford, *Prophetic Identities: Indigenous Missionaries on British Colonial Frontiers, 1850–75* (Vancouver: UBC Press, 2012); and Peggy Brock, "New Christians as Evangelists," in Norman Etherington, ed., *Missions and Empire* (Oxford: Oxford University Press, 2005), 132–52.

39. Balia, "Bridge over Troubled Waters," 78.

40. William Taylor, *Story of My Life* (New York: Eaton and Mains, 1896), 356.

41. Ibid. While Pamla was a creative interpreter, he sided with white missionaries in their condemnation of such African customs as bridewealth and circumcision, which he labeled "an immoral and ruinous custom." See Charles Pamla, *Some Reflections on Native Customs*, pamphlet (n.d.), 6.

42. William Storey, *Guns, Race, and Power in Colonial South Africa* (Cambridge: Cambridge University Press, 2008).

43. Ibid., 213–14.

44. Ibid.

45. Ayliff and Whiteside, *History of the Abambo*, 71–72.

46. Cape of Good Hope, *Petition of Residents of the Kamastone and Oxkraal Locations to Honourable Speaker of the House of Assembly of Cape of Good Hope Signed by Joshua and 441 Others*, A. 11-—1879, Cape of Good Hope; the petition also appeared in the 9 August 1879 issue of the *Cape Argus*, cited in Storey, *Guns, Race, and Power*, 248. Kamastone's resident Wesleyan missionary, Edward Barrett, who assisted with raising Mfengu troops, expressed his skepticism about how loyal Kamastone residents actually were; he stated that they had not enthusiastically volunteered for service in the recent wars and reluctantly handed over their guns at the war's end. Cape of Good Hope, *Report and Proceedings with Appendices of the Government Commission on Native Laws and Customs*, G. 41883 (Cape Town: W. A. Richards and Sons, 1883), 1:301.

47. *Journal* (Grahamstown), 4 June 1887.

48. Andre Odendaal, *The Founders: The Origins of the ANC and the Struggle for Democracy in South Africa* (Auckland Park: Jacana, 2012).

49. Ibid., 96.

50. *Journal* (Grahamstown), 4 June 1887.

51. Odendaal, *The Founders*, 115; *Imvo Zabantsundu*, 1 June 1887. Queenstown area politicians such as Bisset Berry and John Frost were consistently outspoken in opposing the legislation.

52. Petition to Queen Victoria from "the Native Inhabitants of the Location of Oxkraal, July 1887," in Thomas Karis and Gwendolen Carter, eds., *From Protest to Challenge: A Documentary History of African Politics in South Africa, 1882–1964* (Stanford: Hoover Institution Press, 1972), 1:15–16.

53. Cape of Good Hope, *List of Persons Residing in the Electoral Division of Queenstown in the Year 1903* (Cape Town: Cape Times Government Printers, 1903); *Journal* (Grahamstown), 19 January 1888.

54. This discussion heavily relies on the work of Lindsay Braun, "The Cadastre and the Colony: Surveying, Territory and Legibility in the Creation of South Africa, c. 1860–1913" (Ph.D. diss., Rutgers University, 2008), 36–60.

55. *Fort Beaufort Advocate*, 23 March 1870.

56. Braun, "The Cadastre and the Colony," 142.

57. Ibid., 150.

58. Ibid., 153.

59. Ibid., 154.

60. Richard Bouch, "Farming, Capitalization and Labour in a Newly Colonized Area: Queenstown, 1852–1886," paper presented at Cape Slavery and After Conference, 1989. Queenstown became linked to East London by a railway in 1880.

61. Cape of Good Hope, *Report and Proceedings with Appendices of the Government Commission on Native Laws and Customs*, G. 4—1883 (Cape Town: W. A. Richards and Sons, 1883), 2:348–53.

62. Quoted in Colin Bundy, *The Rise and Fall of the South African Peasantry* (Berkeley: University of California Press, 1979), 72.

63. *Cape Argus,* 29 June and 24 July 1875.

64. Bundy, *Rise and Fall,* especially 65–145.

65. *Journal* (Grahamstown), 12 October 1901.

66. *Queenstown Representative,* 2 December 1884.

67. Ibid. He is probably referring to *brandsiekte,* a sheep scab caused by mites.

68. Ibid.

69. Clifton Crais, *Poverty, War, and Violence in South Africa* (Cambridge: Cambridge University Press, 2011), 117.

70. All the quotes are cited in *Report of the Natives Land Commission,* vol. 2, U.G. 22—1916 (Cape Town, 1916), 111–18.

71. Adam Ashforth, *The Politics of Official Discourse in Twentieth-Century South Africa* (Oxford: Clarendon, 1990), 40–47.

72. Timothy Stapleton, "Gathering under the Milkwood Tree: The Development of Mfengu Tribalism in the Eastern Cape (1878–1978)," *New Contree* 41 (1997): 213–16.

73. "Fingo Day," Native Affairs Department, SANA, Cape Town, vol. 432.

74. Rev. E. H. Hurcombe, "Wesleyan Missions Centenary. Notable Personages: Captain Veldtman," *East London Daily Dispatch,* 21 October 1921. On Fingo Day, see also Odendaal, *The Founders,* 154–55.

75. Ayliff and Whiteside, *History of the Abambo,* 73–74.

76. *Journal* (Grahamstown), 28 May 1908.

77. Wright Rulushe, chairman, and William C. Bekwa to Lord Gladstone, Governor General, 25 May 1911, Governor General, NASA, Pretoria, 1160, 50/123. A change in the tone of proclamations came in the 1930s when Fingo Day organizers began injecting their apprehensions about the Hertzog legislation, which aimed to abolish the Cape African vote. The following passage was inserted in the 1931 declaration: "Although we are very sorry to notice that this long enjoyed privilege of franchise, which has never been tampered with and never been abused since 1852, has now become a subject of discussion in the parliamentary debate of this country with a view to changing its original form. If this happens it will never be appreciated by the Native races of South Africa." The 1934 proclamation commented: "Although it is not our usual custom, in such an address to enter into political affairs, we venture to say if the Status Bill, which is agitating to the uttermost the minds of the people of South Africa; and which now almost passed all the stages in the Parliamentary houses will in no way endanger the Native vote, and infringe their welfare, Your humble loyal subjects will ever be thankful." NTS 9816 2/403. And *Imvo Zabantsundu* (31 March 1935) editorialized on the occasion of the 1935 commemoration: "The Bantu races had originally learned to attach credence to a promise, let alone a pledge, given by the Whiteman's government, but the example of the

Government's failure to protect Fingo claims in and outside the courts of law is a sad commentary on the integrity of the European race."

D. D. T. Jabavu, a lecturer at Fort Hare College and the son of John Tengo Jabavu, sought to heal the divisions between Mfengu and Xhosa to create a larger African unity. In an essay published in 1935, a century after the Mfengu exodus, he rejected the notion that the British had liberated the Mfengu from Xhosa oppression and argued instead that they voluntarily left the Gcaleka in search of cattle of their own. That same year, he was a leading figure in the creation of a new national organization, the All African Convention. See D. D. T. Jabavu, "The 'Fingo Slavery' Myth," *South African Outlook* (1 June 1935): 123–24. On Fingo Day commemorations in the 1960s, see Richard Moyer, "Some Current Manifestations of Early Mfengu History," *Collected Seminar Papers on the Societies of Southern Africa in the 19th and 20th Centuries* (University of London Institute of Commonwealth Studies), 3 (1973), 144–54.

78. QDR, 19 May 1910.

79. Several thousand copies of *History of the Abambo* were distributed.

80. Ayliff and Whiteside, *History of the Abambo,* 89.

81. John Tamana, interview by author, Ilinge Resettlement Cape, 4 June 1974. Born at Middledrift about 1896, Tamana was a shepherd who became very close to the Mgijima household. He served as a trustee and evangelist in the Church of God and Saints of Christ in later years. His wife was Dora Tamana, who later became a prominent African National Congress activist.

82. QFP, 2 May 1865 and 31 March 1866.

83. Tamana, interview.

84. Welsh Mgijima, son of Josiah Mgijima, interview by author, Bulhoek,3 June 1974. Charles, fourteen, and Josiah, thirteen, entered Zonnebloem in 1881. Zonnebloem College Admission Register, 1876–1900, Manuscripts Division, African Studies Library, University of Cape Town.

85. Mamtembu died around March 1921. Enoch married Ida sometime between Mamtembu's death and the Bulhoek massacre. They had one daughter, Nobantu. Enoch married another wife, Lillian, around 1924 or 1925.

86. The Israelites often compared Enoch to Moses, who was also a hunter when he was watching the flock of his father-in-law at Midian.

87. Tamana, interview; Gideon Ntloko, interview by author, Queenstown, 9 May 1974.

88. Tamana, interview; Ntloko, interview.

89. Tamana, interview; Ntloko, interview.

90. Sources on Mgijima's relations with the Moravians are *Jahresbericht uber das Missionswerk der Brudergemeine fur das Jahr, 1912,* 42–43; Bishop Ernst van Calker, *Hundert Jahre Kaffernmission der Brudergemeine: 1828–1928* (Herrnhut: Verlag der Missionsverwaltung, 1928), 80–83; W. S. Mazwi, *A History of the Moravian Church in Southeast Africa in Outline* (Morija, 1938); and Walther Bourquin,

"Irrungen und Wirrungen in Silo," *Missionsblatt der Brudergemeine* 77, no. 4 (April 1913): 73–80.

91. *Periodical Accounts Relating to Moravian Missions of the Church of the United Brethren* 8 (September 1912): 353.

92. *Periodical Accounts* 43 (1912): 586.

93. Ibid.

94. *Diarium Shiloh*, 1912, Moravian Archive, Mvenyane, South Africa.

95. Bernhard Krüger, *The Pear Tree Blossoms: A History of the Moravian Mission Stations in South Africa, 1737–1869* (Genadendal: Genadendal Printing Works, 1967), 14.

96. *Periodical Accounts* 34 (1893): 142–43; J. Taylor Hamilton and Kenneth Hamilton, *History of the Moravian Church: The Renewed Unitas Fratrum, 1722–1957* (Bethlehem, PA: Interprovincial Board of Christian Education, Moravian Church in America, 1967).

97. The same kinds of tensions existed at Genadendal, Elim, and Mamre, Moravian mission stations in the western Cape. See Bernhard Krüger and P. W. Schaberg, *The Pear Tree Bears Fruit: The History of the Moravian Church in South Africa West*, II, 1869–1960 (Genadendal: Moravian Book Depot, 1984), 80–88. For an example of how some residents at the Kat River settlement had their land swindled from them in the late nineteenth century, see J. B. Peires, "The Legend of Fenner-Solomon," in Belinda Bozzoli, ed., *Class, Community and Conflict South African Perspectives* (Johannesburg: Ravan, 1987), 65–97.

98. *Annual Report for 1901*, 383. See also *Periodical Accounts* 34 (1887) and *Periodical Accounts* 36 (1893): 142–43.

99. *Moravian Missions* 13 (1915): 44–45.

100. *Periodical Accounts* 42 (1911): 352–53.

101. *QDR*, 11 April 1912.

102. *Diarium Shiloh*, 1912; NTS 138 626/F263.

103. Mdudu was born at Shiloh but had lost his land around 1890 for moral lapses, according to the Moravians, and was not allowed to reclaim it until he paid his taxes in the mid-1890s. This he refused to do. When he joined the Church of England, this signified to the Moravians that he no longer qualified for any mission station land. NTS 138 626/E263.

104. Van Calker, *Hundert Jahre Kaffernmission*, 80–83.

105. *Periodical Accounts* 43 (1912): 587.

106. Walther Bourquin, *Bruder Mensch: 41 Jahre Herrnhuter Mission in Südafrika* (Hamburg: Appel, 1967), 26.

107. Ibid., 27–28; see also Bourquin, "Abschriften von Notizen aus dem Jahr 1912 und 1913 uber En. Mgijima und die bewegung in Silo." I thank Bourquin's son for sharing these writings and Maria Kail for assisting with translations.

108. The Wesleyan missionary at Kamastone, Rev. Joseph Metcalf, appealed to Mgijima to stay in the fold. Mgijima told him "that he was grateful to Rev.

Metcalf for having come to show them the right way when they were going astray, but he said that they would not return to him if they felt that they were following the foot-tracks of Jesus Christ." Statement of M. C. Nkopo, for Keith Hancock's biography of Jan Smuts.

109. Bourquin, *Bruder Mensch,* 27–28; see also Bourquin, "Irrungen und Wirrrungen in Silo."

110. Van Calker, *Hundert Jahre Kaffernmission,* 80–83; *Thirty-First Report of the South African Missionary Society* (Pietermaritzburg, 1913).

111. For detailed analysis of the independent church movement in southern Africa, see Sundkler, *Bantu Prophets;* Shepperson and Price, *Independent African;* Christopher Saunders, "Tile and the Thembu Church," *Journal of African History* 11, no. 4 (1970): 553–70; Norman Etherington, *Preachers, Peasants, and Politics in Southeast Africa* (London: Royal Historical Society, 1978); Bengt Sundkler, *Zulu Zion and Some Swazi Zionists* (London: Oxford University Press,1976); and Elphick, *Equality of Believers,* 89–94.

112. Quoted in Wallace Mills, "The Role of African Clergy in the Reorientation of Xhosa Society to the Plural Society in the Cape Colony, 1850–1915" (Ph.D. diss., University of California, Los Angeles, 1975), 54.

113. Daryl Balia, *Black Methodists and White Supremacy* (Durban: Madiba, 1991), 62; statement of Silwana Nkopo; Mabel Matshoba, daughter of Silwana Nkopo, interview by author, 3 June 1974; L. Mqotsi and N. Mkele, "A Separatist Church: Ibandla Lika-Krestu," *African Studies* 5 (1946): 106–25.

114. James Campbell, *Songs of Zion: The African Methodist Episcopal Church in the United States and South Africa* (New York: Oxford University Press, 1995), 109–10.

115. Elphick, *Equality of Believers,* 89.

116. Frederick Bridgman, "The Ethiopian Movements in South Africa," *Missionary Review of the World* 26, no. 6 (June 1904): 944. Similar sentiments were expressed in J. du Plessis, "The Native Situation in South Africa: A Missionary Point of View," *Missionary Review of the World* 30 (December 1907): 919–26.

117. Emma Green, "Native Unrest in South Africa," *Nineteenth Century* 46, no. 273 (November 1899): 710.

118. South African Native Affairs Commission, *Report of the Commission with Annexures and Appendices, 1903–1905* (Cape Town, 1905), 1:64.

119. Roderick Jones, "Black Problem in South Africa," *Nineteenth Century and After* 57, no. 339 (May 1905): 771.

120. See the resolution in *Report of the Proceedings of the First General Missionary Conference Held at Johannesburg, 13–20 October 1904* (Johannesburg: Argus, 1905), 178. See also Campbell, *Songs of Zion,* 139–40.

121. *Report of the Proceedings of the First General Missionary Society Conference,* 130; "Ethiopianism," *Christian Express,* 1 December 1901, 184.

122. Edwin Neame, "Ethiopianism: The Danger of a Black Church," *Empire Review* 10, no. 1 (1905): 259.

123. The Israelite writer cited this quote from an article in *Abantu Batho* published in *QDR*, 13 October 1920.

124. Ibid.

2. The Prophet's Call

1. Campbell, *Songs of Zion*, 116–17, 136.

2. Besides James Campbell's work on the AME, see Robert Vinson, *The Americans Are Coming: Dreams of African American Liberation in Segregationist South Africa* (Athens: Ohio University Press, 2012); Robert Vinson and Robert Edgar, "Zulus Abroad: Cultural Representations and Educational Experiences of Zulus in America, 1880–1945," *Journal of Southern African Studies* 31, no. 1 (2007): 43–62; Ntongela Masilela, "The Black Atlantic and African Modernity in South Africa," *Research in African Literatures* 27, no. 4 (Winter 1997): 88–95; Hunt Davis, "John L. Dube: A South Exponent of Booker T. Washington," *Journal of African Studies* 1, no. 2 (1975): 497–528; and Richard Ralston, "A Second Middle Passage: African Student Sojourns in the United States during the Colonial Period and Their Influences upon the Character of African Leadership" (Ph.D. diss., University of California, Los Angeles, 1972).

3. Beersheba Crowdy Walker, *Life and Works of William Saunders Crowdy* (Philadelphia: Elfreth J. P. Walker, 1955). Beersheba Crowdy Walker was Crowdy's granddaughter. See also Jesse E. Brown, "Prophet William Saunders Crowdy and the Church of God and Saints of Christ: The Implications of His Life and Thought for the Mission of the Church," Ph.D. diss., Colgate Rochester Divinity School, 1986.

4. We know that Sothoron was the slave owner from the bounty roll records of black soldiers, which list the names of slave owners. Daniel joined the Nineteenth Colored Regiment on 4 December 1863. Comptroller of the Treasury (Bounty Rolls), 1864–1868, Slaves and Owners by U.S. Colored Troops Regiment, S 629/5/4, Maryland State Archives, Annapolis. I thank Amy Richmond of the Southern Maryland Studies Center for referring me to the Bounty Rolls.

5. Barbara Fields, *Slavery and Freedom on the Middle Ground: Maryland during the Nineteenth Century* (New Haven, CT: Yale University Press, 1985), 125. I thank David Anthony for directing me to this source.

6. William Tidwell, *April '65: Confederate Covert Action in the American Civil War* (Kent, OH: Kent State University Press, 1995), 178; Stephen Calhoun, *The Marylanders without Shelter or a Crumb: A Saga of the Fascist Repression of a Family during the American Civil War*, rev. ed. (Westminster, MD: Heritage Books, 2007); Charles Wagandt, *The Mighty Revolution: Negro Emancipation in Maryland, 1862–1864* (Baltimore: Johns Hopkins Press, 1964), especially 116–32.

7. Daniel Crowdy (1842–92) served in the Nineteenth Regiment from 4 December 1863 to 15 January 1867. He suffered from rheumatism contracted

in Brownsville, Texas, in 1866. Eventually he settled in Baltimore, where he married Frances in 1874. He died of phthisis on 3 December 1892.

8. Fields, *Slavery and Freedom*, 139. Several years later Basil Crowdy lodged a complaint about the incident to Maj. S. N. Clark, who was investigating cases for the Freedmen's Bureau. Records of the Assistant Commissioner for the District of Columbia, 20 November 1867, Freedmen's Bureau, http://freedmensbureau .com/washingtondc/outrages.htm. According to the U.S. Census of 1880, Basil, a widower, and a number of family members were then living in Baltimore.

9. On his death in 1892 Daniel's only daughter, Rachel applied for a soldier's invalid payment. She was paid eight dollars a month through November 1896. Application 818234, Box 40223, U.S. National Archives, Washington, D.C.

10. Nell Painter, *Exodusters: Black Migration to Kansas after Reconstruction* (New York: Knopf, 1977), 187.

11. Their children were Mattie Leah, Isaac, and August. In December 1924 Lovey, then living at 1638 Fitzwater Street, Philadelphia, applied for a widow's pension from the U.S. Army. She stated that William Crowdy could have signed up under the names William Crawford or William Crowder, but a search of army records did not turn up a file under any of these names and her application was turned down. William S. Crowdy, file 1223687, National Archives, Washington, D.C.

12. Sonja Woods, "Black Americans and the Lure of Guthrie, 1887–1897," unpublished paper, 12. For her information on Crowdy's activities in Guthrie, Woods drew on the Guthrie Business Directory of 1894, 26. I thank her for sharing her research with me.

13. Peter Hinks and Stephen Kantrowitz, "Introduction: the Revolution in Freemasonry," in Hinks and Kantrowitz, eds., *All Men Free and Brethren: Essays on the History of African American Freemasonry* (Ithaca, NY: Cornell University Press, 2013), 17.

14. Walker, *Life and Works*, 4.

15. The vomit Crowdy referred to is mentioned in Isaiah 28:8.

16. Walker, *Life and Works*, 6.

17. John Msikinya, biographical sketch of William S. Crowdy, *Weekly Prophet*, 28 August 1908. I thank Terry Miller for sharing this document with me.

18. Ibid.

19. Walker, *Life and Works*, 8.

20. *Syracuse Evening Herald*, 18 February 1899.

21. Walker, *Life and Works*, 8.

22. *Columbus Enquirer-Sun*, 13 March 1898; *Fort Scott Fair Play*, 22 July 1898.

23. *Emporia Gazette*, 13 September 1899.

24. *Columbus Enquirer-Sun*, 13 March 1898. Ingersoll died in 1899.

25. *Broad-Ax* (Chicago), 6 August 1898 (column taken from the *Grit*, Williamsport, PA).

26. *Boston Journal*, 4 June 1904.

27. S. F. Collins, "A Peculiar Religious Sect of Colored People Their Prophet, William S. Crowdy, Styled by Many as the 'Black Dowie,'" *Colored American* 9, no. 1 (December 1905): 691–94.

28. *Philadelphia Press*, 13 January 1902; see also *Macon Telegraph* (Georgia), 25 January 1902.

29. *Boston Globe*, 4 June 1904.

30. *Philadelphia Inquirer*, 3 December 1903. See also *Philadelphia Inquirer*, 8 December 1903.

31. *Washington Post*, 25 June 1906.

32. Brown, "Prophet William Saunders Crowdy," 189.

33. *Census of Religious Bodies, 1926: United States Bureau of the Census* (Washington, D.C., 1928). Under Crowdy was a governing executive council, composed of twelve ordained elders and evangelists. Ministers, elders, evangelists, and bishops carried out the church's ministry. Mgijima's church hierarchy was somewhat patterned after Crowdy's church. At the top was the prophet Mgijima. Below him were four bishops who represented the corners of the world, Grandfather Abraham, evangelists (no more than sixteen, who visited local tabernacles), elders, deacons, trustees, and Father Abraham (stewards). All these positions were filled by men. There were several women's auxiliaries, including the daughters of Jerusalem, daughters of mercy, and daughters of the Prophet. They were primarily responsible for home visitation and caring for the sick. They had their own hierarchy—Grandmother Sara, Mother Sara, Mother Rachel, Mother Leah, Sister Mary, and Sister Martha.

34. He predicted that a large battleship would be blown up before the sinking of the *Maine* in Havana harbor in February 1898. *Syracuse Post-Standard*, 3 March 1899. See also Elmer Clark, *Small Sects in America* (Nashville: Cokesbury, 1937), 189; *Boston Journal*, 4 June 1904; *Broad-Ax* (Chicago), 6 August 1898. According to Msikinya's account in the *Weekly Prophet* (28 August 1908), Crowdy met McKinley and gave him the choice of carrying out "the law of God or the law of the nation." McKinley chose the latter, and that sealed his fate.

35. *Syracuse Evening Herald*, 18 February 1899.

36. Yvonne Chireau and Nathaniel Deutsch, eds., *Black Zion: African American Religious Encounters with Judaism* (New York: Oxford University Press, 2000), 16. See also Merrill Singer's chapter, "Symbolic Identity Formation in African American Religious Sects," in the same volume and Allen Callahan, *The Talking Book: African Americans and the Bible* (New Haven, CT: Yale University Press, 2006), especially chapter 5 on Exodus.

37. Albert J. Raboteau, "African Americans, Exodus and the American Israel," in Paul Johnson, ed., *African American Christianity* (Berkeley: University of California Press, 1994), 15. See also Raboteau, *Fire in the Bones: Reflections on*

African-American Religious History (Boston: Beacon, 1995); Eddie Glaude, *Exodus! Religion, Race, and Nation in Early Nineteenth Century Black America* (Chicago: University of Chicago Press, 2000); Cheryl Kirk-Duggan, "Let My People Go! Threads of Exodus in African American Narratives," in Randall Bailey, ed., *Yet with a Steady Beat: Contemporary U.S. Afrocentric Biblical Interpretation* (Atlanta: Society of Biblical Literature, 2003), 123–43; and Robin Kelly, *Freedom Dreams: The Black Radical Imagination* (Boston: Beacon, 2002).

38. *Syracuse Evening Herald,* 18 February 1899.

39. Ibid.

40. Ibid.

41. *Emporia Daily Gazette,* 14 April 1899. Other sources state that the first Passover was held in 1901.

42. Ibid.

43. *Minneapolis Journal,* 14 April 1906.

44. *New York Times,* 14 April 1906.

45. *New York Tribune,* 22 April 1906.

46. CGSC leaders such as H. Z. Plummer and L. S. Plummer were also Masons. Prince Hall had launched Freemasonry among African Americans in Massachusetts in 1784. See William Grimshaw, *Official History of Freemasonry among the Colored People in North America* (New York: Negro Universities Press, 1969); George Crawford, *Prince Hall and His Followers* (New York: AMS Press, 1971); and Sara Stone, "Marching and Related Phenomena in the Church of God and Saints of Christ: a Possible Masonic Connection?," paper presented at the Society for Ethnomusicology, March 1988. See also Stone's dissertation, "Song, Composition, Transmission and Performance Practice in an Urban Black Denomination: The Church of God and Saints of Christ" (Ph.D. diss., Kent State University, 1988).

47. See Proverbs 15:3: "The eyes of the Lord are in every place, beholding the evil and the good."

48. *Washington Bee,* 14 August 1909.

49. Clark, *Small Sects,* 188–89. In the late 1930s, Clark described the several hundred members of the Bellville community as "owning and cultivating one thousand acres of land, operating several small industries, a commissary, schools and homes for orphans and aged." Ibid., 188. For additional details on Israelite beliefs and rituals, see Katesa Schlosser, *Eingeborenenkirchen in Sud- und Sudwestafrika: Ihre Geschichte und Socialstruktur* (Kiel: Kommissionverslag W. G. Muhlau, 1958), chapter 4.

50. Robert Vinson puts the number of West Indians in South Africa in 1905 as five hundred. For more details, see Vinson, *The Americans Are Coming,* 63–81.

51. Terry Miller and Sara Miller, *The Church of God and Saints of Christ in Africa: The First One Hundred Years (1903–2003)* (Kent, OH: printed by the authors, 2008), 9.

52. Reuben Matshaka, interview by author, Uitenhage, June 1974; *Jubilee Year of the Church of God and Saints of Christ, 1903–1963,* handbill supplied to B. A. Pauw by Reuben Matshaka, 1963 (I thank Dr. Pauw for sharing this document with me); Bishop J. R. Grant, Church of God and Saints of Christ, "Our Leaders and Forefathers" (1980).

53. Sampson Msikinya, interview by author, Aliwal North, 23 May 1974; David Msikinya, interview by author, Umtata, 15 June 1974; *Cape Argus,* 25 May 1921. Rev. Allen Lea observed of Msikinya's educational sojourn that "he went to the United States to further his education, but was spoilt and came back with a swollen head." Allen Lea, *The Native Separatist Church Movement in South Africa* (Cape Town: Juta, 1926).

54. *Koranta ea Becoana,* 7 September 1904.

55. *Weekly Prophet,* 29 January 1909.

56. The *Cape,* 18 September 1910, drew a connection between the African American connection and agitators: "These men avowedly belong to an American organisation calling itself the 'church of God and Saints' which appears to be nothing else than the work of a gang of 'educated' American Negroes who find a fruitful source of livelihood in exploiting and deluding the only slightly more ignorant Fingoes."

57. R. Thomson to Resident Magistrate, Uitenhage, 8 January 1910, NTS 1428 28/214; statement of J. Hardaker, Uitenhage School Board, n.d., 3/UIT 8/303, SANA, Cape Town.

58. Office of Civil Commissioner, Alice, to Under Secretary to the Native Affairs Department, Cape Town, 21 June 1910, NTS 1428 20/214.

59. Edward Dower to Magistrate's Office, Peddie, 6 October 1911, NTS 1428 20/214.

60. See Matthew 6:26.

61. Rex v. Mhlabane and Matshaka, 31 August 1910,NTS 1428 20/214.

62. Rex v. John I. Msikinya and 6 Others, 11 August 1920, NTS 1428 20/214.

63. Testimony of Detective James White, Rex v. Mhlabane and Matshaka, 31 August 1910; testimony of James White, Rex. v. John I. Msikinya and 6 Others, 11 August 1910; Report of Capt. W. C. van Ryneveld to Resident Magistrate, Grahamstown, 24 August 1910, NTS 1420 20/214.

64. Evidence of Samuel Matshaka, preparatory examination, trial of Israelites, Queenstown Criminal Circuit Court, 29 June 1921, SANA, Cape Town.

65. Tamana, interview.

66. Ibid.

67. To symbolize the atonement of his sins and his recognition of Mgijima as prophet, Msikinya composed a hymn, "My Sins Are Taken Away."

68. *QDR,* 13 July 1921. Reverend Ntlemeza, a CGSC minister in Uitenhage, supplied this information to the newspaper.

69. Interview by author with group of Israelite women, Shiloh, 29 May 1974; Silwana Nkopo, *History of the Israelites* (n.d.) Gideon Ntloko has compiled additional prophecies of Mgijima in *Ngokubekiesele e bandleni*, copy in possession of author.

70. D. D. T. Jabavu, "Lessons from the Israelite Episode," *South African Outlook* (1 July 1921): 106; statement of M. C. Nkopo of Mceula, collected by Sister Moore of Grahamstown, copy in possession of author. I thank T. R. Davenport for supplying me with this document.

71. Sundkler, *Bantu Prophets*, 325; see also Jane Linden and Ian Linden, "John Chilembwe and the New Jerusalem," *Journal of African History* 12, no. 4 (1971): 629–51.

72. Edward Barrett, Native Affairs Department, Cape Town, to Chief Magistrate, Umtata, Chief Magistrate, Transkei, 3/781, NASA, Cape Town.

73. *Diarium Shiloh,* 1912.

74. *Johannesburg Star,* 17 May 1921; *Cape Argus,* 23 May 1921. It is probably coincidental that Mgijima and Charles Russell, the founder of Watch Tower, both saw 1914 as a significant year for their millennial predictions. Russell had forecast for many years that in 1914, the saints would be carried up to heaven to rule with Christ and that God would cause the breakup of all earthly kingdoms and substitute theocratic rule for the rest of the millennium (Revelation 12). Studies of Watch Tower include Alan Rogerson, *Millions Now Living Will Never Die* (London: Constable, 1969); Barbara Harrison, *Visions of Glory* (New York: Simon and Schuster, 1978); James Penton, *Apocalypse Delayed: the Story of Jehovah's Witnesses* (Toronto: University of Toronto Press, 1997); and Fields, *Revival and Rebellion.* Although the Watch Tower message had a profound impact on central African preachers such as Elliott Kamwana, Jeremiah Gondwe, and John Chilembwe, Watch Tower did not actively proselytize in the eastern Cape until several decades later. However, it is possible Mgijima had access to Watch Tower literature.

75. Evidence, Samuel Matshaka, prep. exam.

76. Ibid.

77. C. P. Mhlabane to Enoch Mgijima, 8 August 1916, Bulhoek Massacre Miscellany, BC 1061, Manuscripts Division, African Studies Library, University of Cape Town.

78. *QDR,* 13 July 1921. Reverend Ntlemeza, a CGSC minister in Uitenhage, supplied this information to the newspaper.

79. The best analysis of Israelite theology is Martin Mandew, "War, Memory and Salvation: The Bulhoek Massacre and the Construction of a Contextual Soterioloy" (Ph.D. diss., University of Natal, 1996). On the attraction of Judaism to Africans, see Bruder, *Black Jews of Africa.*

80. The words are taken from Psalm 137.

81. Michael Walzer, *Exodus and Revolution* (New York: Basic Books, 1985), 4.

82. On Afrikaners see Leonard Thompson, *The Political Mythology of Apartheid* (New Haven, CT: Yale University Press, 1985); and Donald Akenson, *God's People: Covenant and Land in South Africa, Israel and Ulster* (Ithaca, NY: Cornell University Press, 1992).

83. This is in keeping with Hlubi cultural practices, in which it is important for the lamb to be slaughtered in a painless way.

84. Israel Finkelstein and Neil Silberman, *The Bible Unearthed: Archaeology's New Vision of Ancient Israel and the Origin of Its Sacred Texts* (New York: Free Press, 2001).

85. Discussion with Gideon Ntloko, 7 July 2010.

86. Ibid. Juda stood for the Hlubi, Efrayime for the Xhosa, and Josef and brethren for all other peoples.

87. Ezekiel 37:21.

88. Ezekiel 37:27–28

89. Helen Scanlon, *Representation and Reality: Portraits of Women's Lives in the Western Cape, 1948–1976* (Cape Town: HSRC Press, 2007), 170. Scanlon is relying on an interview conducted by Jenny Schreiner with Dora Tamana on 7 March 1977.

90. Ibid., 170–171. See also Tamana, interview; Dora Tamana, "A Short Story of Enoch Mgijima the Prophet," 1 March 1973, Jack and Ray Simons Collection, Women—biographies, Dora Tamana, Manuscripts Division, African Studies Library, University of Cape Town, BC 1081, R 1.9. Dora's father, Joel, and two of her brothers, Richard and Madukela, died in the Bulhoek massacre. John and Dora married in 1923.

91. Statement of Benjamin Duba to P. M. Bell, 2 June 1921, Government Native Labour Bureau 222 169/21/110, NASA, Pretoria. Duba left Ntabelanga in November 1920 for a job in the gold mines. Although he had not returned, his family remained at Ntabelanga through the massacre.

92. Rev. John Kingon, "The Economics of the East Coast Fever as Illustrated by the Transkeian Territories," *South African Journal of Science* 13 (1915): 213–28.

93. *QDR*, 29 October and 6 November 1918; *Report of the Native Affairs Department for the years 1919 to 1921*, U.G. 34—1922; Howard Phillips, *"Black October": The Impact of the Spanish Influenza Epidemic of 1918 on South Africa*, Archives Year Book for South African History (Pretoria: The Government Printer, 1990), 237. For examples of how the pandemic affected other religious movements in southern Africa, see T. O. Ranger, "Plagues of Beasts and Men: Prophetic Responses to Epidemic in Eastern and Southern Africa," in T. O. Ranger and P. Slack, eds., *Epidemics and Ideas: Essays on the Historical Perception of Pestilence* (Cambridge, Cambridge University Press, 1992), 241–68. Ben Carton, "The Forgotten Compass of Death: Apocalypse Then and Now in the Social History of South Africa," *Journal of Social History* 37 (Fall 2003): 200–18 also discusses the impact of rinderpest and HIV-AIDS in addition to the influenza.

94. *Tarka Herald*, 20 August 1919; see also J. L. Bisset's letter, "Distress in the Transkei," *QDR*, 3 January 1920.

95. M. G. Apthorp to J. X. Merriman, 15 December 1919, J. X. Merriman Papers, National Library of South Africa, Cape Town.

96. Peter Walshe, *The Rise of African Nationalism in South Africa: The African National Congress, 1912–1952* (London: C. Hurst, 1970), 61–66.

97. *QDR*, 6 January 1920.

98. Matshoba may have been referring to the strike of forty thousand miners in February 1920.

99. Although the student grievances were over what they considered rotten bread, their protest ended in violence as several buildings were burned. Lovedale officials expelled many students.

100. On the Garvey movement's message reaching South Africa, see Vinson, *The Americans Are Coming*.

101. Letters from Gilbert Matshoba to Enoch Mgijima, Rex v. Israelites. Matshoba (c. 1875–1941) was educated at Healdtown. Besides his employment as a law clerk, he taught at De Aar and Britstown. After the Bulhoek massacre, he worked as an Israelite evangelist at De Aar, Queenstown, and Basutoland. Maria Dinge, daughter of Gilbert Matshoba, interview by author, Queenstown, 1974.

102. Michael Barkun, "Law and Social Revolution: Millenarianism and the Legal System," *Law and Society Review* 6 (1971): 113–41.

103. Cohn, *Pursuit of the Millennium*, 208–18.

104. Kenelm Burridge, *New Heaven, New Earth: A Study of Millenarian Activities* (Oxford: Blackwell, 1969), 61.

3. The Making of a Massacre

1. Evidence of Geoffrey Nightingale, prep. exam., 23 June 1921.

2. Evidence of Samuel Masiza, Israelite evangelist, prep. exam., 21 June 1921; Silwana Nkopo, *History of the Israelites*; G. Nightingale to Resident Magistrate, Queenstown, 27 October 1920, Justice Department, vol. 287, file 2/853/20 (hereafter cited as JD 287, 2/853/20).

3. *Interim and Final Reports of the Native Affairs Commission and Telegram from Commissioner, South African Police, Relative to "Israelites" at Bulhoek and Occurrences in May, 1921*, A. 4—1921.

4. Cape of Good Hope, *Report of the Surveyor-General 1877* (Cape Town, 1878), G. 38–78, 7–8.

5. W. M. Murray, Surveyor-General's Office, Cape Town, to Provincial Secretary, Cape Town, 18 February 1915; Secretary for Native Affairs, Pretoria, to Secretary for Interior, Pretoria, 10 December 1914, vol. 292, Surveyor-General's Office, Cape Town.

6. L. M. Walton, Surveyor, Office of the Native Locations to Surveyor General, Cape Town, 7 October 1911, NTS 6743 184/335.

7. Petition from inhabitants of Bulhoek location for Board of Management, 28 April 1894, Cape Colony, NA 774.

8. John Alf Sishuba to Minister of Interior, Pretoria, 24 December 1914, Surveyor-General's Office, Cape Town, vol. 292.

9. W. M. Murray, Surveyor-General's Office, to Provincial Secretary, 18 February 1915, Surveyor-General's Office, Cape Town, vol. 292.

10. *Report of Native Locations Surveys*, U.G. 42—1922.

11. Ibid. The Kamastone case was not an exception to the rule; land surveys throughout the Ciskei were abysmal failures. Thus few regulations were enforced; most became dead letters. There were few areas where beacons and boundaries were honored, where individuals did not claim two or more allotments, or where there were not infrequent encroachments on the commonage. In 1911 surveys were carried out in a number of the Kamastone sublocations (but not Bulhoek).

An additional complication was that when an individual wished to transfer land to another party, he had to procure a formal transfer deed, which necessitated employing a lawyer and paying legal costs. Often the expense of transferring land was the same and sometimes more expensive than the value of the land itself. Hence it is not surprising that most Africans ignored the transfer process. Echoing the report of the Locations Surveys Commission, the Native Affairs Department concluded in the mid-1920s that "the Ciskeian lands present a deplorable tangle of claims to ownership, defective titles and questions of prescription which cannot be unravelled under the law as it stands to-day." *Report of the Native Affairs Department Years 1922 to 1926*, U.G. 14—1927. See also *Report of the Local Natives Land Committee, Cape Province*, U.G. 8—1918.

12. Lamb H. Brinkman, attorney, to Resident Magistrate, Queenstown, 1 June 1917, prep. exam.

13. Clement Gladwin to Magistrate, Queenstown, 12 June 1917, prep. exam.

14. Evidence of G. Nightingale, prep. exam. Not all Africans escaped prosecution. Edward Maholwana of Zangokwe location was charged with illegal plowing on the commonage without permission of the superintendent of natives. Maholwana admitted he knew he was breaking the law but he thought it was worth the risk. The headman, John Maqutyana, testified: "I know that a number of natives are ploughing Crown lands. I also know that we take these risks, hoping that we will benefit by it, in the acquisition of the land, or at least by the crops harvested therefrom." Fining Maholwana 10s., the judge stated that although this kind of activity had been going on for years, "instructions had been issued by the government to put a stop to this activity." QDR, 14 January 1919.

15. Evidence of G. Nightingale. Enoch also received a summons on 1 September 1920 for not paying a vehicle tax on a wagon and for not having his full name printed on it.

16. Ibid..

17. Saul Dubow, *Racial Segregation and the Origins of Apartheid in South Africa* (Houndmills: Macmillan, 1989), 77.

18. *Imvo Zabantsundu,* 20 September 1910.

19. Charles Mgijima and A. Ntloko to Magistrate, Queenstown, 6 September 1920, prep. exam.

20. Gilbert Matshoba to Enoch Mgijima, September 1920, prep. exam.

21. Enoch Mgijima to Chief E. Mhlambiso, Amatole Basin (translated by Isiah Bud M'belle, interpreter for the Native Affairs Department), prep. exam. The headman of Mhlambiso's location in 1921 was actually Llewellyn Mhlambiso, grandson of Ebenezer, but the government had branded him as a troublemaker and soon replaced him with Alfred Mabuto.

22. Evidence of Charles Mgijima, Rex v. Israelites.

23. The Queenstown newspaper saw events in a very different light, commenting that Mgijima's "misguided" followers were now returning home and that "police reports from Kamastone indicate that everything is quiet and peaceful." *QDR,* 11 September 1920.

24. Evidence of G. Nightingale, Rex v. Israelites; G. Nightingale to E. C. Welsh, Queenstown, 5 September 1920, JD 287 2/85320. Likewise, Sgt. S. Lavery, who assisted in the delivery of summonses to the Israelites on 3 September, observed that "I am not, however, in a position to state what attitude these natives would take up in the event of arrests to be effected." S. Lavery to District Commandant, South African Police, Queenstown, 4 September 1920, and Lavery, South African Police, to District Commandant, South African Police, Queenstown, 4 September 1920, JD 287 2/853/20.

25. *QDR,* 15 September 1920; evidence of G. Nightingale, Rex v. Israelites.

26. Petition of European farmers to Magistrate, Queenstown, September 1920 JD 287 2/853/20. This was ironic because in the nineteenth century Xhosa who regarded missionaries as a divisive force labeled mission stations as "hotbeds of vice" and "haunts of disreputable characters with libertine habits." Fast, "African Perceptions of the Missionaries," 140.

27. *QDR,* 8 October 1920.

28. P. Whitaker to Resident Magistrate, Queenstown, 6 September 1920, JD 287 2/853/20.

29. Evidence, Alfred Ndondolo, prep. exam., 24 June 1921. Alfred Makapela, prep. exam., 27 June 1921.

30. Petition of Kamastone headmen to Nightingale, 4 September 1920, JD 287 2/853/20. A day later, the headmen were visited by two Israelite evangelists, Joseph Tuso and Kosani Nduna, who were actively spreading the message that the time had come when nation would fight against nation and those who sided with whites would suffer as well. Interestingly, Tuso and Nduna also asked the headmen if they had read in the newspapers that Americans

and Indians were proposing to come to Africa. Statements of headmen George Maholwana, Charles Bam, Robson Matshoba, and Alfred Mpateni, 7 September 1920; Nightingale to Magistrate, Queenstown, 9 September 1920, JD 287 2/853/20.

31. Compare Ntabelanga to William Moister's characterization of mission stations: "Every Mission station in Kafferland is an asylum for the oppressed and afflicted . . . and every Missionary is a friend of the persecuted outcast." Moister, *History of Wesleyan Missions*, 250.

32. *QDR*, 29 October 1920.

33. *QDR*, 20 November 1920.

34. Some millennial movements have gained notoriety for antinomian behavior, but the Israelites were if anything morally upright. Nevertheless, European missionaries portrayed the Israelites as a morally bankrupt sect. Rev. D. D. Stormont of Blythswood Institute recorded in his diary that the Israelites were thieves, that Israelite men abused their women and children, that venereal disease was rampant at Ntabelanga, and that Israelite meeting houses were "suites of iniquity." Diary of D. D. Stormont, 22 June 1921, MS 7511, Cory Library, Rhodes University.

35. Charles had previously worked as a magistrate's court interpreter at De Aar. According to S. Nkopo, Enoch's movement reminded Charles of a dream in which he had visited the Hlubi chief Langalibalele. "He saw a star moving from the east. It continued revolving and went back where it came from. All the other stars then gathered round it and then he saw people who were people similar to those at Ntabilanga gathered in the veld." Evidence of Charles Mgijima, Rex v. Israelites: *The Bullhoek Tragedy: The Full Story of the Israelite Settlement at Ntabelanga* (East London: East London Daily Dispatch, 1921), 4; S. Nkopo, *Umprofite Enoch Mgijima*.

36. Ezekiel 5:1 supplied the scriptural basis for the shaven heads, and Luke 22:36 for the swords, which were incorporated into the Israelite uniform around 1916.

37. Nightingale to Welsh, 3 October 1920, JD 287 2/853/20.

38. Nightingale to Resident Magistrate, Queenstown, 20 October 1920, JD 287 2/853/20.

39. Nightingale to Resident Magistrate, Queenstown, 26 November 1920, JD 287 2/853/20.

40. *Bulhoek—Precis Covering the Period 23.8.1920–10.5.21*, South African Police Archive, Pretoria. This view was also put forward by Meschach Pelem, who argued that the Israelites would have left long before but for their fear that Enoch would be arrested and jailed. But the government would not give a guarantee for his safety. *Precis*, 3 November 1920.

41. The complacency of many whites is reflected in a letter of Samuel Clark, secretary of the South African Missionary Society, to the Queenstown paper

after the massacre. He contended the paternalistic native policies of administrators such as Sprigg, Elliott, W. E. Stanford, Sauer, and Moffatt were the best since Africans were still in a stage of childhood in which ignorance, superstition, and barbarism still reigned. "What greater proof can we have of the wisdom and value of present methods than the generally peaceful and industrious condition of the tribes inhabiting the native territories? Where in the world will you find a district with from fifty to eighty thousand native residents successfully governed by a dozen European civil servants, and an equal number of native police?" *QDR*, 21 June 1921.

42. Gary Baines, "South Africa's Amritsar? Responsibility for and Significance of the Port Elizabeth Shootings of 23 October 1920," *Contree* 34 (November 1993), 4.

43. *Cape Times*, 1 November 1920.

44. *Precis*, 6 December 1920.

45. *Interim and Final Reports*, 3.

46. The Israelites were regularly given information about the intentions and strategies of the authorities through a network of Israelites and non-Israelite Africans (especially clerks) who worked in Queenstown. On various occasions Enoch Mgijima had Queenstown Africans come out to Ntabelanga to solicit their support for the Israelite cause. For instance, Nightingale reported that in early December, about a dozen Queenstown Africans attended a meeting at Ntabelanga at which Mgijima asked the non-Israelites to state whether they would give the Israelites support and assistance when the expected trouble happened with the government. An ex-headman, Philip Matshoba, gave his support, saying "he was against the English and the British flag." Another, Baliso Mgijima, stated he would not help the Israelites, whereupon he was asked to leave the meeting. Nightingale to Resident Magistrate, 6 December 1920, Rex v. Israelites.

47. Nightingale to Resident Magistrate, Queenstown, 3 December 1920, JD 287 2/853/20.

48. Evidence of Maj. Edward S. Hutchons, Rex v. Israelites; Silwana Nkopo, *History of Israelites*.

49. Ibid. Hutchons also posted guards at the Queenstown African location since he was concerned about the possibility of trouble breaking out there.

50. Evidence of Capt. Philip Whitaker, Rex v. Israelites. When Whitaker asked some Israelites about their Saturday Sabbath, Charles Mgijima jokingly told him, "You people don't keep the Sabbath; you play tennis and golf." Evidence of Stanford Kati, Native Constable, South African Police, prep. exam., 27 June 1921. Another Israelite reaction to the Port Elizabeth shootings came from a white journalist who went out to Ntabelanga pretending to be a mine recruiter. He asked some Israelites if they had heard about the Port Elizabeth disturbances. The Israelites asked him to relate what had happened, and when

he did, they said, "Oh, it must be the strike." The reporter added he had seen a number of police in Queenstown that day. He was asked if he knew what they were there for, and when he replied that he did not know if they might be for Port Elizabeth or the Israelites, the Israelites laughed. "One of them said they had always earned all they had from the Government, and owed it nothing. They had received nothing from the white man without earning it, and were independent of him." *QDR*, 29 October 1920.

51. Maj. Hutchons to Pretoria, 10 December 1920; *Precis*, 10 December 1920, JD 287 2/853/20.

52. Maj. Hutchons to Pretoria, 10 December 1920; *Precis*, 10 December 1920, JD 287 2/853/20.

53. Tamana, interview; S. Nkopo, *History of the Israelites.*

54. Dora Tamana affirmed that Mgijima never claimed bullets would turn to water, "but it came out of the talk of the people" after the confrontation with the police. Tamana, "A Short Story of Enoch Mgijima."

55. *QDR*, 11 December 1920.

56. Frank Brownlee to W. Merriman, 14 December 1920, Merriman Papers.

57. Sgt. E. Alston, Alice, to District Commandant, South African Police, Cradock, 2 December 1920; A. T. Davie, Acting Deputy Commissioner of Police, Cape Eastern Division, Grahamstown, to Secretary, South African Police, Pretoria, 7 December 1920, JD 289 2/950/19.

58. Davie to Secretary, South African Police, Pretoria, 7 December 1920, JD 289 2/950/19.

59. *QDR,* 8 December 1920.

60. *Precis,* 10 December 1920.

61. J. C. Smuts to A. H. Frost, 13 December 1920, NTS 169 420/13/387. Frost was the successor to Bisset Berry, a longtime political force in the Queenstown area. Frost was a sheep farmer in the Tarkastad district. He had fought in the wars against the Xhosa and in the Anglo-Boer War.

62. *QDR*, 13 January 1921.

63. *QDR*, 21 December, 1921.

64. H. J. Simons and R. E. Simons, *Class and Colour in South Africa* (Harmondsworth: Penguin, 1969), 252.

65. A. T. Davie, Acting Deputy Commissioner of Police, Cape Eastern Division, Grahamstown, to Secretary, South African Police, Pretoria, 7 December 1920, JD 289 2/950/19.

66. Report of W. H. Quirk, South African Police, Eastern Cape Division, to Deputy Commissioner, South African Police, Grahamstown, 5 January 1921 (JD 287 2/853/20).

67. *Daily Dispatch*, 26 October 1921.

68. Mhlabane subsequently died in the Bulhoek massacre.

69. *QDR*, 23 December 1920.

70. *QDR*, 25 October 1921. Mattushek's nephew, Bertie, a hotel proprietor and a former mayor of Queenstown, recollected his uncle's version of the story. His uncle had been having problems with stock thieves and trespassers. One day several Israelites, who were on their way to Lehman's Drift railroad depot, passed through his land. Mattushek fired several warning shots and told the Israelites to go back and take the road. Upon returning to Ntabelanga, the Israelites reported to Enoch, who sentenced Mattushek to twenty-five lashes. Mattushek learned of this and was prepared to defend himself when three Israelites came to his farm. When they rushed him, he shot two of them with a revolver. But they were unfazed and Mattushek began wondering if his bullets were indeed turning into water. The Israelites, however, were actually wearing breastplates, and as Mattushek struggled with them, he shot one in a vulnerable spot and killed him. Then one of the Kloppers unloaded a round of buckshot into another. The third Israelite fled. Bertie Mattushek, interview by author, 8 May 1974.

4. When People Rally Round the Word of God

1. Barrett was appointed secretary of native affairs after J. B. Moffat, formerly chief magistrate of Transkei, suddenly died in January 1919.

2. Edward James Barrett (1840–1932) came to South Africa when he was twenty-four to help an invalid brother. Entering the ministry in 1865, he served mission stations at Glen Grey, Cofimvaba, Butterworth, Kamastone, Annshaw, and Buntingville, where he became blind. A widower, he lived the last two decades of his life at Corn Exchange, Basutoland, "cared for with affectionate devotion by his one daughter, who was his constant nurse and companion."

3. *QDR*, 13 December 1920. Edward Barrett had been in the Native Affairs Department since 1894. A brother, A.L., joined the Native Affairs Department after 1910 and served until his retirement in 1941. The Queenstown newspaper responded to Barrett's comment by editorializing that he and the Native Affairs Department still did not understand the gravity of the situation. "Mr. Barrett speaks glibly on a situation that he doesn't understand, has never understood, and has therefore mishandled from the start." *QDR*, 13 December 1920.

Government officials complained especially about a *Daily Dispatch* correspondent sensationalizing how the government was handling the Israelites (11 December 1920), calling it the "comedy at Queenstown, a comedy which unfortunately may at any moment be converted into a tragedy." The reporter blamed local officials for not intervening aggressively at an early stage when the Israelites were holding their Passover in 1919. As a result, "other natives from elsewhere, attracted by the charms of a workless life, have joined the insurgents" and made it extremely difficult to get rid of the trespassers—even though they were being induced by the promise of free passage home.

4. Other members of the delegation were Welsh, Medford, Lieutenant Strydom, Captain Whitaker, Subinspector Gould, Nightingale, A. Frost, and Halse, the Israelites' attorney.

5. *QDR*, 18 December 1920.

6. Born in 1859 near Middledrift, Pelem was educated at Healdtown Institute, where he qualified as a primary school teacher. He taught at Cradock and Middleburg before venturing to the diamond fields at Kimberley. He later joined the British expeditionary force under Charles Warren that occupied and annexed Bechuanaland in 1885, and he served as an interpreter to Bishop K. Bruce, the Anglican Bishop of Bloemfontein. After returning to the Cape and settling in Queenstown, he launched himself in various businesses, including the ox-wagon trade and operating a boarding house. He recruited African labor for the Railway Administration. He was a leading figure in the Church of the Province of South Africa and served on the governing council of Fort Hare University College. Active in Cape politics, he was selected as a deputy president of the South African Native National Congress on its founding in 1912; in 1919, he founded and served as president of the Bantu Union. He spent his last years in King William's Town running Pelem's Hotel. *Imvo Zabantsundu*, 14 May 1936 and 19 August 1961; T. D. Mweli Skota, *The African Yearly Register* (Johannesburg, 1931), 235. Educated at Blythswood Institution and a well-to-do farmer in the Emgcwe district in the Transkei, Xabanisa was a member of the Nqamakwe local council and the Transkei Territorial General Council from its inception. He served as president of the Transkei Native Farmers' Union. A vice president of the Bantu Union, he participated in the All-African Convention in 1935. The son of a prominent Mfengu chief in the Butterworth area, Veldtman was active in local and general council politics.

7. *Interim and Final Reports*, 4.

8. Evidence of Edward Barrett, Rex v. Israelites; "Rough Notes of a Meeting Held at McComb's Drift, near Bullhoek location, Queenstown, on Friday, 17 December 1920," JD 288 2/853/20.

9. Evidence of Edward Barrett; Nkopo, *History of the Israelites*. The Israelite delegation consisted of Charles Mgijima, Isaiah Kekane, Barrington Mgijima, Edward Booi Mgijima, Edward Mpateni, and Silwana Nkopo.

10. Nkopo, *History of the Israelites*; *QDR*, 18 December 1920.

11. Evidence of Joseph Kekana, Rex v. Israelites.

12. Evidence of Edward Barrett, Rex v. Israelites.

13. Ibid.

14. W. K. Hancock, *Smuts: The Fields of Force, 1919–1950* (Cambridge: Cambridge University Press, 1968), 2:93.

15. Apthorp to J. X. Merriman, 23 December 1920, Merriman Papers.

16. Smuts won the comfortable majority he was seeking as his South African Party gained an additional thirteen seats. Overall the South African Party won 79 seats, National Party 45, Labour 9, and Independent 1.

17. *Tarka Herald,* 21 January 1921.

18. Smuts to A. H. Frost, 13 December 1920, NTS 169 420/13/387.

19. J. C. Smuts to C. P. Crewe, 6 May 1921, Smuts Papers, vol. 102, no. 206, NASA, Pretoria. Smuts was unaware that Halse had stopped representing the Israelites in October. Halse had also grown hostile to the Israelites. Speaking at a meeting of mostly white farmers in Queenstown, he advised the government to act firmly with the Israelites and show no leniency. Otherwise the prestige of whites would diminish in the eyes of Africans. *QDR,* 10 January 1921.

20. For a discussion of African electoral politics, see Stanley Trapido, "African Divisional Politics in the Cape Colony, 1884–1910," *Journal of African History* 9, no. 1 (1968): 79–98.

21. *QDR,* 25 June 1921.

22. *Die Burger,* 1 June 1921. A committed Afrikaner nationalist, Louw later served as South Africa's ambassador to the United States, France, and Portugal in the late 1920s and 1930s and was an unrepentant advocate of apartheid as minister of foreign affairs from the mid-1950s to the mid-1960s.

23. *QDR,* 25 June 1921.

24. The Israelite women played a minimal role in Israelite decision making during the negotiations with the government. For that reason, most of my oral and written documentation on Israelite strategy and responses comes from Israelite men.

25. *QDR,* 25 June 1921.

26. *Die Burger,* 1 June 1921.

27. Louw in turn was sharply criticized for not warning the Israelites of the serious consequences of their defiance.

28. After Frost died the following September, a by election was called to fill his seat. Because of the massacre's impact on the white farming community, the selection of candidates was partly tied to the forthcoming Israelite trial. Writing to Smuts, Charles Crewe warned: "I doubt any local man in Queenstown being strong enough to carry that seat, practically every farmer is credited with having egged on the Govt to break up Bulhoek, and of course there were public meetings at which both farmers and merchants spoke. The candidate must be an Englishmen and in my judgement should be from outside the constituency unconnected with the recent trouble and able to say he disapproved." Charles Crewe to Smuts, 2 October 1921, Prime Minister, NASA, Pretoria, 1/1/434, no. 124/1922, vol. 2, quoted in Noel Garson, "The Cape Franchise in Action: The Queenstown By-Election of December 1921," history workshop paper, Witwatersrand University, 1984. However, the South African Party candidate was Livingstone Moffat, a Tarkastad farmer and grandson of the missionary Robert

Moffat. The National Party candidate again was Louw. This time Moffat won, but with a slightly reduced majority.

29. Tamana, interview.

30. Nightingale to Magistrate, Queenstown, 3 April 1921, JD 287 2/853/20. According to the Israelites the dam was designed to drain swampy land and to guard against excess water spilling over on garden plots.

31. Evidence of John Cranke, prep. exam., 28 July 1921. Typhus and other diseases and illnesses such as pneumonia may have severely struck the Israelites. On 5 June 1921, Cranke found seventy recently dug graves at Ntabelanga. While in jail, thirty to forty Israelites contracted typhus and at least five died.

32. Ibid.

33. Apthorp to Merriman, 10 April 1921, Merriman Papers.

34. Apthorp to Merriman, 6 June 1921, Merriman Papers.

35. Evidence of Oliver Nobuza, prep. exam., 28 July 1921.

36. See the letter from Bhokara, QDR, 16 September 1922.

37. Evidence of Capt. Henry Quirk, Criminal Investigation Department, Eastern Province, Rex v. Israelites; Cape Argus, 26 November 1921.

38. Evidence of Tasman Jaxa, prep. exam., 28 July 1921.

39. Evidence of Lunqwana Mtsha, prep. exam., 29 July 1921; evidence of Lunqwana Mtsha, Rex v. Israelites.

40. Evidence of Tasman Jaxa, prep. exam., 28 July 1921.

41. Ibid.

42. *Report of the Native Affairs Commission for the Year 1921*, U.G. 15—1922 (Cape Town, 1921).

43. Both Roberts and Loram were obvious candidates for the government commission. Roberts had been principal teacher of the training school at Lovedale from 1883 to 1920. An astronomer, he received the first doctoral degree in science in 1899 from the University of the Cape of Good Hope. He served on the Native Affairs Commission from 1920 to 1935 and the Native Church Commission and the Native Economic Commission. He was a senator from 1920 to 1936, but he was not reappointed after he opposed the Hertzog bills in 1936.

Loram was well known for his work on "'native'" education. Born in Pietermaritzburg, he had taken his B.A. at the University of the Cape of Good Hope and an M.A. and LL.B. at Cambridge University. He taught at Leys School, Cambridge, before returning to South Africa as an inspector of schools. In 1913 he left for the United States, where he completed a Ph.D. at Columbia University. His dissertation was entitled "The Education of the South African Native." On his return to South Africa he was made chief inspector of "native" education in Natal. In the 1920s, he participated in the Phelps-Stokes Commission, which investigated African education in southern and eastern Africa. He also served as vice- chairman of the Lovedale government council. In 1931 he left South

Africa to take up an appointment as professor of education at Yale University in the United States.

Keith Hancock suggests Smuts may have included Gen. Lodewyk Arnoldus Slabbert Lemmer because his "earthy common sense" served "as a counterweight to the academic sophistication of his two colleagues." Hancock, *Smuts*, 2:93. A graduate of Stellenbosch, he fought as a burgher in the South African War and eventually rose to the rank of general. During the war, his wife and children were taken to a concentration camp where one of their children died of illness. He served with South African forces in the First World War in South West Africa and as MP for Marico from 1911 until his death in 1944.

44. Roberts to Merriman, 4 September 1920 and 30 August 1921, Merriman Papers.

45. *Tarka Herald*, 28 January 1921.

46. Ibid.

47. Evidence of A. W. Roberts, Rex v. Israelites. Writing to Barrett in March, Clement Gladwin, a former Superintendent of Natives at Kamastone, had recommended granting the Israelites several acres of land for a permanent site for their Tabernacle, but this drew fire from Queenstown officials when they met with the Commission on 7 April. In particular, Welsh opposed giving a site to the Israelites because taking such a step would legalize their occupation. Before leaving, the commission also met with local African and white farmers. *Interim and Final Reports*, 6; C. Gladwin to E. Barrett, 8 March 1921, cited in Sundkler, *Zulu Zion*, 316.

48. Evidence of A. W. Roberts and General Lemmer in *Debates of the House of Assembly*, 23 June 1921, 264.

49. Evidence of Alfred Makapela, prep. exam., 27 June 1921; Alfred Ndondolo, prep. exam., 24 June 1921; Adam Reuters, prep. exam., 27 June 1921; *Debates of the House of Assembly*, 23 June 1921, 264; QDR, 19 May 1921.

50. Testimony of Edward Sokabo, Rex v. Israelites.

51. Bisset Berry to Merriman, 11 January 1921, Merriman Papers.

52. *QDR*, 26 April 1921.

53. *QDR*, 6 May 1921.

54. Enoch Mgijima to Magistrate, Queenstown, 31 March 1921, JD 287 2/85320.

55. Evidence of Charles Mgijima, Rex v. Israelites.

56. PM 418 280/20.

57. *Cape Argus*, 13 May 1921.

58. Evidence of A. W. Roberts, Rex v. Israelites.

59. Ibid.

60. Nkopo, *History of the Israelites*.

61. *Debates of the House of Assembly*, 23 June 1921, 265.

62. Ibid.

63. Prep. exam., Rex v. Israelites.

64. *QDR*, 7 June 1921.

65. *Nongqai* 12 (July 1921): 338.

66. *Nongqai*, 12 (May 1921).

67. *Cape Times*, 24 June 1921.

68. *Debates of the House of Assembly*, 23 June 1921, 265; Secretary for Defence to Minister of Defence, 13 May 1921; Secretary for Defence to Secretary for Native Affairs, 14 May 1921, Defence Archive, Pretoria, box DC 451, file 52002, enclosure 40.

69. Notes on Suggested Alternatives for Dealing with the Israelites, box DC 451, file 52002, enclosure 40.

70. Minister of Defence to Gen. Van Deventer, 18 May 1921, box DC 451, file 52002, enclosure 40.

71. *Johannesburg Star*, 26 May 1921.

72. *Johannesburg Star*, 17 May 1921. The government might have had such sentiments in mind when, in 1922, it used airplanes extensively to brutally put down the rebellion of the Bondelswarts in South West Africa.

73. Evidence of C. M. Dantu, Rex v. Israelites; *Johannesburg Star*, 17 May 1921; *The Bullhoek Tragedy*, 19–20; *Imvo Zabantsundu*, 7 September 1941.

74. *QDR*, 20 May 1921.

75. *Imvo Zabantsundu*, 17 May 1921.

76. *Tarka Herald*, 12 May 1921.

77. *Cape Argus*, 23 May 1921.

78. *Cape Argus*, 20 May 1921.

79. *QDR*, 11 May 1921.

80. *QDR*, 12 May 1921.

81. *Cape Argus*, 24 May 1921.

82. The 1921 government census counted 6,134 Africans, 5,231 whites, and 1,503 Coloureds and Indians in Queenstown.

83. Banana Martins to Enoch Mgijima, May 1921, Rex v. Israelites.

84. Evidence of Banana Martins, Rex. v. Israelites.

85. *QDR*, 2 June 1921.

86. *The Bullhoek Tragedy*, 21.

87. *Cape Argus*, 21 May 1921; *Johannesburg Star*, 21 May 1921.

88. Evidence of James Malumbazo, 3 December, Rex v. Israelites.

89. Tamana, interview.

90. Ibid.

91. Ibid.

92. At least twelve Mgijimas died in the massacre, including Barrington Mgijima. The Israelite view of the last few days before the massacre is drawn from interviews with surviving Israelite participants such as Nondumo Ndike, Edgar Mkumatela, John Tamana, who was wounded in the battle, and Welsh Mgijima and Israelite groups at Shiloh, Queenstown, and Bulhoek.

93. *QDR,* 23 May 1921. For more details on Aggrey's tour, see Edwin Smith, *Aggrey of Africa: A Study in Black and White* (London: Student Christian Movement, 1929).

94. The officers decided to bring their forces in together because they feared the Israelites might attack smaller units sent separately.

95. *QDR,* 2 June 1921.

96. Interview by author with a group of Israelite women, Shiloh, 29 May 1974.

97. Evidence of Ernest Woon and William Henry Quirk, prep. exam., 4 August 1921. The discussion between the police and Israelites took place in isiXhosa.

98. Evidence of Ernest Woon, inquest; *QDR,* 30 May 1921; report of W. H. Quirk, Inspector, South African Police, 26 May 1921, Bulhoek file, South Africa Police Archive, Pretoria; evidence, Theo Truter, inquest; *QDR,* 1 June 1921.

99. Evidence of John Tyobeka, Native Sergeant Detective, East London, prep. exam., 4 August 1921.

100. Report by Subinspector S. Chisholm, "C" Squadron, First Regiment, South African Police, Bulhoek Operations, 25 May 1921, JD 288 2/853/20. For accounts of the shooting, I have relied on police reports filed shortly after the massacre, newspaper accounts, interviews with African and white participants, and several articles that appeared in *Nongqai,* a police magazine. Lt. E. J. Brinton, "A Reminiscence of the Bulhoek Affair," *Nongqai* 13, no. 7 (1922): 389–90; Lt. Col. H. F. Trew, "When the 'Israelites' Rebelled: Personal Recollections of the Native Rising at Bullhoek Fanatical Bravery of the 'Prophets' Disciples," *Nongqai* 21, no. 5 (1930): 331–34.

101. Report by William Quirk, JD 288 2/853/20.

102. Evidence of S. Vanqa, Rex v. Israelites.

103. Evidence of John Sihlahla, Rex v. Israelites.

104. Evidence of Charles Mgijima, Rex v. Israelites.

105. Ibid.

106. Nondumo Ndike, interview by author, Dudumashe location, Nqamakwe, July 1974. Born around 1890 and educated at Lovedale, Ndike came to Ntabelanga around 1919 when he married a daughter of Edward Mgijima. He had previously worked as a clerk at a pass office in Johannesburg, as an interpreter for the Basutoland police, and as a teacher at Umtata and Ngqeleni. He left the Israelites in the early 1930s and joined the Watch Tower movement.

107. Report by S. Chisholm, 24 May 1921, JD 288 2/853/20.

108. *The Bullhoek Tragedy,* 28.

109. Testimony of Colonel Woon, inquest, in *QDR,* 30 May 1921.

110. F. Gardner, interview by author, Whittlesea, 6 May 1974.

111. *QDR,* 30 May and 6 June 1921.

112. *Johannesburg Star,* 25 May 1921.

113. Evidence of Charles Mgijima, Rex v. Israelites; evidence of Charles Mgijima, Rex v. Israelites. See also Tamana, interview; . Tamana suffered a

broken leg and was hit by a bullet in the battle and was taken by rail for treatment at Wynberg Hospital. The bullet stayed in his arm for decades and finally squeezed out on its own around 1953. Dora Tamana, interview by Jenny Schreiner, 17 March 1977.

At an interview with a group of Israelites, I was told that it was significant that they were slaughtered at the same time of day that Christ was believed to have been crucified.

114. Interviews with Israelite women, Shiloh, Queenstown, and Bulhoek; evidence of Nomi Ncwatya, prep. exam., 29 July 1921.

115. *Report of the Native Churches Commission*, U.G. 39—1925 (Cape Town: Government Printers, 1925), 16. Using government documentation, D. H. Makobe of the Documentation Services Directorate of the South African National Defense Force put the number of dead at 225. His figure includes 163 who died during the battle, 37 who died at the dressing station set up at Bulhoek after the battle, 5 who died on the way to Frontier Hospital in Queenstown, and 17 who died at Frontier Hospital, 2 at Roberts Military Hospital, and 1 at Wynberg Military Hospital. See Makobe, "The Price of Fanaticism," 41.

116. *QDR*, 2 June 1921.

117. Trew, "When the 'Israelites' Rebelled," 332.

118. Ibid.

119. *The Bullhoek Tragedy*, 28. The Israelites later constructed a memorial on the largest mass grave and inscribed the stone markers with five scriptures: John 11:25, Revelation 7:15–17, Revelation 14:12–13, Revelation 12:17, and Psalms 83:3–4. The latter two speak directly to the massacre. Revelation 12:17: "And the dragon was wroth [angry] with the woman, and went off to make war with the remnant of her seed, which keep the commandments of God, and have the testimony of Jesus Christ." Psalms 83:3–4: "They have said, Come, and let us cut them off from being a nation, that the name of Israel may be no more in remembrance." I have used the King James version for these scriptures.

120. Because of space limitations at the Queenstown hospital more than one hundred of the Israelite wounded were taken around 10 June for treatment by train to the Roberts Heights military hospital in Wynberg, Cape Town. "List of Wounded Israelites," South African Police Archives, Pretoria.

121. John Andrew, "The Warrior Who Survived at the Last Stand of the Israelites," *Sunday Times*, 26 July 1992.

122. *QDR*, 26 May 1921.

123. Saul Dubow, "South Africa and South Africans: Nationality, Belonging, Citizenship," in Robert Ross, Anne Kelk Mager, and Bill Nasson, eds., *Cambridge History of South Africa* (New York: Cambridge University Press, 2011), 2:45.

124. James C. Scott, *Domination and the Arts of Resistance: Hidden Transcripts* (New Haven, CT: Yale University Press, 1990).

125. Ibid., 2.

126. Ibid., xii.

127. Ibid., 4.

128. Ibid., 8.

129. Evidence of G. Nightingale, prep. exam.

130. Ibid.

131. Catherine Wessinger, *How the Millennium Comes Violently: From Jonestown to Heaven's Gate* (New York: Seven Bridges, 2000), xii. See also her edited volume, *Millennialism, Persecution, and Violence: Historical Cases* (Syracuse, NY: Syracuse University Press, 2000).

132. Trew, "When the 'Israelites' Rebelled," 332.

5. The Bulhoek Aftermath

1. The heading of this section comes from a letter to the *Cape Times* (4 July 1921) by S. B. Napi-Nfihlela, in which he commented that many Africans were "dead shocked" at the massacre. For coverage of additional newspaper commentary on the Bulhoek massacre, see Frederick Hale, "Fear and Support of an African Independent Church: Reactions to the Bulhoek Massacre of 1921," *Fides et Historia Journal of the Conference on Faith and History* 26, no. 1 (1994): 68–84.

2. *Imvo Zabantsundu,* 31 May 1921.

3. *Umteteli,* 4 June 1921.

4. *Umteteli,* 11 June 1921.

5. *QDR,* 1 June 1921.

6. *Abantu Batho,* 23 June 1921.

7. *Abantu Batho,* 2 June 1921.

8. *Abantu Batho,* 9 June 1921; *QDR,* 27 May 1921.

9. *Ilanga lase Natal,* 3 June 1921.

10. *Abantu Batho,* 2 June 1921.

11. *Abantu Batho,* 23 June 1921.

12. *Cape Argus,* 27 May 1921.

13. *Cape Times,* 21 and 23 July 1921.

14. *QDR,* 1 and 8 June 1921; *Cape Argus,* 6 June 1921; *Abantu Batho* 30 June 1921.

15. *Chicago Defender,* 4 June 1921.

16. I thank Robert Vinson for informing me about this piece.

17. Editorial, "Negro Martyrs," *Negro World,* 7 January 1922. This belief that Mgijima visited America remains current among some members of the American Church of God and Saints of Christ.

18. In Russia news of the massacre reportedly caused much anxiety among Jews, who believed the killing of the "Israelites" was part of a pogrom. *QDR,* 1 September 1921.

19. *QDR,* 5 December 1921.

20. *Het Westen,* 25 May 1921.

21. *Cape Times,* 30 June 1921.

22. S. C. Cronwright, letter to *Cape Times,* 30 June 1921.

23. *Cape,* 27 May 1921.

24. *Cape,* 7 June 1921.

25. *Cape,* 3 June 1921.

26. *Southern Cross,* quoted in *Ilanga lase Natal,* 1 July 1921.

27. Deputy Commissioner of Police to Colonel Truter, 15 June 1921, South African Police Archive, Pretoria.

28. *Cape Argus,* 7 June 1921.

29. Some insight into what was included in the film footage comes from photographs from Africa Film Productions that appeared in *South African Pictorial,* 4 June 1921, 10.

30. Office of Commissioner of Police, Pretoria, to Secretary for Justice, Cape Town, 4 June 1921, South African Police Archive. The government had to move quickly because the film was due to be shown at a Queenstown cinema on 7 and 8 June and a negative had been sent to England. The latter was returned. As a result of the decision to ban the film, the government compensated the film company £211 for the costs of production. On the controversy of the showing of the newsreel of the Jack Johnson–Jim Jeffries fight, see Vinson, *The Americans Are Coming,* 24–27.

31. A. Weisbecker, for Provincial Secretary, Cape Town, 1 June 1921, to Secretary, Board of Film Inspectors, Cape Town, NTS 7659 9/332; General Manager, African Film Productions, to Colonel Truter, South African Police, Pretoria, 6 June 1921; Office of Commissioner of Police, Pretoria, to Secretary for Justice, Cape Town, 4 June 1921; R. Barlow Coulthard, African Film Productions, Johannesburg, to Col. G. D. Gray, Office of the Commissioner, Bulhoek file, South African Police Archive, Pretoria; *Cape Times,* 7 June 1921.

32. *Abantu Batho,* 23 June 1921.

33. Millin, *General Smuts,* 328; *Cape Times,* 26 May 1921.

34. Roy Campbell, *Adamastor* (London: Faber and Faber, 1930).

35. Roy Campbell, *The Wayzgoose: A South African Satire* (London: Jonathan Cape, 1928), 12.

36. *Cape Times,* 24 June 1921.

37. See the speeches of Arthur Barlow, J. M. Mushet, and J. B. M. Hertzog on 15, 23, and 24 June 1921, *Debates of the House of Assembly.*

38. J. B. M. Hertzog, *Debates of the House of Assembly,* 24 June 1921.

39. Ibid.

40. F. S. Malan, *Debates of the House of Assembly,* 24 June 1921.

41. *Cape Times,* 8 September 1921.

42. *Daily Dispatch,* 15 October 1921; Wilfrid Harrison, *Memoirs of a Socialist in South Africa, 1903–1947* (Cape Town: W. H. Harrison, 1947).

43. *Daily Dispatch,* 26 October 1921; *QDR,* 25 October 1921. Judge Graham dismissed the case against John Nkelenjane, who had not responded to a subpoena in the case against Mattushek. Graham accepted the explanation that Nkelenjane had been injured in the Mattushek fracas and was unable to find transport to attend the court session.

44. *QDR,* 2 June 1922.

45. One of those who contributed a token donation to the ICU Bulhoek Tragedy Fund was General Hertzog, who for a brief period courted the support of the ICU leader, Clements Kadalie. Clements Kadalie, *My Life and the ICU* (London: Frank Cass, 1970).

46. At an 8 January meeting of Queenstown area whites Halse had informed the crowd that he had represented the Israelites until 2 October 1920, but after that he had advised the government that if it showed any leniency toward the Israelites, the prestige of whites would be diminished. *QDR,* 10 January 1921. However, after the Israelite trial, Queenstown whites showed their resentment of Halse representing the Israelites at all, and at their trial some even thought he was the deus ex machina behind the Israelites. The white community ostracized him, and eventually he left the Queenstown area.

47. Bisset Berry to John X. Merriman, 30 Nov. 1921, Merriman Papers.

48. *QDR,* 21 November, 1921.

49. *QDR,* 1 September 1921.

50. *QDR,* 22 November 1921.

51. Ibid.

52. Ibid.

53. Ibid.

54. Ibid.

55. *Daily Dispatch,* 6 December 1921.

56. *QDR,* 1–3 December 1921.

57. Ibid.

58. E. Barrett, Secretary for Native Affairs, to Sec. for Justice, 3 September 1921, Bantu Affairs Department 6645 29/331.

59. George Brebney, Smuts's secretary, to P. A. Brown, chairman, South Africa Party, Queenstown district; *QDR,* 10 January 1921.

60. *QDR,* 5 December 1921.

61. *QDR,* 6 December 1921.

62. *Daily Dispatch,* 6 December 1921.

63. *QDR,* 26 January 1922; *Daily Dispatch,* 6 December 1921.

64. *QDR,* 19 January and 27 September 1923; Director of Prisons to Secretary for Native Affairs, 31 March 1924, JD 288 2/853/20. Before he died, Charles reportedly was heard praying, "Lord, if it be your will to do something to my family, do it to me. Send this one [Enoch] to go back and put things right."

65. This was a variation on the custom of *ukungena,* or levirate, that provided for cases where a man died before his wife gave birth to an heir. A younger brother then could enter into a union with his wife to produce children who would be accepted as the children of the dead husband.

66. Dora Tamana, "A Short Story of Enoch Mgijima."

67. *QDR,* 5 March 1929.

68. Gideon Ntloko, *Prophecies and Sayings by Prophet Enoch J. Mgijima* (c. 2006).

69. *Report of the Native Churches Commission.* See Joel Cabrita's analysis of the commission in *Text and Authority in the South African Nazaretha Church* (Cambridge: Cambridge University Press, International African Library, 2014), 301–4.

70. *Daily Dispatch,* 17 October 1922.

71. *Blythswood Review* 2, no. 13 (1925): 3.

72. *South African Police Annual Report,* 1922, U.G. 9—1924.

73. Maj. W. E. Earle, Office of the Deputy-Commissioner, Pietermaritzburg, to Secretary, South African Police, Pretoria, 20 September 1921, JD 334 4/567/21.

74. Elizabeth Gunner, *The Man of Heaven and the Beautiful Ones of God: Writings from Ibandla lama Shembe Nazaretha, a South African Church* (Leiden: Brill, 2002): 23–24.

75. Ibid., 37.

76. Surprisingly there are few scholarly examinations of the history of Lekganyane's church. One of the few is Elias Lukhaimane, "The Zion Christian Church of Ignatius (Engenas) Lekganyane, 1924–1948: An African Experiment with Christianity" (master's thesis, University of the North, 1980).

77. The story of Nontetha Nkwenkwe is recounted in Robert Edgar and Hilary Sapire, *African Apocalypse: The Story of Nontetha Nkwenkwe, a South African Prophetess* (Athens: Ohio University Press, 2000).

78. Clement Gladwin to Maj. T. Hutchons, King William's Town, 25 April 1923, JD 268 2/950/19.

79. "Communism in the Union of South Africa," 7 June 1923, JD 289 3/1064/18, part 3.

80. Edgar and Sapire, *African Apocalypse,* 86–89.

81. Much of the material presented in this section comes from my article "Garveyism in Africa: Dr. Wellington and the American Movement in the Transkei," *Ufahamu* 6, no. 3 (1976): 31–56. Since it appeared, major works have appeared on Garveyism in South Africa and Wellington Butelezi and the American movement. See Robert Hill and Greg Pirio, "Africa for the Africans: The Garvey Movement in South Africa, 1920–1940," in Shula Marks and Stanley Trapido, eds., *The Politics of Race, Class and Nationalism in Twentieth-Century South Africa* (New York: Longman, 1987), 209–53; Helen Bradford, *A Taste of Freedom: The ICU in Rural South Africa, 1924–1930* (New Haven, CT: Yale University Press, 1987), 213–40; Sean Redding, *Sorcery and Sovereignty: Taxation,*

Power, and Rebellion in South Africa, 1880–1963 (Athens: Ohio University Press, 2006), 133–46; and Vinson, *The Americans Are Coming*.

82. Chief Native Commissioner, 348 1919/271 and 348 1929/1, NASA, Pietermaritzburg.

83. File 348 1919/271, NASA, Pietermaritzburg; Sworn affidavit of B. H. Wellington, Rex v. Wellington, 224/1926, NASA, Cape Town.

84. On Thaele, see Vinson, *The Americans Are Coming*, 94–102.

85. Vinson, *The Americans Are Coming*, 13–33.

86. Smith, *Aggrey of Africa*, 180–81.

87. Government officials stated that Butelezi also used such aliases as Pontier Hansford Wellington, Wellington Kalinda, and Wellington Kampara.

88. Edgar, "Garveyism in Africa," 39.

89. Letter, F. J. Rumsey, 21 March 1927, *Cowley Evangelist*, June 1927, 143. In 1930 a plane making an emergency landing at Ravenscroft, Tabankulu, in the Transkei soon attracted a crowd of several hundred people chanting "*Amelika, Amelika* [the Americans, the Americans]."

90. Robert Edgar, "African Educational Protest in South Africa: The American School Movement in the Transkei in the 1920's," in Peter Kallaway, ed., *Apartheid and Education* (Johannesburg: Ravan, 1984), 184–91.

91. Bradford, *Taste of Freedom*, 219.

92. Redding, *Sorcery and Sovereignty*, 141.

93. *Matatiele Mail*, 29 March 1927.

94. *Negro World*, 30 July 1927.

95. William Beinart and Colin Bundy, *Hidden Struggles in Rural South Africa: Politics and Popular Movements in the Transkei and Eastern Cape, 1890–1930* (Berkeley: University of California Press, 1987), 251–55.

96. Paul Gulwa, interview by author, Tsolo, July 1974; Tamana, interview; Ndiki, interview.

97. Jongile Peter, interview by author, Ndwindwa location, 1 June 1974.

98. *Round Table* 11, no. 44 (September 1921): 950.

99. Manfred Nathan, *South Africa from Within* (London: John Murray, 1926), 176.

100. James Rose Innes, *Autobiography* (London: Oxford University Press, 1949), 283.

101. *Die Burger*, 30 May 1921. On Slagter's Nek, see Leonard Thompson, *The Political Mythology of Apartheid* (New Haven, CT: Yale University Press, 1985).

102. Vuyani Leonard Mqingwana, "The Israelite Movement and the Bulhoek Episode" (master's thesis, Northwestern University, 1976), 84.

103. Nelson Mandela, *Nelson Mandela Speaks: Speeches, Statements and Articles by Nelson Mandela* (London: Publicity and Information Bureau, African National Congress, c. 1970), 42. See also Mandela, *Long Walk to Freedom* (New York: Little, Brown, 1994), 294.

104. Edward Roux, *Time Longer Than Rope: A History of the Black Man's Struggle for Freedom in South Africa* (Madison: University of Wisconsin Press, 1964), 135. Roux's work was a guidebook for me as I was led to researches on Edwin Mofutsanyana and the Communist Party of South Africa and Lekhotla la Bafo, an anticolonial political movement in Lesotho.

105. Lionel Forman, "The Bullhoek Massacre," *New Age* 19 (October 1961), 5.

106. Sabine Marschall, *Landscape of Memory: Commemorative Monuments, Memorials and Public Statuary in Post-Apartheid South-Africa* (Boston: Brill, 2010); Annie Coombes, *History after Apartheid: Visual Culture and Public Memory in a Democratic South Africa* (Durham, NC: Duke University Press, 2003).

107. A table listing post-apartheid memorials is found in Marschall, *Landscape of Memory*, 387–89. The most comprehensive treatment of resistance heritage sites is Gregory Houston et al., *The Liberation Struggle and Liberation Heritage Sites in South Africa* (Pretoria: Human Sciences Research Council, 2013).

108. To commemorate its one hundredth anniversary the *Sunday Times* initiated a Heritage Project in 2006–7, in which it commissioned several art works to remember several dozen individuals and events at sites around the country. The newspaper commissioned a statue that was placed at the main Israelite Tabernacle in the Queenstown location. Because of splits among the Israelites, the statue was defaced, and barbed wire had to be placed around it to protect it.

109. This and subsequent quotations from speeches at the ceremony are from the program of the eightieth anniversary of the Bulhoek massacre, 24 May 2001 (copy in possession of author).

110. Ibid.

111. Ibid.

112. Ibid.

113. *Daily Dispatch*, 1 February 2016.

114. Sam Matiase, "The Significance of the Bulhoek Massacre Today," Politicsweb, http://www.politicsweb.co.za/news-and-analysis/the-significance-of-the-bulhoek-massacre-today.

115. Ibid.

6. The Lost Ark

1. Several edited collections treat the challenges other social scientists have dealt with in their field research. See Carolyn Adenaike and Jan Vansina, eds., *In Pursuit of History: Fieldwork in Africa* (Portsmouth, NH: Heinemann, 1996); and Susan Thompson, An Ansoms, and Jude Murison, eds., *Emotional and Ethical Challenges for Field Research in Africa* (New York: Palgrave Macmillan, 2013).

2. Permit under 24 (1) of Act No. 18 of 1936. Original in possession of author.

3. An African police detective at Shiloh mission station kept tabs on my movements. The political climate in May and June 1974 also complicated my

interviewing. The Portuguese military coup on 25 April 1974 had overthrown the Salazar regime, and many black South Africans began anticipating that the independence of Angola and Mozambique could be a harbinger of major change in their own country. The expectations for change were great, but for some blacks who held positions in the apartheid system, it increased their suspicions of strangers. For instance, several Transkei headmen expressed their concern to me that I might be a scout for one of the liberation movements.

4. When I was invited to talk about my research at Federal Theological Seminary, I received a grilling from the audience. I later learned that in the audience was the executive committee of the South African Student Organization that had been meeting at the seminary.

5. Enoch Mgijima to Magistrate, Queenstown, 29 January 1925, South African Police Archive, Pretoria.

6. Denver Webb and Wouter Holleman, "Sins of the Father: Cultural Restitution and the Bulhoek Massacre," *South African Museums Association Bulletin* 23, no. 1 (1997): 16–19.

7. W. C. Nienaber and M. Steyn, "Archaeology in the Service of the Community: Repatriation of the Remains of Nontetha Bungu," *South African Archaeological Bulletin* 57, no. 156 (2002): 80–84. The Eastern Cape Heritage Office has called on these archaeologists on other occasions to exhume the remains of political prisoners who had been executed by the government and buried in Pretoria cemeteries and return them to their homes.

Bibliography

Principle Archives Consulted

Cory Library, Rhodes University
    Abantu Batho file on Bulhoek massacre
    Diary of D. D. Stormont
Defence Archives, Pretoria
Maryland State Archives, Annapolis, Maryland
Moravian Archives, Mvenyane
National Library of South Africa, Cape Town
    J. X. Merriman Papers
South African National Archives
    Cape Town
        Chief Magistrate Records, Transkei
        John Ayliff Diary
        Native Affairs Department
    Pretoria
        Office of Governor General
        Government Native Labour Bureau
        Jan Smuts Papers
        Justice Department
        Department of Native Affairs
        Office of Prime Minister
South African Police Archives, Pretoria
Surveyor General's Office, Cape Town
United States National Archives
University of Cape Town, Manuscripts Division
    Bulhoek Massacre Miscellany
    Jack and Ray Simons Papers

Cape Colony Publications

List of Persons Residing in the Electoral Division of Queenstown in the Year 1903.
   Cape Town: Cape Times Government Printers, 1903.
Petition of Residents of the Kamastone and Oxkraal Locations to Honourable
   Speaker of the House of Assembly of Cape of Good Hope signed by Joshua
   and 441 others (A. 11—1879).
*Reports and Proceedings with Appendices of the Government Commission on Native
   Laws and Customs* (G. 4—1883). Cape Town: W. A. Richards and Sons.
Report of the Surveyor-General 1877 (G. 38—1878).
South African Native Affairs Commission. *Report of the Commission with Annex-
   ures and Appendices, 1903–1905.*

Union Government Publications

*Interim and Final Reports of the Native Affairs Commission and Telegram from Com-
   mission on South African Police, Relative to "Israelites" at Bulhoek Occurrences
   in May, 1921* (A. 4—1921).
Report of the Native Affairs Department for the Years 1919 to 1921 (U.G. 34—
   1922).
Report of the Native Affairs Department for the Year 1921 (U.G. 15—1922).
Report of the Native Affairs Department for the Years 1922 to 1926 (U.G. 14—1927).
Report of the Native Churches Commission (U.G. 39—1925).
Report of the Natives Land Commission, vol. 2 (U.G. 22—1916).
Report of the Natives Land Committee, Cape Province (U.G. 8—1918).
Report of the Native Locations Survey (U.G. 42—1922).

Books and Articles

Adenaike, Carolyn, and Jan Vansina, eds. *In Pursuit of History: Fieldwork in Af-
   rica.* Portsmouth, NH: Heinemann, 1996.
Akenson, Donald. *God's People: Covenant and Land in South Africa, Israel, and
   Ulster.* Ithaca, NY: Cornell University Press, 1992.
Alexander, James. *Narrative of a Voyage of Observation among the Colonies of
   Western Africa in the Thalia, and of a Campaign in Kaffirland on the Staff of the
   Commander-in-Chief.* Vol. 2. London: Henry Colburn, 1837.
Ashforth, Adam. *The Politics of Official Discourse in Twentieth-Century South Af-
   rica.* Oxford: Clarendon, 1990.
Ayliff, John. *Memorials of the British Settlers of South Africa.* Grahamstown: R.
   Godlonton, 1845.
Ayliff, John, and Joseph Whiteside. *History of the Abambo: Generally Known as
   the Fingos.* Butterworth: Gazette, 1912.

Bailey, Randall, ed. *Yet with a Steady Beat: Contemporary U.S. Afrocentric Biblical Interpretation*. Atlanta: Society of Biblical Literature, 2003.

Baines, Gary. "South Africa's Amritsar? Responsibility for and Significance of the Port Elizabeth Shootings of 23 October 1920." *Contree* 34 (November 1993): 1–10.

Balia, Daryl. *Black Methodists and White Supremacy*. Durban: Madiba, 1991.

———. "Bridge over Troubled Waters: Charles Pamla and the Taylor Revival in South Africa." *Methodist History* 30, no. 2 (1992): 78–90.

Bank, Leslie, and Benedict Carton. "Forgetting Apartheid: History, Culture and the Body of a Nun." *Africa* 86, no. 3 (2016): 472–503.

Barkun, Michael. "Law and Social Revolution: Millenarianism and the Legal System." *Law and Society Review* 6 (1971): 113–41.

Beinart, William, and Colin Bundy. *Hidden Struggles in Rural South Africa: Politics and Popular Movements in the Transkei And Eastern Cape, 1890–1930*. Berkeley: University of California Press, 1987.

Bouch, Richard. "Farming, Capitalization and Labour in a Newly Colonized Area: Queenstown, 1852–1886." Paper presented at Cape Slavery and After Conference, 1989.

Bourquin, Walther. *Bruder Mensch: 41 Jahre Herrnhuter Mission in Sudafrika*. Hamburg: Appel, 1967.

———. "Irrungen und Wirrrungen in Silo." *Missionsblatt der Brudergemeine* 77, no. 4 (April 1913): 73–80.

Bozzoli, Belinda, ed. *Class, Community and Conflict: South African Perspectives*. Johannesburg: Ravan, 1987.

Bradford, Helen. *A Taste of Freedom: The ICU in Rural South Africa, 1924–1930*. New Haven, CT: Yale University Press, 1987.

Bradford, Tolly. *Prophetic Identities: Indigenous Missionaries on British Colonial Frontiers, 1850–75*. Vancouver: UBC Press, 2012.

Braun, Lindsay. "The Cadastre and the Colony: Surveying, Territory and Legibility in the Creation of South Africa, c. 1860–1913." Ph.D. diss., Rutgers University, 2008.

Bredekamp, Henry. "The Dead Bones of Adam Kok." In Annari van der Merwe and Paul Faber, eds., *Group Portrait South Africa: Nine Family Histories*, 132–55. Cape Town: Kwela Books, 2003.

Bridgman, Frederick. "The Ethiopian Movements in South Africa." *Missionary Review of the World* 26, no. 6 (June 1904): 934–45.

Brinton, Lt. E. J. "A Reminiscence of the Bulhoek Affair." *Nongqai*, 13, no. 7 (1922): 389–90.

Brock, Peggy. "New Christians as Evangelists." In Norman Etherington, ed., *Missions and Empire*, 132–52. Oxford: Oxford University Press, 2005.

Brown, Jesse E. "Prophet William Saunders Crowdy and the Church of God and Saints of Christ: The Implications of His Life and Thought for the

Mission of the Church." Ph.D. diss., Colgate Rochester Divinity School, 1986.

Bruder, Edith. *The Black Jews of Africa: History, Religion, Identity.* Oxford: Oxford University Press, 2011.

The Bullhoek Tragedy: The Full Story of the Israelite Settlement at Ntabelanga. East London: East London Daily Dispatch, 1921.

Bundy, Colin. *The Rise and Fall of the South African Peasantry.* Berkeley: University of California Press, 1979.

Burridge, Kenelm. *New Heaven, New Earth: A Study of Millenarian Activities.* Oxford: Blackwell, 1969.

Cabrita, Joel. *Text and Authority in the South African Nazaretha Church.* Cambridge: Cambridge University Press, International African Library, 2014.

Callahan, Allen. *The Talking Book: African Americans and the Bible.* New Haven, CT: Yale University Press, 2006.

Calhoun, Stephen. *The Marylanders without Shelter or a Crumb: A Saga of the Fascist Repression of a Family during the American Civil War,* rev. ed. Westminster, MD: Heritage Books, 2007.

Campbell, James. *Songs of Zion: The African Methodist Episcopal Church in the United States and South Africa.* New York: Oxford University Press, 1995.

Campbell, Roy. *Adamastor.* London: Faber and Faber, 1930.

———. *The Wayzgoose: A South African Satire.* London: Jonathan Cape, 1928.

Carton, Ben. "The Forgotten Compass of Death: Apocalypse Then and Now in the Social History of South Africa." *Journal of Social History* 37 (Fall 2003): 200–18.

Casalis, Eugene. *The Basutos, or Twenty-Three Years in South Africa.* Morija: Morija Museum and Archives, 1992.

Cavanagh, Edward. *The Griqua Past and Present and the Limits of South African History, 1902–1994.* New York: Peter Lang, 2011.

Chireau, Yvonne, and Nathaniel Deutsch, eds. *Black Zion: African American Religious Encounters with Judaism.* New York: Oxford University Press, 2000.

Clark, Elmer. *Small Sects in America.* Nashville: Cokesbury, 1937.

Cohn, Norman. *Cosmos, Chaos and the World to Come: The Ancient Roots of Apocalyptic Faith.* New Haven, CT: Yale University Press, 1993.

———. *The Pursuit of the Millennium: Revolutionary Messianism in Medieval and Reformation Europe and Its Bearing on Modern Totalitarian Movements.* Fairlawn, NJ: Essential Books, 1957.

Collins, S. F. "A Peculiar Religious Sect of Colored People Their Prophet, William S. Crowdy, Styled by Many as the 'Black Dowie.'" *Colored American* 9, no. 1 (December 1905): 691–94.

Coombes, Annie. *History after Apartheid: Visual Culture and Public Memory in a Democratic South Africa.* Durham, NC: Duke University Press, 2003.

Crais, Clifton. *The Politics of Evil: Magic, State Power and the Political Imagination in South Africa.* Cambridge: Cambridge University Press, 2002.

———. *Poverty, War, and Violence in South Africa.* Cambridge: Cambridge University Press, 2011.

Crais, Clifton, and Thomas McClendon. *The South Africa Reader: History, Culture, Politics.* Durham, NC: Duke University Press, 2014.

Crawford, George. *Prince Hall and His Followers.* New York: AMS, 1971.

Davis, Hunt. "John L. Dube: A South African Exponent of Booker T. Washington." *Journal of African Studies* 1, no. 2 (1975): 497–528.

Docherty, Jayne. *Learning Lessons from Waco: When the Parties Bring Their Gods to the Negotiation Table.* Syracuse, NY: Syracuse University Press, 2001.

Dubow, Saul. *Racial Segregation and the Origins of Apartheid in South Africa.* Houndmills: Macmillan, 1989.

———. "South Africa and South Africans: Nationality, Belonging, Citizenship." In Robert Ross, Anne Kelk Mager and Bill Nasson, eds., *Cambridge History of South Africa,* 2:17–65. New York: Cambridge University Press, 2011.

Du Plessis, J. "The Native Situation in South Africa: A Missionary Point of View." *Missionary Review of the World* 30 (December 1907): 919–26.

Edgar, Robert. "African Educational Protest in South Africa: The American School Movement in the Transkei in the 1920's." In Peter Kallaway, ed., *Apartheid and Education,* 184–91. Johannesburg: Ravan, 1984.

———. "The Fifth Seal: Enoch Mgijima, the Israelites and the Bulhoek Massacre." Ph.D. diss., University of California, Los Angeles, 1977.

———. "Garveyism in Africa: Dr. Wellington and the American Movement in the Transkei." *Ufahamu* 6, no. 3 (1976): 31–56.

Edgar, Robert, and Hilary Sapire. *African Apocalypse: The Story of Nontetha Nkwenkwe, a South African Prophetess.* Athens: Ohio University Press, 2000.

Edgar, Robert, and Christopher Saunders. "A. A. S. Le Fleur and the Griqua Trek of 1917: Segregation, Self-Help, and Ethnic Identity." *International Journal of African Historical Studies* 15, no. 2 (1982): 201–20.

Elphick, Richard. *The Equality of Believers: Protestant Missionaries and the Racial Politics of South Africa.* Charlottesville: University of Virginia Press, 2012.

Elphick, Richard, and Rodney Davenport, eds. *Christianity in South Africa: A Political, Social and Cultural History.* Berkeley: University of California Press, 1997.

Etherington, Norman. *The Great Treks: The Transformation of Southern Africa, 1815–1854.* London: Longman, 2001.

———. *Preachers, Peasants, and Politics in Southeast Africa.* London: Royal Historical Society, 1978.

Fast, Hildegarde. "African Perceptions of the Missionaries and Their Message: Wesleyans at Mount Coke and Butterworth, 1825–35." Master's thesis, University of Cape Town, 1991.

———. "'In at One Ear and Out at the Other': African Response to the Wesleyan Message in Xhosaland 1825–1835." *Journal of Religion in Africa* 23, no. 2 (1993): 147–74.

Fields, Barbara. *Slavery and Freedom on the Middle Ground: Maryland during the Nineteenth Century.* New Haven, CT: Yale University Press, 1985.

Fields, Karen. *Revival and Rebellion in Colonial Central Africa.* Princeton, NJ: Princeton University Press, 1985.

Finkelstein, Israel, and Neil Silberman. *The Bible Unearthed: Archaeology's New Vision of Ancient Israel and the Origin of Its Sacred Texts.* New York: Free Press, 2001.

Forman, Lionel. "The Bullhoek Massacre." *New Age* 19 (October 1961): 5.

Frankel, Philip. *An Ordinary Atrocity: Sharpeville and Its Massacre.* New Haven, CT: Yale University Press, 2001.

Freeman, Charles. *A New History of Early Christianity.* New Haven, CT: Yale University Press, 2011.

Fry, Poppy. "Allies and Liabilities: Fingo Identity and British Imperialism in South Africa's Eastern Cape, 1800–1935." Ph.D. diss., Harvard University, 2007.

Garson, Noel. "The Cape Franchise in Action: The Queenstown By-Election of December 1921." History workshop paper, Witwatersrand University, 1984.

Glaude, Eddie. *Exodus! Religion, Race, and Nation in Early Nineteenth-Century Black America.* Chicago: University of Chicago Press, 2000.

Gordon, David M. *Invisible Agents: Spirits in a Central African History.* Athens: Ohio University Press, 2012.

Gordon, Ruth E. *Shepstone: The Role of the Family in the History of South Africa, 1820–1900.* Cape Town: A. A. Balkema, 1968.

Green, Emma. "Native Unrest in South Africa." *Nineteenth Century* 46, no. 273 (November 1899): 708–716.

Grimshaw, William. *Official History of Freemasonry among the Colored People in North America.* New York: Negro Universities Press, 1969.

Gunner, Elizabeth. *The Men of Heaven and the Beautiful Ones of God: Writings from Ibandla lama Shembe Nazaretha, a South African Church.* Leiden: Brill, 2002.

Hale, Frederick. "Fear and Support of an African Independent Church: Reactions to the Bulhoek Massacre of 1921." *Fides et Historia Journal of the Conference on Faith and History* 26, no. 1 (1994): 68–84.

Hamilton, Carolyn, ed. *The Mfecane Aftermath: Reconstructive Debates in Southern African History.* Johannesburg: Witwatersrand University Press, 1995.

Hamilton, Carolyn, V. Harris, M. Pickover, R. Reid, and J. Taylor, eds. *Refiguring the Archive.* Boston: Kluwer Academic, 2002.

Hamilton, J. Taylor, and Kenneth Hamilton. *History of the Moravian Church: The Renewed Unitas Fratrum, 1722–1957.* Bethlehem, PA: Interprovincial Board of Christian Education, Moravian Church in America, 1967.

Hancock, W. K. *Smuts: The Fields of Force, 1919–1950.* Vol. 2. Cambridge: Cambridge University Press, 1968.

Harrison, Barbara. *Visions of Glory.* New York: Simon and Schuster, 1978.

Harrison, Wilfrid. *Memoirs of a Socialist in South Africa, 1903–1947.* Cape Town: W. H. Harrison, 1947.

Hill, Robert, and Greg Pirio. "Africa for the Africans: The Garvey Movement in South Africa, 1920–1940." In Shula Marks and Stanley Trapido, eds., *The Politics of Race, Class, and Nationalism in Twentieth-Century South Africa,* 209–53. New York: Longman, 1987.

Hinks, Peter P., and Stephen Kantrowitz. "Introduction: the Revolution in Freemasonry." In Hinks and Kantrowitz, eds., *All Men Free and Brethren: Essays on the History of African American Freemasonry,* 1–20. Ithaca, NY: Cornell University Press, 2013.

Hinks, Peter P., and Stephen Kantrowitz, eds. *All Men Free and Brethren: Essays on the History of African American Freemasonry.* Ithaca, NY: Cornell University Press, 2013.

Hodgson, Janet. "The Battle for Sacred Power: Christian Beginnings among the Xhosa." In Richard Elphick and Rodney Davenport, eds., *Christianity in South Africa: A Political, Social and Cultural History,* 66–88. Berkeley: University of California Press, 1997.

———. *Ntsikana's Great Hymn: A Xhosa Expression of Christianity in the Early 19th Century Eastern Cape.* Cape Town: Centre for African Studies, University of Cape Town, 1980.

Houston, Gregory, Mojalefa Dipholo, Hangwelani Magidimisha, Shepi Mati and Elme Vivier. *The Liberation Struggle and Liberation Heritage Sites in South Africa* Pretoria: Human Sciences Research Council, 2013.

Innes, James Rose. *Autobiography.* London: Oxford University Press, 1949.

Jabavu, D. D. T. "The 'Fingo Slavery' Myth." *South African Outlook* (1 June 1935): 123–24, 134–35, 195–96.

———. "Lessons from the Israelite Episode." *South African Outlook* (1 July 1921): 106.

Jones, Roderick. "Black Problem in South Africa." *Nineteenth Century and After* 57 (May 1905): 760–76.

Kadalie, Clements. *My Life and the ICU.* London: Frank Cass, 1970.

Karis, Thomas, and Gwendolen Carter. *From Protest to Challenge: A Documentary History of African Politics in South Africa, 1882–1964.* Stanford, CA: Hoover Institution Press, 1972.

Kawa, Richard. *Ibali lamaMfengu.* Lovedale: Lovedale, 1929.

Kelly, Robin. *Freedom Dreams: The Black Radical Imagination.* Boston: Beacon, 2002.

Kingon, John. "The Economics of the East Coast Fever as Illustrated by the Transkeian Territories." *South African Journal of Science* 13 (1915): 213–28.

Kirk-Duggan, Cheryl. "Let My People Go! Threads of Exodus in African American Narratives." In Randall Bailey, ed., *Yet with a Steady Beat: Contemporary U.S. Afrocentric Biblical Interpretation,* 123–44. Atlanta: Society of Biblical Literature, 2003.

Krüger, Bernhard. *The Pear Tree Blossoms: A History of the Moravian Mission Stations in South Africa, 1737–1869.* Genadendal: Genadendal Printing Works, 1967.

Krüger, Bernhard, and P. W. Schaberg. *The Pear Tree Bears Fruit: The History of the Moravian Church in South Africa West (II), 1869–1960.* Genadendal: Moravian Book Depot, 1984.

Landau, Paul. *Popular Politics in the History of South Africa, 1400–1948.* New York: Cambridge University Press, 2010.

Landes, Richard. *Heaven on Earth: The Varieties of the Millennial Experience.* New York: Oxford University Press, 2011.

Lanternari, Vittorio. *Religions of the Oppressed: A Study of Modern Messianic Cults.* London: MacGibbon and Kee, 1973.

Lea, Allen. *The Native Separatist Church Movement in South Africa.* Cape Town: Juta, 1926.

Linden, Jane, and Ian Linden. "John Chilembwe and the New Jerusalem." *Journal of African History* 12, no. 4 (1971): 629–51.

Lodge, Tom. *Sharpeville: An Apartheid Massacre and Its Consequences.* Oxford: Oxford University Press, 2011.

Lukhaimane, Elias. "The Zion Christian Church of Ignatius (Engenas) Lekganyane, 1924–1948: An African Experiment with Christianity." Master's thesis, University of the North, 1980.

Maclennan, Ben. *Proper Degree of Terror: John Graham and the Cape's Eastern Frontier.* Johannesburg: Ravan, 1986.

Makobe, D. H. "The Price of Fanaticism: The Casualties of the Bulhoek Massacre." *Militaria* 26, no. 1 (1996): 38–41.

Mandela, Nelson. *Long Walk to Freedom.* New York: Little, Brown, 1994.

———. *Nelson Mandela Speaks: Speeches, Statements and Articles by Nelson Mandela.* London: Publicity and Information Bureau, 1970.

Mandew, Martin. "War, Memory and Salvation: The Bulhoek Massacre and the Construction of a Contextual Soterioloy." Ph.D. diss., University of Natal, Pietermaritzburg, 1996.

Marschall, Sabine. *Landscape of Memory: Commemoration Monuments, Memorials and Public Statuary in Post-Apartheid South-Africa.* Boston: Brill, 2010.

Marks, Shula, and Stanley Trapido, eds. *The Politics of Race, Class, and Nationalism in Twentieth-Century South Africa.* New York: Longman, 1987.

Masilela, Ntongela. "The Black Atlantic and African Modernity in South Africa." *Research in African Literature* 27, no. 4 (Winter 1997): 88–95.

Mazwi, W. S. *A History of the Moravian Church in Southeast Africa in Outline.* Morija, 1938.

Mears, Gordon. "Charles Pamla." *Methodist Missionaries,* no. 2. Rondebosch: Methodist Missionary Department, 1959.

Miller, Terry, and Sara Miller. *The Church of God and Saints of Christ in Africa: The First One Hundred Years (1903–2003).* Kent, OH: printed by the authors, 2008.

Millin, Sarah Gertrude. *The Coming of the Lord*. London: Constable, 1928.

———. *General Smuts*. Boston: Little, Brown, 1938.

Mills, Wallace. "The Role of African Clergy in the Reorientation of Xhosa Society to the Plural Society in the Cape Colony, 1850–1915." Ph.D. diss., University of California, Los Angeles, 1975.

Moister, William. *A History of Wesleyan Missions in All Parts of the World from the Commencement to the Present Time*. London: Elliot Stock, 1871.

Moodie, J. W. D. *Ten Years in South Africa: Including a Particular Description of the Wild Sports of That Country*. London: Richard Bentley, 1835.

Mostert, Noel. *Frontiers: The Epic of South Africa's Creation and the Tragedy of the Xhosa*. New York: Knopf, 1992.

Moyer, Richard. "A History of the Mfengu of the Eastern Cape, 1815–1865." Ph.D. diss., University of London, 1976.

———. "The Mfengu, Self-Defence and the Cape Frontier Wars." In Christopher Saunders and Robin Derricourt, eds., *Beyond the Cape Frontier*, 101–26. London: Longman, 1974.

———. "Some Current Manifestations of Early Mfengu History." *Collected Seminar Papers on the Societies of Southern Africa in the 19th and 20th Centuries*. University of London Institute of Commonwealth Studies, 3 (1973): 144–54.

Mqingwana, Leonard Vuyani. "The Israelite Movement and the Bulhoek Episode." Master's thesis, Northwestern University, 1976.

Mqotsi, L., and N. Mkele. "A Separatist Church: Ibandla Lika-Krestu." *African Studies* 5 (1946): 106–25.

Nathan, Manfred. *South Africa from Within*. London: John Murray, 1926.

Neame, Edwin. "Ethiopianism: The Danger of a Black Church." *Empire Review* 10, no. 1 (1905): 256–65.

Newport, Kenneth. *The Branch Davidians of Waco: The History and Beliefs of an Apocalyptic Sect*. Oxford: Oxford University Press, 2006.

Newport, Kenneth, and Crawford Gribben. *Expecting the End: Millennialism in Social and Historical Context*. Waco, TX: Baylor University Press, 2006.

Nicol, Mike. *This Day and Age*. New York: Knopf, 1992.

Nienaber, W. C., and M. Steyn. "Archaeology in the Service of the Community: Repatriation of the Remains of Nontetha Bungu." *South African Archaeological Bulletin* 57, no. 156 (2002): 80–84.

Ntloko, Gideon. *Ngo kubekiesele e bandleni*. Printed by the author, n.d.

———. *Prophecies and Sayings by Prophet Enoch J. Mgijima*. Printed by the author, 2006.

Odendaal, Andre. *The Founders: The Origins of the ANC and the Struggle for Democracy in South Africa*. Auckland Park: Jacana, 2012.

O'Leary, Stephen, and Glen McGhee, eds. *War in Heaven / Heaven on Earth: Theories of the Apocalyptic*. Oakville, CT: Equinox, 2005.

Painter, Nell. *Exodusters: Black Migration to Kansas after Reconstruction.* New York: Knopf, 1977.

Pamla, Charles. *Some Reflections on Native Customs.* Pamphlet. N.p.: n.p., n.d.

Peires, J. B. *The Dead Will Arise: Nongqawuse and the Great Xhosa Cattle-Killing Movement of 1856–7.* Bloomington: Indiana University Press, 1989.

———. *House of Phalo: A History of the Xhosa People in the Days of Their Independence.* Johannesburg: Ravan, 1981.

———. "The Legend of Fenner-Solomon." In Belinda Bozzoli, ed., *Class, Community and Conflict: South African Perspectives,* 65–97. Johannesburg: Ravan, 1987.

Penton, James. *Apocalypse Delayed: The Story of Jehovah's Witnesses.* Toronto: University of Toronto Press, 1997.

Phillips, Howard. *"Black October": The Impact of the Spanish Influenza Epidemic of 1918 on South Africa.* Archives Year Book for South African History. Pretoria: The Government Printer, 1990.

Plaatje, Solomon T. *Native Life in South Africa, before and since the European War and the Boer Rebellion.* 2nd ed. London: P. S. King and Son, 1917.

Raboteau, Albert J. "African Americans, Exodus and the American Israel." In Paul Johnson, ed., *African-American Christianity: Essays in History,* 1–17. Berkeley: University of California Press, 1994.

———. *Fire in the Bones: Reflections on African-American Religious History.* Boston: Beacon, 1995.

Ralston, Richard. "A Second Middle Passage: African Student Sojourns in the United States during the Colonial Period and Their Influences upon the Character of African Leadership." Ph.D. diss., University of California, Los Angeles, 1972.

Ranger, T. O. "Plagues of Beasts and Men: Prophetic Responses to Epidemic in Eastern and Southern Africa." In T. O. Ranger and P. Slack, eds., *Epidemics and Ideas: Essays on the Historical Perception of Pestilence,* 241–68. Cambridge: Cambridge University Press, 1992.

Ranger, T. O., and P. Slack, eds., *Epidemics and Ideas: Essays on the Historical Perception of Pestilence.* Cambridge: Cambridge University Press, 1992.

Redding, Sean. *Sorcery and Sovereignty: Taxation, Power, and Rebellion in South Africa, 1880–1965.* Athens: Ohio University Press, 2006.

Reeves, Ambrose. *Shooting at Sharpeville: The Agony of South Africa.* Boston: Houghton Mifflin, 1961.

Report of the Proceedings of the First General Missionary Conference Held at Johannesburg, 13–20 1904. Johannesburg: Argus, 1905.

Rogerson, Alan. *Millions Now Living Will Never Die.* London: Constable, 1969.

Rosenfeld, Jean. *Island Broken in Two Halves: Land and Renewal Movements among the Maori of New Zealand.* University Park: Pennsylvania State University Press, 1999.

Ross, Robert, Anne Mager, and Bill Nasson, eds. *Cambridge History of South Africa.* 2 vols. New York: Cambridge University Press, 2011.

Roux, Edward. *Time Longer Than Rope: A History of the Black Man's Struggle for Freedom in South Africa.* Madison: University of Wisconsin Press, 1964.

Saunders, Christopher. "Tile and the Thembu Church." *Journal of African History* 11, no. 4 (1970): 553–70.

Saunders, Christopher, and Robin Derricourt, eds. *Beyond the Cape Frontier.* London: Longman, 1974.

Scanlon, Helen. *Representation and Reality: Portraits of Women's Lives in the Western Cape, 1948–1975.* Cape Town: HSRC, 2007.

Schlosser, Katesa. *Eingeborenenkirchen in Sud-und Sudwestafrika: Ihre Geschichte und Socialstruktur.* Kiel: Kommissionverslag W. G. Muhlau, 1958.

Scott, James C. *Domination and the Arts of Resistance: Hidden Transcripts.* New Haven, CT: Yale University Press, 1990.

Shepperson, George, and Thomas Price. *Independent African John Chilembwe and the Origins, Setting and Significance of the Nyasaland Native Rising of 1915.* Edinburgh: Edinburgh University Press, 1958.

Simons, H. J., and R. E. Simons. *Class and Colour in South Africa.* Harmondsworth: Penguin, 1969.

Singer. Merrill. "Symbolic Identity Formation in African American Religious Sects: The Black Hebrew Israelites." In Yvonne Chireau and Nathaniel Deutsch, eds., *Black Zion African American Religious Encounters with Judaism,* 55–72. New York: Oxford University Press, 2000.

Skota, T. D. Mweli. *The African Yearly Register.* Johannesburg, 1931.

Smith, Edwin. *Aggrey of Africa: A Study in Black and White.* London: Student Christian Movement, 1929.

Stapleton, Timothy. "Gathering under the Milkwood Tree: The Development of Mfengu Tribalism in the Eastern Cape (1878–1978)." *New Contree* 41 (1997): 209–25.

Stone, Sara. "Marching and Related Phenomena in the Church of God and Saints of Christ: A Possible Masonic Connection?" Paper presented at the Society for Ethnomusicology, March 1988.

———. "Song, Composition, Transmission and Performance Practice in an Urban Black Denomination: The Church of God and Saints of Christ." Ph.D. diss., Kent State University, 1988.

Storey, William. *Guns, Race, and Power in Colonial South Africa.* Cambridge: Cambridge University Press, 2008.

Sundkler, Bengt. *Bantu Prophets in South Africa.* 2nd ed. London: Oxford University Press, 1961.

———. *Zulu Zion and Some Swazi Zionists.* London: Oxford University Press, 1976.

Tabor, James, and Eugene Gallagher. *Why Waco? Cults and the Battle for Religious Freedom in America.* Berkeley: University of California Press, 1995.

Taylor, William. *Story of My Life.* New York: Eaton and Mains, 1896.

Thompson, Leonard. *The Political Mythology of Apartheid.* New Haven, CT: Yale University Press, 1985.

Thompson, Susan, An Ansoms, and Jude Murison, eds., *Emotional and Ethical Challenges for Field Research in Africa.* New York: Palgrave Macmillan, 2013.

Tidwell, William. *April '65: Confederate Covert Action in the American Civil War.* Kent, OH: Kent State University Press, 1995.

Trapido, Stanley. "African Divisional Politics in the Cape Colony, 1884–1910." *Journal of African History* 9, no. 1 (1968): 79–98.

Trew, H. F. "When the 'Israelites' Rebelled: Personal Recollections of the Native Rising at Bullhoek Fanatical Bravery of the 'Prophets' Disciples." *Nongqai* 21, no. 5 (1930): 331–34.

Van Calker, Ernst. *Hundert Jahre Kaffernmission der Brudergemeine, 1828–1928.* Herrnhut: Verlag der Missionsverwaltung, 1928.

Van der Merwe, Annari, and Paul Faber, eds. *Group Portrait South Africa: Nine Family Histories.* Cape Town: Kwela Books, 2003.

Vinson, Robert. *The Americans Are Coming: Dreams of American Liberation in Segregationist South Africa.* Athens: Ohio University Press, 2012.

Vinson, Robert, and Robert Edgar. "Zulus Abroad: Cultural Representations and Educational Experiences of Zulus in America, 1880–1945." *Journal of Southern African Studies* 31, no. 1 (2007): 43–62.

Voss, Megan. "Urbanising the North-eastern Frontier: The Frontier Intelligentsia and the Making of Colonial Queenstown, c. 1859–1877." Master's thesis, University of Cape Town, 2012.

Wagandt, Charles. *The Mighty Revolution: Negro Emancipation in Maryland, 1862–1864.* Baltimore: Johns Hopkins Press, 1964.

Walker, Beersheba Crowdy. *Life and Works of William Saunders Crowdy.* Philadelphia: Elfreth J. P. Walker, 1955.

Walshe, Peter. *The Rise of African Nationalism in South Africa: The African National Congress, 1912–1952.* London: C. Hurst, 1970.

Walzer, Michael. *Exodus and Revolution.* New York: Basic Books, 1985.

Webb, Denver, and Wouter Holleman. "Sins of the Father: Cultural Restitution and the Bulhoek Massacre." *South African Museums Association Bulletin* 23, no. 1 (1997): 16–19.

Webster, Alan. "Unmaking the Fingo: The War of 1835 Revisited." In Carolyn Hamilton, ed., *The Mfecane Aftermath: Reconstructive Debates in Southern African History,* 240–76. Johannesburg: Witwatersrand University Press, 1995.

Wells, Julia. *Rebellion and Uproar: Makhanda and the Great Escape from Robben Island.* Pretoria: University of South Africa Press, 2007.

Wessinger, Catherine. *How the Millennium Comes Violently: From Jonestown to Heaven's Gate.* New York: Seven Bridges, 2000.

————, ed. *Millennialism, Persecution, and Violence: Historical Cases*. Syracuse, NY: Syracuse University Press, 2000.

Whiteside, J. *History of the Wesleyan Methodist Church of South Africa*. London: Elliot Stock, 1906.

Woods, Sonja. "Black Americans and the Lure of Guthrie, 1887–1897." Unpublished paper.

Worsley, Peter. *The Trumpet Shall Sound: A Study of "Cargo Cults" in Melanesia*. London: MacGibbon and Kee, 1957.

Wright, John. "Turbulent Times: Political Transformations in the North and East." In Carolyn Hamilton, Bernard Mbenga, and Robert Ross, eds., *The Cambridge History of South Africa*, 1:211–52. Cambridge: Cambridge University Press, 2010.

Wright, John, and Andrew Manson. *The Hlubi Chiefdom in Natal-Zululand: A History*. Ladysmith: Ladysmith Historical Society, 1982.

Wright, Stuart, ed. *Armageddon at Waco: Critical Perspectives on the Branch Davidians*. Chicago: University of Chicago Press, 1995.

Young, Samuel. *A Missionary Triumph of Grace; As Seen in the Conversions of Kafirs, Hottentots and Fingoes*. New York: Lane and Scott, 1849.

Index

Matomela, 12
Matshaka, Adonis, 59–60
Matshaka, Andrew, 57
Matshaka, Peter, 57, 63
Matshaka, Samuel, 57, 60, 63
Matshikiza, 108
Matshoba, Gilbert, 71, 103, 137, 141
Matshoba, Samuel, 162, 170
Matthew, 54, 64
Matthews, Z. K., 154
Mattushek, John, 91–92, 135–36
Mazwi, B. S., 35, 89–90
Mbuzini, 155
Mceula, 74, 76
Merriman, John X., 39, 95, 132
Mfecane, 11–12
Mfengu, 3, 118; alliance with British,
    24, 28; disarmament by Cape gov-
    ernment, 25–26; Fingo Emanci-
    pation Day, 32–35; involvement
    in Cape politics, 27; land holdings,
    28; migrations during Mfecane,
    12–13; relations with British
    missionaries, 13–15; relations with
    British officials, 13–17, 21; rela-
    tions with Gcaleka Xhosa, 12–13;
    settlement at Kamastone, 20–24;
    triple covenant with missionaries,
    17, 35, 37
Mgijima, 12, 20, 21
Mgijima, Barrington, 111–12
Mgijima, Charles, 10, 35, 78, 80, 83,
    95, 98, 101–5, 115, 116, 121, 137,
    139, 141
Mgijima, Enoch, 1, 2, 8, 11, 20, 29,
    40, 44, 45, 79, 82, 83, 87, 95, 98,
    110, 120, 128, 129, 130, 145, 146,
    153, 154, 155; Bulhoek massacre,
    108–10, 111, 113, 115, 117–19; call
    to Ntabelanga, 67–68, 70, 121;
    death, 142–43; early life, 35–36;
    family history, 12–13, 21, 35; Israel-
    ites, 64–67, 141–42; Israelite trial,
    137, 139, 141; legacy, 157, 162, 170;
    negotiations with government offi-
    cials, 74–75, 77–79, 84, 121; prison,

141; relations with Church of God
    and Saints of Christ, 41, 46, 57,
    60–61; relations with Eric Louw,
    98–99; relations with Moravians,
    37–41; relations with Wesleyan
    Methodists, 37, 41–42; visions and
    prophecies, 35–37, 61–63, 71–73,
    101
Mgijima, Hezekiah, 68
Mgijima, Innes, 112
Mgijima, Jonas Mayekiso, 12, 16, 21,
    35
Mgijima, Mamtembu, 36
Mgijima, Mekeswa, 35
Mgijima, S. P., 112, 161
Mgijima, Timothy, 35
Mhlabane, Charles, 59, 60, 63
Mhlabane, Philip, 86, 91, 135–36
Mhlambiso, 12, 20, 21
Mhlambiso, Ebenezer, 79, 80
Middledrift, 146
milkwood tree, 17, 24, 33
Millin, Sarah Gertrude, 7, 174n2
Mini, Vuyusile, 158
Missions Stations and Communal
    Reserves Act (1909), 39
Moister, William, 18, 194n31
Mokone, Mangena, 45
Mokrawuzana, Tobi, 167
Moodie, Dunbar, 19
Moravia, 38
Moravian mission, 4, 36–40, 43, 62,
    74, 120, 160
Mordecai, 66
Moriah, 146
Moses, 49, 53, 64
Moshoeshoe, 12, 18
Motlabane, Charles, 57
Mount Ayliff, 149
Mount Carmel, 6
Mount Fletcher, 149, 151
Moyer, Richard, 13
Mpateni, Alfred, 94
Mpateni, Edward, 84, 86, 94, 95,
    112–15
Mphahlele, Moses, 128

Wesleyan Methodist Church, 4, 14,
    15, 17–19, 21–24, 35, 36, 41, 42, 57,
    93, 120, 126, 147, 152
Whitaker, Philip, 81, 85, 87
White, Eben, 47
Whiteside, Joseph, 34
Whittlesea, 21, 32
Wicks, Sergeant, 112–13
Wilberforce Institute, 57
Wilberforce University, 46, 57
William, Archibald, 90
Winterveld, 2
Wodehouse, Philip, 27
Wood, Yankee, 46

Woon, Ernest, 113, 116, 117
World War I, 62, 69, 70, 90, 94, 109,
    131

Xabanisa, Patrick, 94, 198n6
Xerxes, 66
Xhosa, 2, 11–15, 18, 19

Young, Samuel, 19

Zazulwana, 33
Zion Christian Church, 146
Zonnebloem, 35
Zulu, Chief, 31

Reconsiderations in Southern African History

Milton Shain, *The Roots of Antisemitism in South Africa*

Timothy Keegan, *Colonial South Africa and the Origins of the Racial Order*

Ineke van Kessel, *"Beyond Our Wildest Dreams": The United Democratic Front and the Transformation of South Africa*

Benedict Carton, *Blood from Your Children: The Colonial Origins of Generational Conflict in South Africa*

Diana Wylie, *Starving on a Full Stomach: Hunger and the Triumph of Cultural Racism in Modern South Africa*

Jeff Guy, *The View across the River: Harriette Colenso and the Zulu Struggle against Imperialism*

John Edwin Mason, *Social Death and Resurrection: Slavery and Emancipation in South Africa*

Hermann Giliomee, *The Afrikaners: Biography of a People*

Tim Couzens, *Murder at Morija: Faith, Mystery, and Tragedy on an African Mission*

Diana Wylie, *Art and Revolution: The Life and Death of Thami Mnyele, South African Artist*

David Welsh, *The Rise and Fall of Apartheid*

John Edwin Mason, *One Love, Ghoema Beat: Inside the Cape Town Carnival*

Eric Allina, *Slavery by Any Other Name: African Life under Company Rule in Colonial Mozambique*

Richard Elphick, *The Equality of Believers: Protestant Missionaries and the Racial Politics of South Africa*

Hermann Giliomee, *The Last Afrikaner Leaders: A Supreme Test of Power*

Meghan Healy-Clancy, *A World of Their Own: A History of South African Women's Education*

Ruramisai Charumbira, *Imagining a Nation: History and Memory in Making Zimbabwe*

Jeffrey Butler, edited by Richard Elphick and Jeannette Hopkins, *Cradock: How Segregation and Apartheid Came to a South African Town*

Hermann Giliomee, *Historian: An Autobiography*

Robert R. Edgar, *The Finger of God: Enoch Mgijima, the Israelites, and the Bulhoek Massacre in South Africa*